T3-AKB-356

AGING

AGING

*Strategies for Maintaining
Good Health and Extending Life*

by
JAMES A. GOLCZEWSKI

McFarland & Company, Inc., Publishers
Jefferson, North Carolina, and London

Cover photo: R.C. "Buck" Mitchell. Photo by Lynn Worth, used by permission. Photo courtesy of *The Alleghany News* (Sparta, North Carolina).

British Library Cataloguing-in-Publication data are available

Library of Congress Cataloguing-in-Publication Data

Golczewski, James A., 1945–
    Aging : strategies for maintaining good health and extending life
/ by James A. Golczewski.
        p.   cm.
    Includes bibliographical references and index.
    ISBN 0-7864-0412-4 (sewn softcover : 50# alkaline paper) ∞
    1. Longevity.   2. Aging.   3. Medicine, Preventive.   4. Health
I. Title.
RA776.75.G646   1998
613 — dc21   98-10801
                                                                CIP

Manufactured in the United States of America

McFarland & Company, Inc., Publishers
  Box 611, Jefferson, North Carolina 28640

To Gretel

It is often necessary to make a decision on the basis of knowledge sufficient for action but insufficient to satisfy the intellect.

— Kant

Often you have to decide when the data are not as good as you would like.

— Donald Kennedy

Contents

Preface

So many books have been written on health and longevity in recent years that one might naturally wonder: Why another?

There are several reasons.

First, in my opinion, no one has fully and accurately addressed all aspects of the subject.

Second, the best books on the subject are now around ten years old; in such a rapidly changing field, much information needs to be added or updated.

Third, much of what has been written is undocumented opinion. In contrast, I have tried to reference all recommendations and to point out areas where the data do not permit a definite conclusion. In such cases some recommendation is still needed, since we all have to follow some course in our lives, even if the course is simply to continue our current behavior. But I have tried in all instances to show how and why I came to my conclusions and recommendations.

Fourth, even the best recommendations in the world are useless if one cannot follow them with a reasonable consistency. I will present several alternatives consistent with a healthy lifestyle. I hope there will be some factors conducive to a long and healthy life that appeal to everyone.

The aim of this book is to provide practical information on delaying aging, avoiding disease, and extending life. I will discuss the free radical theory of aging and biological damage due to oxidation, since these topics have generated a considerable amount of interest in recent years. But I do not discuss other theories of aging in any detail, primarily because it is not the book's aim to do so, but also because there is very little evidence to support any of the current theories, let alone a consensus as to which of them is most likely valid.

As noted above, I will provide the scientific background and reasoning behind all recommendations in this book. Aside from other considerations, it is usually easier to follow a recommendation if you can see the rationale behind it. To make these explanations clear and useful to as many readers as possible, I have included both advanced and somewhat elementary material in the references and appendices. This book does not assume anything beyond the most basic scientific knowledge. I will explain possibly unfamiliar scientific terms when they are first introduced in the text; a glossary explaining such words and terms, plus others that may be encountered in this field, is also provided.

Chapter 1 describes some of the basic ideas and terminology relevant to aging and life extension.

Chapter 2 discusses the nature of the evidence in this field. How certain can we be that something will extend or shorten life? How can we determine what and whom to believe? While I consider these questions of great importance, this chapter is not critical to understanding the rest of the book. If you prefer, it can be skimmed over or skipped altogether.

Chapters 3 through 8 consider the current most promising methods of avoiding disease and extending life and youth, plus some factors implicated in shortening life. Diet and nutrition, dietary supplements, exercise, and various lifestyle or behavioral factors are discussed. Methods of extending a good quality of life into later years are also considered. In other words, we will be concerned with prolonging our more youthful years, not our old age. We will therefore discuss such topics as preventing osteoporosis (loss of bone mass), preserving vision, preventing aging of the skin, and maintaining overall vitality.

I will then discuss some of the trade-offs involved in putting together a life extension program, give my own recommendations, and describe my own program. Finally, we will go over some recipes, tips, and other matters to make your life extension regimen as enjoyable and as practical as possible.

ONE. Basic Concepts of Aging

A common way of looking at aging of a certain population, or cohort, of animals is to plot a survival curve for that group. In its simplest terms, this means plotting the number, or the fraction, of animals still alive as the group ages. Put another way, we are plotting the percentage of animals surviving versus time. If we did this for a population living in good conditions, such as laboratory animals maintained in a germ-free environment or people in the present-day United States or other developed countries, we might typically get the type of curve shown in Figure 1.1. It is somewhat idealized and neglects infant mortality, but is otherwise quite like plots of actual survival curves of both people and animals. We start off, by definition, with the entire cohort, or 100 percent, alive. As the cohort ages, we can see that the fraction surviving decreases, slowly at first, then with increasing speed. This is just a consequence of the common observation that the death rate increases as people get older. Mathematically, the death rate increases exponentially after maturity. Consequently, at present in the developed countries the probability of dying doubles about every eight years after the age of 30. (The rate of increase actually slows somewhat in old age.) Eventually the cohort reaches an age at which half of its members have died; this is the definition of the *median*, one common measure of the average life span of the group. As you can see on the graph, from this point on the animals die off rather rapidly. The maximum life span for the group can be defined as simply the age at which the oldest survivor dies, or put another way, where the survival curve reaches zero. The specific numbers on the horizontal axis depend of course on the particular species and subspecies, ranging from days for some microscopic creatures, to months for some small mammals, to many years for humans and some large animals. Scientifically, the distinction between maximum life span and average life span is very important; it is less so in a practical sense for the individual, for reasons I will try to make clear.

The maximum life span of a species is the maximum age to which any member of that species has lived. For example, the maximum authenticated age to which a human being has lived is 120 years. Similarly, we can determine the maximum life span of any species or group for which we have accurate records. In actual fact, we have life span records for only a small minority of the species on earth. These are primarily companion animals like cats and dogs, some zoo animals, and some species used in laboratory research. Another problem with this definition of maximum life span is that it is dependent on the last few survivors, or even the very last survivor, of a group — hardly a good statistical sample. What can be done to circumvent this difficulty is to define maximum life span in a way to preserve the original idea of it

3

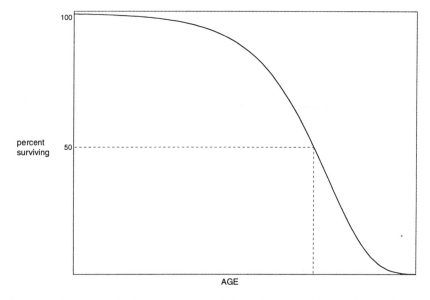

Figure 1.1 **Typical survival curve for a population of animals living under good conditions, in which the deaths are primarily age related.**

as the age of the last few survivors, while including more of them. For example, we can call it the average age of the last 10 percent of survivors. This means that it will no longer be the maximum age attained by a member of that species or group, but it will give a good indication of the age to which the very oldest live.

Almost all measures of physiologic function decline after maturity. These include vital capacity (the volume of air that can be expelled from the lungs after a maximum inhalation), cardiac output (the volume of blood pumped by the heart per unit time), muscle strength, kidney function, and so on (Figure 1.2). Interestingly, while the rate of decline varies widely, depending on the specific function and how it is measured, this decline is usually roughly linear with age, in contrast to the exponentially increasing death rate. Keep in mind that these plots are average values of a population. The actual value of a physiologic function that a particular person has at a particular age may be very different from this average. Figure 1.3 illustrates this point for a typical function, cardiac index, a measure of cardiovascular fitness. The points plotted on the graph are measurements of cardiac index for each individual in the sample population; the line represents the decline in this function for the sample population as a whole. As you can see, some older individuals have greater function than younger individuals. This sort of distribution is common. A physically fit 60-year-old can easily have the same or greater vital capacity or muscle strength as an out-of-shape 20-year-old.

The incidence of most diseases and mortality due to them also increases rapidly after maturity, like the overall death rate. Which diseases kill off the most animals depends on the species and the living conditions of the group studied. If

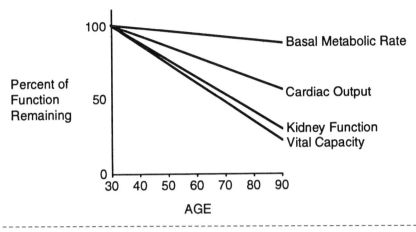

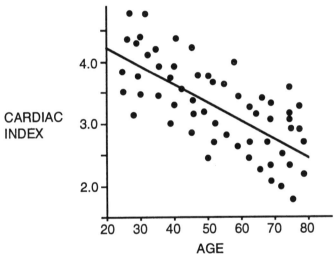

Top: Figure 1.2 Decline of typical physiologic functions with age in humans. *Bottom:* Figure 1.3 Variation in the decline of a typical physiologic function with age among a human population. Cardiac index, the volume of blood pumped by the heart per unit time divided by body surface area (liters per minute per square meter) is plotted on the vertical axis, each point representing one individual whose age is given on the horizontal axis. The solid line represents a statistical measure of the average decline in this function with age.

living conditions are poor (crowding, poor sanitation, malnutrition, etc.), more of the animals will die at a relatively young age, giving us a survival curve like A in Figure 1.4. Such conditions, and such survival curves, are in fact obtained for the populations of many present-day poor countries in Asia and Africa. This type of plot is also obtained for the population of the United States around the beginning of the twentieth century. Infectious diseases like tuberculosis and pneumonia are

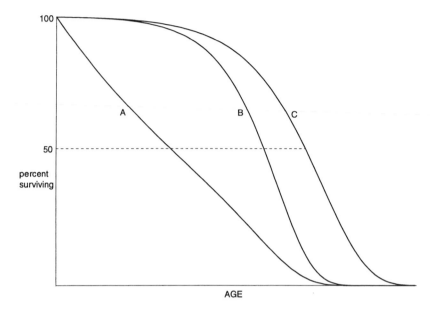

Figure 1.4 Survival curves for 3 populations of the same animal. Under poor living conditions, as in A, more animals die at younger ages; under better conditions (B), average life is greater (the age at which 50 percent have died increases) but maximum life span is about the same. For a population in which the aging process has been delayed (C), both average and maximum life span are greater.

frequently the major causes of death in these populations. If we plotted the survival curve for the present-day United States on the same graph, we would obtain a curve like B in Figure 1.4. Note that the average life span of the population has increased; if we measure this by median life span, we can see from the graph that the age at which 50 percent of the population has died off is clearly greater in B. Note, however, that the maximum life span has not changed. A few individuals still lived to the very oldest ages under poor conditions; it's just that far fewer people made it to old age. One could make statistical quibbles about this, since by some definitions of maximum life span, fewer people surviving to the oldest ages decreases the average of the last 10 percent (or whatever) of survivors. Furthermore, with fewer people surviving to old age, there is a decreased chance of anyone living to the actual maximum attainable life span for the species. These do not change the basic idea: With better living conditions, the average life span increases significantly, but the maximum age attained by any member of that group or species changes little if at all. So in the present-day United States, the odds of living to 75 are much better than in the year 1900, but the odds of living to 110 are about the same.* There actually has been some increase in the life expectancy (the average number of years remaining) for people even at advanced old age. Percentagewise, the increase looks good, but it amounts to only a few years at best because the average amount of life remaining at such an age is so small (i.e., two years added to eight years still isn't very much).

This "squaring" of the survival curve in going from A to B in Figure 1.4 has been observed many times in many populations of people and animals as their living conditions are improved. If the actual aging rate of a population is slowed, you get a shift in the survival curve to C in Figure 1.4. The animals start to die off from age-related diseases later because their aging process itself has been delayed, and the maximum life span is increased. This last is a crucial point, since it is never seen with the more common environmental improvement. The survival curve has essentially shifted to the right. This type of shift is rarely seen; it probably never occurs naturally and there are only a few laboratory manipulations that can accomplish it, primarily with non-warm-blooded animals.

A similar situation confronts individuals trying to increase their life expectancy. They can avoid the diseases likely to kill them before they have reached the maximum life span of their species, or they can — theoretically at least — adopt a lifestyle or strategy that increases their maximum life span. The second is much harder to do; there is, in fact, only one known method of increasing the maximum life span of mammals — caloric restriction, which we shall discuss in a later chapter. We have seen how all the combined improvements in public health over the past century have not increased the maximum age attained by a few people. This still leaves us a lot of room for improvement, however, even if we don't slow the basic aging process, and, as we shall see, to some extent that also can be done. The average life span in the United States is now about 75 years (72 years for males and 78 years for females; among mammals, females almost always live longer). The difference between current average age at death and the maximum life span of humans (120 years) is 45 years. If we can prolong some aspects of youth and make those added years healthy, enjoyable ones, who would not take them?

Decreasing our risk of serious disease and maintaining some youthful qualities into old age is not trivial, but is definitely possible. There are in fact many strategies that we will discuss to do just that. Furthermore, there is nothing incompatible between increasing average and maximum life span (at least none that we will discuss here), as we shall see. At the risk of stating the obvious, I would mention that nothing can guarantee a long life. There is an element of chance in determining the age at which any given animal dies. If you look at the survival curves in Figure 1.4, you see that even under good conditions, there is considerable variation in age at death. Interestingly, this type of curve is obtained even for identical animals living under identical conditions. Many of the mouse and rat strains used in aging research are *syngeneic*; that is, the animals have been inbred over many generations so that they have become genetically identical, like so many identical twins. Even when housed in laboratory cages under conditions as nearly the same as possible, their survival curve looks like Figure 1.1 or B in Figure 1.4 — there is still significant variation of age at death.

In 1900, people over 65 constituted 4 percent of the population; by 1988 they had increased to 12.4 percent. This percentage is expected to rise to 13 by the year 2000 and 22 percent by 2030.

TWO. Evidence

I would like at the outset to discuss the difficult question of how to judge what is likely to extend your life: what supplements to take, what daily amounts of these supplements are optimal, what other lifestyle changes are most likely to insure a long life. It is a question that I was frequently asked by the students in my nutrition class. There is not, of course, any definitive answer to this; I don't think there is any foolproof way to determine truth in nutrition or biomedicine any more than there is in any field. Ideally, one would like studies of large populations of people over their entire lifetimes, in which each of the supplements or other factors is changed one at a time and the resultant effect on life span noted. Obviously, this is impractical and will probably never happen. However, there have been such studies of animals over their entire lives. There are also epidemiologic studies. These consist of studies of various human populations (for example, Americans, Japanese, Seventh-Day Adventists, vegetarians) to determine how they differ and what factors cause them to differ. These are more difficult to draw conclusions from because groups of people usually differ in so many ways that it is not clear what factors are causing what results. However, techniques have been developed over the years to do just that. Epidemiologic studies have the advantage of eliminating the question of whether results obtained with animals apply to people. They can also examine the entire life of a population, or at least large portions of it. This is usually quite cumbersome to do in an animal. When you consider that the common short-lived laboratory animals, rats and mice, can live for up to four years or more, you can appreciate the effort involved in conducting life span experiments with them.

Studies on factors affecting immunity, cancer, cardiovascular disease, and the incidence of other diseases have all provided evidence related to life prolongation and will be referenced where applicable. There have been innumerable studies particularly on cardiovascular disease and cancer, which are, respectively, the first and second leading causes of death in the United States and many industrialized countries. This presents another problem for this book: What studies should be referenced in support of the recommendations? It is not really feasible to list all the relevant studies on a topic (the number of papers on heart disease or vitamin E, for example, could run into the thousands), nor would it be very helpful to the reader. No one is going to look up hundreds of references, and there would be no way of deciding beforehand which were most important. On the other hand, most people want to see at least some kind of evidence, to serve as a starting point and to illustrate the reasoning behind the recommendations. I have adopted what I hope is a common-sense approach to this problem — citing what I regard as representative studies, or the best studies, or review articles, or sometimes a combination of these. Interested readers can easily get to other references and more information from there.

News reports, anecdotes, and testimonial evidence are all notoriously unreliable and I have not relied upon them at all. At best, such reports can provide examples to illustrate a point. Problems arise, however, even with studies published in peer-reviewed scientific journals. One of the main problems in drawing conclusions from such studies in the biomedical field is that they frequently have contradictory conclusions, at least on the face of it. For example, some studies may indicate that saccharine can cause cancer, while others find no such effect. There are a number of reasons for this. The studies may have used slightly different experimental conditions (different doses of saccharine, a different strain of mice), or there may be hidden differences that are only revealed by a close inspection of the conditions (e.g., different lots of saccharine from the same manufacturer may differ). Or the experiments may not have been conducted or reported properly.

Theoretically, this last possibility should not happen; in the real world, it does. Having worked in this area in many labs over many years, I can tell you from first-hand experience that there are many studies in the biomedical field that are completely worthless. With the current cutthroat competition for grants and positions and the emphasis on quantity of data and publications, some researchers have taken to grinding out as many publications as possible with little regard for their reliability. After all, if discrepancies do arise, they can always be blamed on slightly different conditions! Publication in a refereed journal, where the manuscript is first approved by other researchers in the field, cannot and does not eliminate this problem. Reviewers can only spot obvious discrepancies or errors in an experiment; they can't look into the laboratory to determine whether what is described in the manuscript is an accurate and faithful account of what was done.

Eventually, all of these sources of error are sorted out. If experiments can't be repeated, or contradictory results are reported, or the ramifications of certain results aren't found, the correct conclusions will eventually become evident as more and more studies are reported. The self-correcting mechanisms of science do work *in the long run*. However, the old saw was never more applicable than here: In the long run, we are all dead. It can take many years before we can say with any certainty which factors will lengthen or shorten life expectancy. In the real world, we usually do have to decide when the evidence is not as good as we would like. This involves evaluating the studies done on whatever it is we are considering doing (adding vitamin E, exercising, and so on). Are the studies well designed, are they relevant to people, are there studies showing negative effects, what amounts caused what effects, are there a number of reports with the same or similar conclusions? Especially in life extension we want to be conservative; we want to avoid doing something that might shorten life at least as much as doing something to extend life. But this does *not* mean that doing nothing, or making no change in our life style, is the most conservative action when the evidence is not clear.

For example, if you eat the typical American diet, you are getting something like 35 to over 40 percent of your calories from fat. There is considerable evidence linking various diseases, especially cardiovascular disease and several cancers, to a high fat intake. This evidence is not at all definitive in many cases, however; for example, some studies have not found any difference in the incidence of breast cancer related to women's fat intake. But since there is considerable evidence for negative consequences from a high-fat diet and little or no evidence for negative consequences from a low-fat diet, the most prudent course is to reduce the amount of fat in your diet. The questions then become: By how much? What sort of fat is worse? What impact will it have on your quality of life? It is these and many similar questions that we will try to answer in the following chapters.

THREE. Caloric Restriction

The only method that has been actually proven to extend both average and maximum life span in mammals is caloric restriction. This consists of feeding the animal a diet complete with all the vitamins, minerals, and other nutrients essential for that animal's health while significantly reducing the total calories in the diet. Caloric restriction has extended the life of many strains of mice and rats, fish, insects, rotifers, and protozoa[1, 2]—in fact, just about every species studied when applied properly. A study is in progress examining caloric restriction in monkeys, but, because of their relatively long life span, no definitive results are in from this yet. While this doesn't prove with absolute certainty that it works for humans, it would be very difficult to see why it would work for such a wide variety of animals and not work for people. Furthermore, as Walford has pointed out,[3] there is some evidence that human populations that naturally consume fewer calories, such as the people of Okinawa, do in fact have a longer-than-average life span.[4]

When begun soon after birth, this method has been found to increase life span by up to 100 percent. This would be equivalent to a human being living to about 240 years. More typical figures are 20 to 80 percent, depending on the degree of caloric restriction and the age of the animal when it is begun. The extent of life extension increases roughly with the amount of restriction;[5, 6] even a small reduction in calories (about 10 percent) results in a small but significant increase in life span. Furthermore, it seems to be the more youthful, healthy portion of life that is extended; restricted animals have stronger immune systems and other more youthful characteristics compared to fully fed animals of the same age. Their incidence of cancer and other diseases is lower. Compared to control animals, the survival curve for calorie-restricted animals is shifted as from B to C in Figure 1.4. This is exactly the type of change we would expect if the basic aging process has been slowed. Essentially, the portion of the curve with a low death rate is extended into later ages. Note that not just average or median life span is increased; maximum life span is also lengthened.

Equally important, thanks to the pioneering work of Roy Walford, in recent years it has been shown that caloric restriction can extend life even if begun at maturity or middle age.[6, 7] However, the mature animal must be gradually switched to the restricted diet. Life expectancy can be actually decreased if the change is too sudden. In the classic experiment of this type, adult male mice of two already long-lived strains were gradually switched to a calorie-restricted diet at the age of 12–13 months. This is equivalent to about a 26-year-old man in one strain and about a 36-year-old in the second. Control groups continued to have unrestricted

11

diets. Mice in the restricted groups consumed 44 percent fewer calories per day than those in the control group. Restricted mice of both strains had increased average and maximum life spans, the increase being about 10 percent in the first strain and 28 percent in the second. In human terms, this would be roughly equivalent to 7 and 20 years, respectively, added to a man's average (median) life expectancy.

An animal's caloric intake can be reduced by simply feeding it fewer calories daily, or by not feeding it every day (e.g., feeding it every other day or three days a week).[5, 8] But it is calories that must be limited; just reducing a particular component of the diet (protein, fat, carbohydrates, etc.) without reducing overall calories doesn't seem to work.[5, 9, 10] As I mentioned, the change to a restricted diet should be gradual; a normal adult who chooses this option should take at least a year to complete the changeover, even longer for the more restricted diets. The extent of life extension depends on the degree of caloric restriction: The life span of rodents has increased with greater restriction up to levels of 60 percent (i.e., animals fed only 40 percent of the calories of controls). Most people are probably neither able nor willing to subject themselves to that great a reduction in calories, and it probably would not be advisable even if they could. There are just too many unknowns here to allow us to extrapolate the more extreme regimens in animals quantitatively to humans. As I've said, we want to be conservative in our approach; we want to first avoid doing anything that might decrease our life expectancy.

I'll address two criticisms of caloric restriction that I have seen in print. First, it has been argued that if caloric restriction works in humans, some populations around the world who live at near-starvation levels would show this increase in life span. This criticism shows a misunderstanding of what caloric restriction is. Restricting calories means *only* reducing the number of calories consumed while ensuring that all the other nutrients are adequate. This is entirely different from the malnutrition found in many countries, in which not only the caloric intake is low, but one or more vitamins, minerals, protein, and other essential nutrients are inadequate. Even if you simply reduce total calories in an otherwise reasonably balanced diet, the levels of certain nutrients are likely to be too low. In fact, the situation is far worse; in areas where food is scarce people frequently subsist on just a few staple foods that provide inadequate or marginal nutrition even when enough is available. Second, it has been argued that in experiments in which calorie-restricted animals outlive unrestricted animals, it is the unrestricted animals who have their lives shortened, not the calorie-restricted animals who have their lives lengthened. As far as applying caloric restriction in people, this is not correct; in the developed countries, people essentially have unrestricted access to food, just as the unrestricted control animals in the experiments do. So people who choose to restrict their caloric intake do in fact correspond to the restricted animals in the experiments.

If you choose to undertake caloric restriction, you would gradually reduce your caloric intake while monitoring your body weight. It is in one sense more accurate to gauge your progress from your actual calorie intake; this is what must be permanently reduced in order for the program to work. It has been suggested that, as an alternative, body weight can be monitored, since this can be measured much more easily.[3] However, body weight often changes in strange ways when the number of calories consumed is reduced, sometimes creeping back upward even with a continued lower calorie intake. This is one of the reasons that some people have trouble losing weight and keeping it off permanently. So I would recommend at least trying to calculate your present caloric intake and how you plan to change your diet to meet your goal of reducing it. This is not all that hard; all packaged food has calorie content (as well as other required nutritional information) listed on the label, and similar information for nonpackaged food is now even available in the supermarket produce section, as well as in many references (including Appendix 2 in this volume). It's just a matter of taking the time to put all the information together to come up with a reasonable estimate, then planning what reductions to make to gradually lower total calories. You would continue to lower your calorie intake until you had reduced it by 20 to 30 percent over the course of about a year. Your weight will probably drop by about 10 to 30 percent. The optimal amount to reduce your weight depends on your weight now. If you are already on the thin side, it's probably better to aim for a reduction of around 10 percent; if you're heavy, closer to 30 percent. Again, some people may not see a dramatic permanent reduction in weight, but as long as calorie intake is kept reduced, they will obtain the same beneficial effects.

It should be emphasized that on a calorie-restricted diet, care must be taken to insure an adequate intake of essential nutrients. This can be done by taking a good multivitamin tablet daily, some multimineral preparation, and eating a variety of foods to help insure a sufficient consumption of known and unknown trace elements. It is not a good idea to take too much of certain minerals, such as iron, so I favor a multivitamin with a variety of minerals four days a week, and a multivitamin without minerals (like *Theragran* or equivalent) the other three days.

The second point is worth repeating: You must eat a variety of foods to help insure an adequate nutrient intake; it is not sufficient to rely on vitamin/mineral supplements to do this. I do not believe, however, that it is necessary to go through extensive food analysis such as computer-generated diet plans. It's true that if you were to rely on diet alone to supply all known vitamin, mineral, and nutrient needs, it becomes very tricky to come up with the variety of foods to do this while still maintaining low calorie levels. But this is neither necessary nor desirable. You can, by taking good multivitamin and multimineral plus some individual supplements, insure a more than adequate intake of the known nutrients. If a nutrient is unknown, you are no more likely to guarantee adequate intakes by extensive analysis than by simply eating a variety of foods. You wouldn't know what to look for in the first place, and such a finely detailed analysis of the composition of food is not available. The primary requirement is to eat a variety of whole grains, vegetables, and fruits. These are the most nutrient-dense, healthiest foods and should make up the bulk of your diet. Depending on your individual tastes and inclinations, legumes, skim milk and skim-milk products, and a number of other types of food can be included to round out a varied and healthy diet. There is more on the details of recommended diets in the next chapter; these recommendations would not differ for calorie-restricted diets.

References to Chapter Three

1. C. H. Barrows, L. M. Roeder: Nutrition. In: *Handbook of the Biology of Aging*, C. E. Finch & L Hayflick, eds. Van Nostrand, New York, 1977.

2. R. Weidruch, R. L. Walford: *The Retardation of Aging by Dietary Restriction*, Raven Press, New York, 1987.

3. R. L. Walford: *The 120 Year Diet*. Simon and Schuster, New York, 1986.

4. Y. Kagawa: Impact of westernization on the nutrition of Japanese: changes in physique, cancer, longevity and centenarians. *Preve Medi* 7:205–217, 1978.

5. E. J. Masoro: Dietary restriction and metabolic diseases. In: *Nutritional Intervention in the Aging Process*, H. J. Armbrecht, J. M. Prendergast, R. M. Coe, eds. Springer Verlag, New York, 1984.

6. R. Weidruch, R. L. Walford, S. Fliegiel, D. Guthrie: The retardation of aging in mice by dietary restriction. *J Nutr* 116:641–654, 1986.

7. R. Weidruch, R. L. Walford: Dietary restriction in mice beginning at one year of age. *Science* 215:1415–1418, 1982.

8. C. L. Goodrick, D. K. Ingram, M. A. Reynolds: Differential effects of intermittent feeding and voluntary exercise on body weight and life span in adult rats. *J Gerontol* 38:36–45, 1983.

9. B. P. Yu, E. J. Masoro, C. A. McMahan: Nutritional influences on aging of Fisher 344 rats. *J Gerontol* 40:657–670, 1985.

10. K. Iwasaki, C. A. Gleiser, E. J. Masoro et al.: Influence of the restriction of individual dietary components on longevity and age-related disease of Fisher 344 rats. *J Gerontol* 43:B13–21, 1988.

FOUR. Diet

In this chapter we will look at various foods and other substances that should or should not be included in putting together a healthy diet.

Fat is probably the single major dietary component most closely linked to disease. Fats and oils are essentially the same thing, by the way; they are both in the class of chemicals called triglycerides. Each molecule of fat contains three fatty acids that can be saturated, unsaturated, or polyunsaturated. (A more detailed discussion of fats and fatty acids is provided in Appendix 1.) An oil is just a fat that is liquid at room temperature. Generally speaking, the more unsaturated the fat and the shorter its fatty acids are, the more liquid it will be. For some time it was thought that saturated fats (as in butter and beef) led to increased blood cholesterol and incidence of heart disease, that polyunsaturated fats (as in soybean oil and margarine) decreased blood cholesterol and consequently the incidence of heart disease, and that monounsaturated fats (as in olive oil) were neutral in this respect. It is now known that the effects of dietary fat are not as simple as this, and there are in fact different types of cholesterol. One type, the high-density lipoprotein, or HDL, is associated with lower risk of disease; low-density lipoprotein, or LDL, is associated with higher risk. LDL is thought to transport cholesterol to the sites of disease in the arteries; HDL is thought to help clear cholesterol from such sites by transporting it to the liver where it is broken down for excretion. It is the ratio of HDL to LDL (or, what is similar, the ratio of HDL to total cholesterol) that is the best predictor of cardiovascular disease.[1] In a detailed, well-designed study that measured total cholesterol, LDL, triglycerides, and HDL, along with the actual narrowing of the coronary arteries in men and women, "HDL cholesterol was the most powerful independent variable associated with the presence and severity of [coronary artery disease]"[2] after age and gender. That is, the risk and severity of heart disease increased with the person's age, or if the person was male (factors obviously beyond our control), but after that the person's HDL level was the best indicator of whether disease was present, as well as the extent of the disease, higher HDL being associated with decreased risk. The study also found that in patients with total cholesterol less than 200mg/dL (i.e., normal levels), 79 percent had some degree of coronary artery disease. Therefore, blood cholesterol can be, and frequently is, in the normal range when a person has heart disease. Other recent studies have reported similar findings — it is the level of blood HDL, or the ratio of HDL to LDL (or HDL to total cholesterol) that is most closely associated with (decreased) risk of cardiovascular disease. Or put the other way, low HDL and high cholesterol to HDL ratios are associated with increased risk. While different studies

15

have come up with somewhat different numbers, an HDL less than 25mg/dL would certainly be considered dangerous; below 35 a risk factor; 40 to 45 about normal; and above 45 associated with increasingly below-average risk of coronary disease. A total cholesterol to HDL ratio above 5.5 is a serious warning sign, 4.5 to 5.5 is within the range of normal values, and below 4.5 is good.

The ratio HDL/LDL is not as easy to change as total cholesterol; diet and other lifestyle changes (exercise, smoking) don't seem to increase it in every person. In a practical sense, then, to reduce our risk of heart disease, we must undertake a strategy of adopting lifestyle changes that increase HDL and/or the HDL/total cholesterol ratio, while monitoring both. This last is not difficult, by the way; HDL and the ratio HDL/cholesterol are now routinely measured in a standard complete blood test.

It has long been known that diet has a considerable influence on blood cholesterol and triglycerides. (The latter is also related to heart disease in ways not well understood.) While dietary cholesterol, common in animal products like meat, eggs, and whole milk, has a moderate effect, dietary fats can raise or lower cholesterol levels considerably.[3] The old rule that saturated fats increase blood cholesterol and polyunsaturated fats decrease it has some validity, but is not always true. The effect (raising, lowering, or neutral) depends to a large extent on the specific fatty acids in the fat consumed. Dietary fats typically contain a number of different fatty acids. The fat is labeled saturated, monounsaturated, or polyunsaturated depending on which types of fatty acids predominate. For example, butterfat has mostly saturated fatty acids and few polyunsaturated fatty acids, so we say it is saturated. Some saturated fatty acids (e.g., stearic acid, found in cocoa butter and beef) don't seem to raise cholesterol. There is evidence that some kinds of polyunsaturated fatty acids, such as are found in fish, have an especially beneficial effect on cholesterol and other blood lipids. This has less practical significance than you might think. As I mentioned, the fatty acids found in common foods are almost always mixtures of various types of fatty acids, so we usually cannot eat only beneficial or neutral ones in choosing a particular food. For example, the stearic acid in beef might be neutral, but beef still contains lots of palmitic acid, which strongly raises cholesterol.

Polyunsaturated fats have their own potential for harm. Such fats easily react chemically with oxygen; indeed, antioxidants such as BHT (butylated hydroxytoluene) are frequently added to them to prevent this oxidation. There is considerable evidence linking such oxidized fats to increased incidence of cancer and possibly other diseases. This type of chemical reaction, which is the common way fats go rancid, can occur whenever the fat is exposed to air, and even after it is eaten. It becomes more likely, however, as the temperature increases. Therefore, cooking, especially frying polyunsaturated fat, can result in the formation of potentially dangerous compounds. Oxidation also occurs with monounsaturated and saturated fats, but to a lesser extent because of their chemical nature. One could address this problem (as many people have) by taking large quantities of various antioxidants (i.e., substances that prevent the fat from reacting with oxygen). These include BHT and BHA (butylated hydroxyanisole), both of which are commonly added to commercial foods such as soybean oil and cereals for this purpose, and a number of naturally occurring antioxidants. Among these are vitamin E, which functions in the body as an antioxidant, selenium, an essential component of the glutathione peroxidase system (an intracellular antioxidant and protective system), and beta-carotene (a precursor of vitamin A and also a potent antioxidant). There is evidence that the incidence of cancer and possibly other diseases can be reduced by such antioxidants.[4-6] But antioxidants probably cannot provide complete protection against the oxidation of polyunsaturated fats. However, substituting monounsaturated fatty acids for dietary saturated fatty acids reduces cholesterol while maintaining a very favorable ratio of HDL to LDL.[1, 3, 7-9] Table 4.1 lists the fatty acid composition of a number of common fats. Olive oil is one of the most common sources of monounsaturated fatty acids. It is rather unique in being composed overwhelmingly of monounsaturated fatty acids, with only small amounts of saturated and polyunsaturated ones. You therefore avoid the cholesterol-raising effects of saturated fats and the high susceptibility to oxidation of polyunsaturated fats. Olive oil consumption may well be at least partially responsible for the low incidence of heart disease and certain cancers in southern Italy and other Mediterranean countries.[10, 11] Since it has a long tradition in cooking, it is already included in many recipes and can easily be made part of almost anyone's diet. Canola oil (rapeseed oil) is another monounsaturated fat that has become quite common in recent years. It is somewhat blander and less expensive than olive oil and seems to have similar effects, but has been studied less.

Other dietary factors possibly affecting cardiovascular disease include omega-3 fatty acids. These are polyunsaturated fatty acids found in many fish and marine animals. (Chemically, they differ from the omega-6 fatty acids common in vegetable oils in that the first unsaturated bond is the third from the end of the fatty acid chain instead of the sixth. Again, interested readers can find further details in Appendix 1.) A number of fish, especially cold-water fish like salmon, mackerel, and herring, are rich in them. It was first noticed that Eskimos had low rates of coronary disease despite a high-fat diet. Subsequent epidemiologic studies generally (but not always) confirmed the finding that fish-eating populations had less coronary disease compared to non-fish-eating populations. A fair amount of evidence has now accumulated linking omega-3 fatty acids to a decreased risk of heart attack.[12] The two main omega-3 fatty acids found in fish are called eicosapentaenoic acid (EPA) and docosahexaenoic acid (DHA). It is thought that EPA and DHA play a role in atherosclerosis (hardening of the arteries), inflammation, immunity, high blood pressure, and the formation of blood clots through several of the body's metabolic pathways. The actual composition of the fat in your body, including that in the membranes surrounding each of your body's cells, depends to a large extent on the kind of fat you eat. Several studies have shown that omega-3 fatty acids influence this composition in a favorable manner. However, you may have to eat a substantial amount of omega-3 fatty acids daily to obtain effective long-term benefits. In laboratory studies, fairly high intakes of fish oil (around 100g, or 3.5 oz. a day) were needed to significantly reduce blood cholesterol. The most consistent

Fat	Saturated	Monounsaturated	Polyunsaturated
almond oil	8	70	17
avocado oil	12	71	14
beef tallow	50	42	4
butterfat	62	29	4
canola oil	7	59	30
chicken fat	30	45	21
cocoa oil	60	33	3
coconut oil	87	6	2
corn oil	13	24	59
cottonseed oil	26	18	52
fish oil, cod liver	23	47	23
fish oil, herring	21	57	16
fish oil, salmon	20	29	40
lard, pork	39	45	11
linseed oil	9	20	66
oat oil	20	35	41
olive oil	14	74	8
palm kernel oil	82	11	2
palm oil	49	37	9
peanut oil	17	46	32
poppyseed oil	14	20	62
safflower oil, regular	9	12	75
sesame oil	14	40	42
soybean lecithin oil	15	11	45
soybean oil	14	23	58
sunflower oil, regular	10	20	66
turkey fat	29	43	23
walnut oil	9	23	63
wheat germ oil	19	15	62

Table 4.1 Saturation of fatty acids in common fats and oils. All values are grams of fatty acids per 100 grams of fat or oil, rounded to nearest whole number. Source: U.S. Dept. of Agriculture Nutrient Database

effect of dietary fish oil is a lowering of blood triglycerides. Other researchers have reported that small to moderate amounts of omega-3 fatty acids had no significant effects on cholesterol nor did they improve HDL, LDL or the ratio of HDL to LDL.[13, 14] These studies suggest that high intakes, approaching the 5 to 10 grams of omega-3 fatty acids consumed daily by Eskimos, are required for any significant beneficial effects.

OMEGA-3 FATTY ACIDS

Food	Total Fat	LNA	EPA	DHA	Cholesterol
herring, Atlantic	9.0	0.1	0.7	0.9	60
herring oil	100.0	0.6	7.1	4.3	570
mackerel, Atlantic	13.9	0.1	0.9	1.6	80
salmon, Atlantic	5.4	0.2	0.3	0.9	63
salmon oil	100.0	1.0	8.8	11.1	485
chicken fat	99.8	1.0	0	0	85
canola oil	100.0	9.3	–	–	0
linseed oil	100.0	53.3	–	–	0
olive oil	100.0	0.6	0	0	0
soybean oil	100.0	6.8	0	0	0
walnut oil	100.0	10.4	0	0	0
wheat germ oil	100.0	6.9	0	0	0

Table 4.2 Omega-3 fatty acids and other fat components in some common foods and oils. All values are grams per 100 grams edible portion except for cholesterol, which is in milligrams. (A dash indicates data not available.) Source: U.S. Dept. of Agriculture Nutrient Database.

Alternative sources of omega-3 fatty acids include linseed oil (flaxseed oil), walnut oil, canola oil, wheat germ oil, and soybean oil. The main omega-3 fatty acid in such plant sources is alpha-linolenic acid (LNA), not the DHA and EPA found in fish oils. LNA can be converted into DHA and EPA by the body after ingestion. Linseed oil in particular has also been suggested as an important source of omega-3 fatty acids.[15] It is rather special in this respect, as you can see from Table 4.2, which lists amounts of the major omega-3 fatty acids in a number of common fats and foods containing significant amounts. Cholesterol content is also listed; it's instructive to see how much dietary cholesterol would be consumed along with substantial quantities of any fish oil. (As with Table 4.1, these are average figures.) Being of plant origin, linseed oil also does not contain the cholesterol associated with all fish oils.

These fatty acids share the same problem as other polyunsaturated fats: They are subject to degradation by oxidation. It is even more of a problem with fish oils than vegetable oils because they are generally composed of long, highly unsaturated fatty acids, and therefore have more chemical bonds that are susceptible to oxidation.[16] Note also the relatively small amounts of omega-3 fatty acids even in oily fish; this is one reason why some researchers question whether it is feasible to consume sufficient quantities of fish to have significant health benefits. Substantial amounts *are* present in *purified fish oils,* along with substantial levels of cholesterol and calories.

Fat has also been linked to cancer. In particular, there is evidence that cancers of the prostate, colon, rectum, and possibly the breast are related to dietary fat.[6, 17, 18] The link to breast cancer is more controversial; while some studies have reported a definite relation, others have not.[19] Cancer of the prostate may be associated with dietary animal fat and protein.[20] The causal relation of fat to cancer does not appear to be as strong as its relation to cardiovascular disease, but it's more than enough to be concerned about. It's particularly difficult in the epidemiologic studies to disentangle the differential effect of low to high fat diets from those due to a diet low or high in fruits and vegetables, which seem to protect against cancer, or other dietary factors. Low-fat diets are usually low in animal products and frequently high in fruits and vegetables. The protective effect of green or yellow-green vegetables against many common cancers, including stomach, esophageal, oral, lung, and bladder, has been established; a similar, smaller effect seems to exist for fruits.[6, 21] The mechanism behind this effect is not known but it is thought that carotenoids, a large group of substances common in plants, may be responsible.[22-27] These include the well-known beta-carotene as well as the lesser known but still common alpha-carotene, canthaxanthin, xanthophyll, lutein, and lycopene. This will be discussed further in the next chapter on dietary supplements.

Fats have something of a double negative effect. There is a good correlation between number of calories consumed and the incidence of many diseases.[28, 29] This might be expected from the data on caloric restriction and life span, but has been seen in experiments quite independent of such severe caloric restriction studies. Fat has over twice the calorie density of protein and carbohydrates. There are four calories per gram of protein or carbohydrate, but nine calories per gram of fat. Alcohol, the only other common source of calories, has seven per gram.* So it becomes harder to keep your total calorie intake within proper limits as fat constitutes a greater percentage of your diet. It also becomes harder to maintain proper body weight, and there seems to be negative health effects of overweight independent of excessive calorie consumption — although these two factors are usually closely related in any practical sense.

It has been suggested that animal protein, or animal product consumption in general, is related to cardiovascular disease, cancer, and other diseases. In an extensive study of over 27,000 Seventh-Day Adventists over a 20-year period,[30] Snowdon reported that "meat consumption was positively associated with mortality because of all causes of death combined (in males), coronary heart disease (in males and females), and diabetes (in males). Egg consumption was positively associated with mortality because of all causes combined (in females), coronary heart disease (in females), and cancers of the colon (in males and females combined) and ovary."

---

*A calorie is a unit of energy, and the units by which the energy extractable from food is usually measured. In the strict scientific use of the term, a calorie is the amount of energy needed to raise the temperature of one gram of water one degree Celsius. What is commonly called a calorie in talking about food (on food package labels, in recipes, etc.), is actually a thousand calories, or a kilocalorie (kcal). This is the unit you will see used in scientific discussions of nutrition. Since this book is intended for a general audience and most people already have a rough idea of how much a calorie is, I will follow the common usage of the term calorie.

This study also found a correlation between milk consumption and prostate cancer mortality, while cheese consumption did not have a clear relationship with any cause of death. Breast cancer and stroke were not related to these products in this study. Consumption of meat, milk, eggs, and cheese was never associated with lower mortality from any cause of death. Evidence from animal studies also suggests that animal products are not conducive to long life. In a life span experiment with rats,[31] animals fed soy protein lived significantly longer (average, or median, life span 844 days) than those fed the same amount of the animal protein casein (average life span 730 days).

There is considerable evidence that dietary fiber helps to prevent several serious diseases, including cancer and heart disease. By definition, *fiber* is the indigestible part of food. It is common in grains, vegetables, and fruits, and essentially absent in meats and animal products. There are several major types of common fibers — cellulose, hemicellulose, lignin, pectins, and gums. Fibers can also be divided into two major groups both by their physical properties and reputed health benefits: insoluble fibers and soluble fibers. The "soluble" here refers to their solubility in water. Insoluble fibers include cellulose, lignin, most types of hemicellulose, and some kinds of pectin. Soluble fibers include most forms of pectin and gums, and some hemicellulose. With the exception of lignin, fibers are carbohydrates, but they cannot be significantly broken down by the body's digestive secretions, as nutritional carbohydrates like starch are. Cellulose is the main structural material of plant cell walls and is therefore present in almost all foods derived from plants. There are significant amounts in many vegetables and most brans. Bran refers to the covering or shell on grains such as wheat, oats, and rye. It is removed along with the germ when whole grains are processed into white flour. Lignin is a woody substance that becomes more abundant in vegetables as they age; it is the only noncarbohydrate fiber. Insoluble fiber, as is found in wheat bran, increases stool bulk and decreases the time it takes for food to move through the digestive tract, thereby exerting a significant natural laxative effect. Table 4.3 lists the different fibers present in a number of common foods. There is considerable evidence that insoluble fibers afford some protection against cancer — primarily colon cancer. This would be no trivial protection: Colorectal cancer is one of the major causes of death in the developed countries. It is the third leading cause of cancer death in both men and women in the United States, ranking behind lung and prostate cancer in men, and lung and breast cancer in women.[32] The mechanism behind this is unknown; it may just be due to the diluting effect fiber has on any carcinogens, or the reduction in the length of time they are in contact with the intestine's cells. It has also been suggested that fiber binds to carcinogens, thereby inactivating them or pulling them out of the body before they can do any harm.

The soluble fibers, as are found in oats and beans, lower total cholesterol and LDL and thereby afford some protection against cardiovascular disease.[33-36] Substantial reductions in blood cholesterol have been obtained by the addition of oats or beans to the diet. In one study,[37] 100 grams of oat bran or 115 grams of beans daily (dry weight of each) lowered cholesterol by 19 percent in men with initial

Food	Total Fiber	Soluble Fiber	Insoluble Fiber		
			Total	Cellulose	Lignin
wheat bran, raw	42.5	3.3	39.2	5.3	5.6
oat bran, raw	17.0	6.5	10.5	1.0	3.5
oatmeal, uncooked	10.6	3.9	6.7	0.6	1.0
oatmeal, cooked	1.9	0.7	1.2	0.1	0.5
bread, Italian	3.8	0.9	2.9	0.9	0.7
apple, unpeeled	2.4	0.3	2.1	0.8	0.2
banana	1.7	0.5	1.2	0.3	0.6
blueberries	2.7	0.3	2.4	0.4	0.9
pear, unpeeled	2.8	0.4	2.4	0.7	0.4
strawberries, fresh	1.8	0.4	1.4	0.4	0.5
asparagus, canned	1.6	0.4	1.2	0.4	0.2
broccoli, raw	3.3	0.3	3.0	1.1	0.3
carrots, raw	2.5	0.2	2.3	0.8	0.1
corn, canned	1.9	0.1	1.8	0.7	0.5
green beans, canned	1.9	0.5	1.4	0.5	0.2
kidney beans, canned	5.2	1.1	4.1	2.2	0.3
peas, canned	4.3	0.3	4.0	2.8	0.1

Table 4.3 Percentage of various fibers in some common foods. These percentages apply to the edible portion of the foods, as noted. Calculated and adapted from USDA data and J. A. Marlett, Content and composition of dietary fiber in 117 frequently consumed foods. *Journal of the American Dietary Association* 92:175–186, 1992.

levels of 260mg/dL or above. LDL was reduced by a somewhat greater percentage. Note, however, that this is a substantial dietary intake; it would amount to nearly 20 percent dry weight of an average diet. When dietary intakes have been closer to practical levels, consisting of a bowl of oat-based cereal per day, small but significant decreases were obtained in cholesterol (2.2 percent) and LDL (4.6 percent) even in people with normal initial cholesterol readings.[38]

A study supposedly showing that oat bran did not in itself lower blood cholesterol received considerable attention in the general news media a few years ago.[39] This was a very small study, involving only 20 people, 16 of whom were women. It compared the effect of adding a small amount of fiber (as oat bran) with the effect of simply replacing dietary fat with a low-fat, low-fiber food like farina. The study reported no significant differences in blood cholesterol in people on these two diets. But oat fiber did lower cholesterol and the changes involved in this experiment were very small. This was because the subjects had normal cholesterol levels to begin with and the amount of fiber or low-fat food added was small. There were other differences between the two groups — namely higher fat and calorie intake in the oat bran group — that could explain the results, but all the numbers involved, including the size of the study, make it almost totally meaningless. As I have mentioned, other, better-designed studies have shown a cholesterol-lowering effect due to oat bran even when the amount added was small,[38] but you have to be careful in the design of the experiment to make it clear in such a case.

Many of the soluble fibers form a gel that inhibits absorption of digested food from the intestine. Guar gum appears particularly effective at this. This property may make these fibers useful in regulating the blood sugar response of diabetics or others with impaired insulin response, or just that of normal people seeking to control their appetite. Such fibers bind to bile in the intestine. The bile is then excreted along with the fiber instead of being reabsorbed, as it normally would. Significant amounts of fat may also be excreted in this way. This process depletes the body's supply of sterol, the molecule used by the liver to make both bile and cholesterol, which may be the reason that soluble fibers decrease blood cholesterol.

But the evidence for protective effects of fiber is not as clear as is sometimes claimed. Some studies have reported no effects; some have reported that fiber increased cancer incidence.[29] Most studies have demonstrated that wheat bran and cellulose exert a protective effect against cancer, whereas some have reported that pectin, corn bran, alfalfa, and a few other fibers enhance cancer. Usually this enhancement was observed with soluble fibers. It is interesting that it is usually the soluble fibers that are fermented most by bacteria in the large intestine. Pectin, which also lowers blood cholesterol and is common in fruits, is fermented almost completely in the colon. In contrast, cellulose is fermented little and lignin not at all. This fermentation can produce considerable intestinal gas and an uncomfortable bloated feeling. It also produces a more acid environment in the colon, which is associated with precancerous conditions.[40] Similar precancerous changes have been reported for tissue in the stomach.[41] There is also some epidemiologic evidence of a correlation between high-fiber diets and the incidence of stomach cancer.[42] The incidence of stomach cancer has undergone a dramatic decrease in the United States and many countries during the past century, but it is still a major cause of death in many parts of the world. In Japan, it is five times as common as in the United States and causes more deaths than all other types of cancer.

In the face of the uncertainty about the effects of various fibers, some best judgments are called for. My own feeling is that the data are clear enough with regard to the beneficial effects of the insoluble, nonfermentable fibers like cellulose and lignin. Wheat bran is one of the most useful sources of these. It is now available in many packaged cereals, or, in lesser amounts, in whole wheat cereals and breads. I have serious reservations about adding large amounts of soluble fiber to a diet. Moderate amounts, however, are probably beneficial, especially when combined with insoluble fiber that speeds their passage through the digestive tract. By moderate amounts, I mean up to roughly 15 grams per day. This is probably as much as most people would care to add in any case. Oat bran, while usually considered a source of soluble fiber, actually has a nice balance between soluble and insoluble (Table 4.3).

Happily, the recommendations from the several dietary practices we have just discussed point in the same direction. Increasing the fiber content of your diet is likely to decrease your consumption of total fats and your total calories. Fruits and vegetables have relatively few calories, contain substantial quantities of fiber, and probably contain inherent protective substances. Whole grains have similar beneficial qualities. The conclusions in terms of practical changes to make in your diet would be similar: Replace the high-fat foods with lots of grains, especially whole grains, fruits, and vegetables. Appendix 2 lists the nutritional content of most of the best foods in terms of the criteria we have just discussed. While whole grains are preferable because of their additional fiber and other nutrients, there is nothing actually wrong with products made from refined white flour. White bread, spaghetti, farina, bagels, and similar products are usually quite low in fat as they are made almost entirely from white flour, which has a negligible fat content. Occasionally you will see these products made with added fat and cholesterol (fresh spaghetti is sometimes made with eggs, and there are egg bagels), but these are the exception and are easily avoided. One also has to be careful of high-fat additions to these foods, such as meat sauces to spaghetti, and butter or margarine to bread. Low-fat alternatives are almost always available.

Nuts are sometimes suggested as a significant source of nutrients. Nuts do contain considerable amounts of fiber, protein, and other nutrients. But they are murderously high in fat and calories (with the exception of chestnuts; water chestnuts, by the way, are not a nut but a vegetable). They therefore can be included in a healthy diet to a minor extent, but not as a staple.

It's probably best to reduce fat to as low a percentage of the diet as possible, and to use monounsaturated fat like olive oil whenever possible. Humans do have a requirement for three unsaturated fatty acids (linoleic, linolenic, and arachidonic), but only linoleic acid is a true dietary essential fatty acid because the body can synthesize the others from it.[43] The adult RDA is estimated to be about three to six grams a day.[44] Fortunately, linoleic acid is one of the most common fatty acids in plants. It constitutes 58 percent of corn oil, 55 percent of wheat germ oil, 51 percent of soybean oil, 20 percent of canola oil, and 8 percent of olive oil (USDA Nutrient Database). Even oats have a significant amount. One tablespoon (15mL) of soybean oil contains seven grams, which exceeds the RDA. You can also easily exceed the RDA just from eating a reasonable amount of whole grains like wheat.

The question is sometimes asked: If we replace meat, eggs, cheese, and the like with vegetables, fruits, and grains, will we get enough protein? Won't we be overloading with carbohydrates? The U.S. Recommended Dietary Allowance for protein is 0.8 grams of protein per kilogram of body weight per day.[44] This amounts to 56g for a 70kg (154 lb) adult. These guidelines recommend that 15 to 20 percent of the calories in your diet come from protein, but they further state that, since there are no benefits and possibly some risks in consuming more protein than needed, no more than twice that amount (i.e., 1.6g per kg of body weight) be consumed. These recommendations are not the minimum requirement for protein but allow for a significant safety margin. But would additional protein above the minimum be beneficial? To the contrary, there are good theoretical and experimental reasons for thinking it would be harmful. Protein — or actually the amino acid components of protein — must be metabolized in the liver and excreted by the kidneys. Normally, there is no problem with this. However, it has been suggested that over longer periods of time a protein intake significantly higher than normal or needed could strain and gradually damage these organs.[45, 46] Animals fed high-protein diets have undergone this overload effect, seen in enlargement of their livers and kidneys. There is also actual life span evidence from a study of rats that compared the effects of caloric restriction, protein restriction without caloric restriction, and normal feeding.[47] Animals fed the same number of calories but only 60 percent of the protein of controls lived about 13 percent longer. (This was still less than rats that consumed 60 percent of the calories of the control group.) This and similar studies suggest that there is certainly nothing beneficial in eating more protein than necessary, and it is probably even harmful.

Table 4.4 lists the percentage of calories from protein in a number of common vegetables, grains, and fruits. One can see that while fruits are rather low in protein, many vegetables and grains have a percentage within and even above the 15 to 20 percent guideline. The items in this table were chosen as typical examples, but if one calculates an average including most common vegetables, one still gets about 27 percent calories from protein. A rough average for the common grains is 15 percent. The point is that protein malnutrition is just not going to be a serious problem on any kind of reasonable diet.

Food	Percent Calories from Protein
asparagus	40.0
broccoli	42.6
corn	12.2
lettuce, romaine	40.5
peas	26.7
potatoes	10.5
squash, zucchini	33.1
oats, rolled	16.7
spaghetti, cooked	19.8
wheat, whole, flour	16.2
wheat, white, flour	11.3
apricots	11.7
oranges	8.0
peaches	6.5

Table 4.4 Percentage of calories from protein in selected vegetables, grains, and fruits. Source: U.S. Dept. of Agriculture Nutrient Database.

The other question that arises is about the quality of the protein. Proteins are composed of various amino acids; it is these that the body uses to build its own proteins. If some of the essential amino acids are missing (there are nine so-called essential amino acids that humans must have supplied in the diet), this synthesis cannot take place. Plant sources are frequently low in one or more of the essential amino acids. This requirement can be met by including some acceptable, low-fat animal protein or by a variety of plant protein. Just three cups of skim milk (about 0.7 liter; a reasonable amount if you total the milk in cereal, coffee, tea, etc.) provide half the RDA. This is not really a problem if you eat a variety of foods. What is low in one food is likely to be high in others, so that the overall protein intake is balanced. Also, some plant sources such as legumes (e.g., kidney beans, soybeans, peas, lentils) do have protein with a well-balanced amino acid composition. As was mentioned earlier, there is some evidence that vegetable protein is healthier than animal protein; in one experiment, rats fed soy protein lived significantly longer than rats fed the same amount of animal protein.[31] High consumption of protein, especially animal protein, also increases the body's excretion of calcium; this can contribute to osteoporosis (loss of bone mass).

My own feeling is that the RDA for protein is somewhat high; in fact, the RDA is formulated to allow for a margin of safety.[44] While I can see the reasons for this, if you judge protein intake by what is most likely to lead to a longer and still healthy life, my best judgment would be to set the percent of calories from protein to at most the low side of the RDA's 15 to 20 percent.

The protein requirements that we have been discussing are for normal adults. Special circumstances may require greater amounts. Protein needs in pregnancy and lactation are up to 15 percent higher than normal. Young children require more protein for growth. Those convalescing from a serious illness, surgery, or trauma may also need more. Athletics, even strenuous athletic activities, do not generally add to our protein requirements unless it involves the actual buildup of tissue as in weight lifting and bodybuilding.[44]

A number of other dietary components have come into question as either positive or negative factors. Some will be dealt with in the next chapter on supplements. Sugar, salt, alcohol, calcium, and caffeine will be discussed here, since they are more like components of an ordinary diet.

Let me first briefly review what sugars are. Carbohydrates, one of the broad nutritional groupings, include the simple sugars and molecules that consist of one of the simple sugars linked together to form a chain. The kind of binding between the sugars, what type of sugar, and whether the chain has branches determine what type of carbohydrate is formed; this ranges from cellulose, which is completely indigestible, to common starch. The long chains are therefore called polysaccharides (poly=many, for many sugars). The single links on the chain, the simple sugars, are called monosaccharides; the most common of these are glucose, fructose, and galactose. Glucose (also called dextrose) is the sugar found in your blood, and common in many fruits, honey, and other natural products. Fructose, or fruit sugar, as the name implies, is abundant in fruits, along with other sugars. Galactose, the least common, is a component of milk sugar. These three monosaccharides bind together two at a time in various combinations to form disaccharides. The most common of these are 1) sucrose (glucose+fructose), which is ordinary table sugar; 2) maltose (glucose+glucose), frequently formed as polysaccharides are broken down into smaller chains; and 3) lactose (glucose+galactose), the sugar that constitutes the carbohydrate in milk. Fructose is the sweetest of the sugars, followed in order by sucrose, glucose, maltose, and lactose. Carbohydrates are abundant in almost all foods derived from plants, either as the simple sugars, as polysaccharides like starch, or both. Digestion of carbohydrates is rapid and begins in fact in the mouth, where enzymes in saliva start the process. During digestion, they are broken down into their component simple sugars and absorbed into the bloodstream as such. Fructose is absorbed much more slowly than glucose, but is converted to glucose soon after absorption into the blood. Glucose is then utilized throughout the body for energy or converted into the body's own storage polysaccharide until needed. Our bodies normally produce the hormone insulin, which drives glucose from the blood into cells whenever the blood level becomes high. On the face of it, then, it does not seem that the simple sugars would have any different effects on the body than more complex carbohydrates. However, some people have hypothesized that simple sugars are absorbed very quickly into the bloodstream, since they do not have to be broken down much further, if at all, by digestion. It was suggested that this could lead to a rapid, sharp increase in blood sugar levels, which would in turn have harmful effects in terms of the development of heart disease and possibly diabetes.[48-50] There is some evidence that persistently high *blood* sugar is detrimental. Diabetics, who cannot regulate blood glucose very well, have various problems, among which are symptoms of accelerated aging. A sharp insulin response due to absorption from the intestine of large amounts of sugar was suggested as another possible and reasonable mechanism for the supposed harmful effects. However, measurements of blood glucose in people after they consumed various types of foods gave some rather surprising results.[51] The rise in blood sugar after eating pure sucrose was not particularly great, and was less than that from many common vegetables like carrots or potatoes. Even sugar-rich foods like ice cream did not produce a high response. The greatest rise in blood sugar came not from candy and ice cream but from the simple sugars glucose and maltose, as you might expect, followed by honey and several vegetables. Apparently, simple sugars cause a sharp increase in blood sugar only when consumed alone. They do not have any particularly dramatic effect when eaten as part of or with other foods.

A few studies have attempted to find a link between sugar and cancer, particularly colorectal cancer.[52] They are not very convincing, especially since sugars are totally absorbed in the small intestine. Starch may have, if anything, the opposite effect.[53]

While a few scientists continue to believe that dietary sugar is a major factor in the development of cardiovascular and possibly other serious diseases,[50] most studies have not found evidence for such a link,[54] and the overwhelming consensus is that sugar does not constitute a significant health risk when consumed in moderation. This is the position taken by the American Dietetic Association[56] and the Royal Society of Medicine.[57] I agree with this general view. There is scant evidence to implicate sugar to disease. It would be very difficult to see why sugars would have effects so much different from other carbohydrates when they and complex carbohydrates rapidly take the same form after ingestion and are absorbed at much the same rate.

Sugars, by the way, do not have any more calories than any other carbohydrate; it is still four calories per gram. They are a more concentrated source of calories only in the sense that, for refined dry sugar for example, there is no associated water and no fiber, so that a gram of table sugar would be very close to an actual gram of carbohydrate, containing four calories, whereas a gram of apple is mostly water, plus some fiber, and so has only 0.6 calories. Because of this, refined sugars are frequently said to have "empty calories"; they provide no other nutrients, fiber, or anything of benefit. For this and other reasons, it is probably wise to limit refined sugar intake to "moderate" levels. It has been suggested that the current average consumption in the United States of 80 grams a day of total sugars, including naturally occurring sugars (but minus lactose, which has quite different characteristics), while at the high end of what can be considered moderate, is still safe.[55] It is also prudent to avoid sharp increases and high levels of blood glucose. This can most practically be done by combining the carbohydrates most likely to cause a sharp rise, like sucrose and glucose, with foods containing fiber, protein, or fat. There is little reason to choose one sugar over another from a nutritional standpoint. Brown sugar, turbinado sugar, and raw sugar are almost identical to ordinary table sugar: They are all sucrose. Fructose is slightly sweeter and is absorbed much more slowly; there is some evidence that it raises blood cholesterol and triglyceride levels, but the reports to date have been too inconsistent to draw any conclusions about this. Honey consists mainly of glucose and fructose, plus water and negligible amounts of other nutrients. High fructose corn syrup, widely used now in place of sucrose to sweeten soft drinks and other packaged foods, is also primarily fructose and glucose.

The artificial sweeteners aspartame and saccharine are also safe and useful in this respect.[55] Aspartame (marketed under the brand name NutraSweet) especially has been thoroughly studied. It is in fact essentially just a combination of two naturally occurring amino acids (the components of protein). The criticism that is sometimes heard — that it is dangerous because methanol (wood alcohol) is produced during its digestion — is absurd. Far more methanol is produced from a glass of tomato juice than from the same amount of aspartame-sweetened diet soda.[57] Such trivial amounts are no cause for concern.

Salt, or sodium, is often mentioned as one of the dietary factors involved in the control and prevention of hypertension (high blood pressure), itself a very significant risk factor in the development of heart disease, atherosclerosis, stroke, kidney disease, and possibly other serious diseases. However, dietary salt is a significant factor only in certain people, not everyone, at least not within reasonable limits. Most people, even those with hypertension, will have little or no change in blood pressure in response to a reduction in dietary salt.[58, 59] Given this, it does not seem justifiable to recommend a salt-restricted diet for everyone. Blood pressure is something that should be routinely monitored in any case. Your doctor will measure it as part of any visit, and you can buy an inexpensive pressure gauge and cuff and easily learn to do it yourself. To determine if you are salt sensitive, you would decrease your dietary salt intake for a month or so while monitoring the effect on blood pressure. It is best to take a number of readings over several days at least, since other factors can affect blood pressure. The reduction in salt intake can be achieved by eliminating salty foods like potato chips and decreasing the amount of salt added to food during preparation, cooking, and at the table. How best to achieve a reduction depends to a large extent on your normal diet. That is, what are the high-salt items you eat at present and what can you do without? If you find that salt reduction does lower your blood pressure significantly, it would be wise to incorporate permanently as much of a reduction as you can live with. Even if your blood pressure is not high now, it's been found that the rise in blood pressure that usually occurs with age can be eliminated in salt-sensitive people by reducing their sodium consumption.

I said that, for non-salt-sensitive people, dietary salt had little or no effect within "reasonable" limits. Populations with significantly higher than normal sodium intakes, as in Japan, do have a relatively high incidence of stroke, even though the cardiovascular disease rate is low, and Japan has the highest life expectancy in the world.[32, 60]

While dietary sodium can raise blood pressure, potassium, calcium and magnesium can lower it.[58, 59, 61] In fact, these minerals may be associated with the prevention of several serious diseases. Calcium may reduce the risk of colorectal cancer.[62] Calcium and potassium can help prevent osteoporosis, or loss of overall bone mass.[63-65] This process may begin as early as the 20s in women. It continues throughout life, accelerating after menopause. A similar process occurs in men, but usually not beginning until their 40s or 50s, and usually of lesser severity. It has been estimated that at least 10 percent of women over 50 years of age suffer from bone loss severe enough to cause fractures and major orthopedic problems. Other studies have estimated that 25 to 30 percent of postmenopausal women have significant osteoporosis.[66] The cessation of hormone production at menopause is known to be a major causative factor in this disease. Bone loss accelerates to 2 percent to 5 percent per year immediately before and for about ten years after menopause. Dietary calcium alone cannot stop this loss of bone mass, whereas estrogen (the female hormone) plus calcium can completely prevent it in most cases. In addition to diet, prevention and treatment of osteoporosis involves other factors that will be discussed later.

Calcium, of course, is essential to the formation of bone, making up 38 percent of its mineral composition. The body of a 70kg (154 lb.) adult contains 1.2kg (2.6 lbs.) of calcium, 99 percent of it in the skeleton. A dietary deficiency of this mineral, or a metabolic imbalance (greater excretion than intake) can be crucial to the development of osteoporosis. Bone is constantly being broken down and reformed, even in adults. About 700mg of calcium enter and exit the skeleton every day; this is why an adequate calcium intake must be maintained throughout life. Potassium is thought to reduce excretion of calcium, while phosphorus increases it.[67, 68] Dietary surveys suggest that the average postmenopausal woman in the United States ingests only about 60 percent of the recommended allowance of 800 milligrams of calcium per day. It has been estimated that this degree of calcium imbalance could lead to a bone loss of about 1.5 percent per year.[69] Poor absorption of dietary calcium in postmenopausal women exacerbates this problem. A number of experts in this area have recommended a daily intake of 1,200 to 1,500mg of (elemental) calcium per day. Milk and milk products have the highest calcium content of all foods. Milk (whole or skim) contains about 300mg per cup (237mL). The calcium content of cheese ranges from 90mg per 100g (3.5 ounces) of cottage, to 1,140mg per 100g of parmesan; most cheeses, of course, have much too high a fat content to serve as dietary staples. It would take over a quart of milk a day to obtain 1,200 to 1,500mg, if you obtained no calcium from other sources. However, around 40 percent of a typical person's calcium intake comes from nondairy sources. A calcium supplement is a reasonable alternative if you feel that you cannot obtain these recommended amounts in your diet. Potassium is widely distributed in foods. Many fruits, especially bananas, apricots, melons, peaches, and oranges, are good sources; squash, tomatoes, and rhubarb also have substantial amounts. Magnesium is also found in a wide variety of foods; raw wheat bran contains 611mg per 100g, whole wheat 130mg per 100g, and spinach 80mg per 100g, but many other common foods have respectable amounts.

Vitamin D is essential for proper calcium absorption and metabolism, but a deficiency of this vitamin is not thought to be one of the major causes of osteoporosis in the general population. Vitamin D can have serious toxic effects in high doses. The RDA is currently set at 5µg (200 I.U.) for those 25 years and older. The prudent course is to insure an intake at around 5 to 10µg (200 to 400 I.U.), but not more than that. *Excessive* caffeine or coffee consumption (note that I emphasize *excessive*) may be related to osteoporosis. Caffeine is a weak diuretic (increases the volume of urine) and increases urinary excretion of sodium, magnesium, and calcium.[70, 71] Epidemiologic studies of young women have found no correlation between caffeine consumption and bone density, but some of the studies on older women have reported adverse effects of caffeine on calcium excretion and bone.[70] Up to about 500mL (2.1 cups; one measuring cup equals 237mL, about one normal-size coffee mug) of coffee a day seems to have little if any effect even in older women, but 1,000mL (4.2 cups) or more could result in significantly greater calcium excretion. It is thought that young women can compensate for disturbances in their metabolism caused by caffeine, whereas older women cannot. Adequate amounts of dietary calcium can negate the extra excretion.[70]

Attempts to link coffee or caffeine to other serious diseases like cancer and heart disease have been generally unsuccessful. An extensive study in Norway involving nearly 14,000 men and 3,000 women found *no* significant correlations between consumption and total mortality, or death from any major cause, including any form of cancer or heart disease.[72] There were actually several statistically significant *inverse* relationships between coffee and several types of cancer (i.e., the coffee drinkers had lower incidence of those cancers), but the differences of any kind were small. Almost all recent studies have found that coffee and caffeine have no effect on blood lipids or blood pressure, at least within fairly high levels of consumption of up to a liter a day (4.2 cups).[73, 74] Decaffeinated coffee does not seem to afford any health benefits over regular; in fact, several studies have reported slight negative effects from decaffeinated when there were none associated with regular coffee. My own assessment is that the two or three cups of coffee a day that most of us drink pose no health risk, even when combined with a similar amount of tea and cola, both of which contain lesser amounts of caffeine. (Cocoa and chocolates contain trivial amounts.) While tea leaves contain more caffeine than coffee grounds, much more is extracted into the liquid in making coffee. The caffeine content of all three beverages varies widely, depending upon method of preparation, brand, brewing time, and so on. Very roughly, coffee has about twice as much caffeine as tea, which has about twice as much as the average cola.

Colas and other sodas also contain phosphoric acid, a source of phosphorus. As I mentioned earlier, phosphorus increases excretion of calcium. This is something to keep in mind, but it generally will not be a problem unless a person's calcium intake is low or overall calcium balance is marginal.

Heavy consumption of alcoholic beverages is related to increased mortality from a number of causes. But epidemiologic evidence has been building that light to moderate alcohol consumption is associated with decreased risk of heart disease, and probably overall lower mortality, although the latter is somewhat controversial. One such study of 20 industrialized countries[75] examined consumption of fat, cholesterol, types of fat (saturated or unsaturated), alcohol, and type of alcohol (beer, wine, or spirits). As one might expect, there was a strong correlation between heart disease and saturated fat, and a slight inverse correlation with polyunsaturated fat. It found an even stronger inverse correlation between total alcohol consumption and the death rate from heart disease. France has received the most publicity in this regard, with a heart disease rate far below the United States and the United Kingdom, despite nearly equal saturated fat consumption, but the correlation fits fairly well for most countries if all three factors (saturated and polyunsaturated fat and alcohol consumption) are taken into account. Other studies of populations within the same country (e.g., the United States and New Zealand) have reached the same conclusion: Light to moderate alcohol consumption reduces the risk of heart disease.[76, 77] The U.S. (California) study examined 129,000 persons from diverse backgrounds and corrected for other various confounding factors such as smoking, body weight, and so on. It found that heavy drinkers, especially women, were at greater risk of death from noncardiovascular causes, but lighter drinkers (one to two drinks a day) had a decreased risk of heart disease and a slightly decreased overall mortality. A "drink" was defined in this study, as it usually is, as either a standard 12-ounce (350-mL) bottle of beer, or a glassful of wine, or the usual, smaller glass of spirits. All have, very roughly, the same amount of alcohol on average. The New Zealand study of several hundred men and women found that, up to more than 56 drinks per week, people had a 40 percent reduction in fatal and nonfatal heart disease compared to those who never drank.

The mechanism through which alcohol protects against heart disease is not known with any certainty; regular consumption of small amounts of alcohol increases blood HDL levels (the "good cholesterol"), but other effects, such as dilation of the blood vessels and the prevention of blood clots, may also be at work.

The issue becomes more clouded when total mortality is considered, especially for women. Even moderate drinkers have higher mortality from cirrhosis of the liver,[77] although death from this is still rare, so it does not affect the overall mortality rate much. For women, light drinkers had a slightly higher cancer death rate. Other studies[78] suggest a link between breast cancer and drinking. High consumption of alcohol is associated with increased risk of several cancers, particularly of the mouth, larynx, and esophagus.[79] Again, this is *high* consumption; it is doubtful whether light to moderate consumption increases cancer risk in itself when other confounding factors are accounted for. Ethanol (ordinary drinking alcohol) is not carcinogenic in itself. It is thought that alcohol can act as a cancer promoter, enhancing the cancer-causing effects of other substances. This is believed to be true particularly for ethanol and smoking.

Many substances found in food (usually in trace amounts) are known or suspected carcinogens. Aflavtoxins are highly carcinogenic toxins produced by a fungus that grows on peanuts and many other foods. This fungus is widely distributed and has been found in animal feed and fish meal. Aflavtoxins are known to cause tumors in the livers of rats, fish, mice, monkeys, and several other species. They are quite toxic directly in high enough doses. Fungi and molds, which can grow on a variety of foods, produce a number of suspected carcinogens. Many other potentially dangerous substances, like the known human carcinogen benzene, occur naturally in many foods. Bruce Ames, inventor of the Ames test, which screens for potential carcinogens, published a survey a few years ago[80] on just how widespread they are. Black pepper, mushrooms, cottonseed oil (and products such as eggs, meat, and milk from animals fed cottonseed), potatoes, fava beans, and browned or burned food all contain significant levels of substances that are known carcinogens in animals, suspected carcinogens in humans, or both. Generally speaking, these do not warrant completely avoiding any specific foods. Our bodies do have mechanisms to deal with and detoxify a wide variety of potentially harmful substances. It is prudent to avoid foods that have begun to go stale, certainly if there is evidence of any mold or fungus on them, but this is something that's advisable and is commonly done in any case. Some compounds that warrant attention can be formed during the processing of food. Nitrites used in curing meats can react to form N-nitroso compounds, some of which cause cancer in animals. Charred or fried meats especially are thought to be sources of these. The actual levels of suspected carcinogens are low; however, if such foods were consumed regularly, it's quite possible that a cumulative effect would occur. In fact, the epidemiologic evidence shows just such an effect in several cases. Consumption of salted, pickled, or smoked foods has been linked to cancer of the esophagus, stomach, and liver, diseases that are almost always fatal. Cancers of the stomach and liver are uncommon in the United States but are major killers in some parts of the world. Liver cancer is widespread in many areas of Africa, China, and Southeast Asia. Stomach cancer used to be common in the United States and developed countries, but its incidence declined steadily and significantly through the twentieth century. It is still common in China, Japan, and South America, though it's not clear whether this is due to consumption of salted, pickled, and smoked foods, the lack of fresh fruits and vegetables containing protective substances such as vitamin C, or to other factors.[81]

I have occasionally been asked whether spices are potentially harmful or beneficial. Spices include a highly diverse group of substances, so one can't generalize too much. A number of common spices are antioxidants. In a survey of 32 spices in simple oil-in-water emulsions, many were found to protect the emulsion from oxidation. Cloves were the most effective; allspice, cinnamon, ginger, mace, nutmeg, oregano, rosemary, sage, thyme, and several others all had significant antioxidant activity.[82, 83] They therefore may well help protect food from oxidative damage, and it's thought they were in fact used as crude preservatives in past centuries; it's unknown whether this effect would continue after consumption. Garlic and onions (spices from related plants) have been reported to have several beneficial effects. Garlic may inhibit cancer and atherosclerosis, but the quantities needed for any significant effects are beyond normal dietary levels. One or two spices, like black pepper, contain carcinogens,[80] that are probably not significant at ordinary dietary levels.

References to Chapter Four

1. D.L. Tribble, R.M. Krauss: HDL and coronary artery disease. *Adv Intern Med* 38:1–29, 1993.

2. P.A. Romm, C.E. Green, K. Reagan, C.E. Rackley: Relation of serum lipoprotein cholesterol levels to presence and severity of angiographic coronary artery disease. *Am J Cardiol* 67:479–483, 1991.

3. P.M. Kris-Etherton, D. Krummel, M.E. Russel et al.: The effect of diet on plasma lipids, lipoproteins, and coronary heart disease. *J Am Diet Assoc* 88:1373–1400, 1988.

4. A.T. Diplock: Antioxidant nutrients and disease prevention: an overview. *Am J Clin Nutr* 53:189S–193S, 1991.

5. K. Imaida, S. Fukushima, K. Inone et al.: Modifying effects of concomitant treatment with butylated hydroxyanisole or butylated hydroxytoluene on N,N-dibutylnitrosamine-induced liver, forestomach and urinary bladder carcinogenesis in F344 male rats. *Cancer Lett* 43:167–172, 1988.

6. J.H. Weisburger: Nutritional approach to cancer prevention with emphasis on vitamins, antioxidants, and carotenoids. *Am J Clin Nutr* 53:226S–237S, 1991.

7. D.M. Dreon, K.M. Vranizan, R.M. Krauss et al.: The effects of polyunsaturated vs. monounsaturated fat on plasma lipoproteins. *JAMA* 263:2462–2466, 1990.

8. G.M. Wardlaw, J.M. Snook, M. Lin et al.: Serum lipid and apolipoprotein concentrations in healthy men on diets enriched in either canola oil or safflower oil. *Am J Clin Nutr* 54:104–110, 1991.

9. F.H. Mattson: A changing role for dietary monounsaturated fatty acids. *J Am Diet Assoc* 89:387–391, 1989.

10. C. LaVecchia, R.E. Harris, E.L. Wyander: Comparative epidemiology of cancer between the United States and Italy. *Cancer Res* 48:7285–7293, 1988.

11. L.H. Kushi, E.B. Lenart, W.C. Willet: Health implications of Mediterranean diets in light of contemporary knowledge. 2. Meat, wine, fats, and oils. *Am J Clin Nutr* 61(suppl): 1416S–1427S, 1995.

12. A.P. Simopoulis: Omega-3 fatty acids in health and disease and in growth and development. *Am J Clin Nutr* 54:438–463, 1991.

13. D.M. Davidson, K.V. Gold: Cardiovascular effects of n-3 fatty acids. *N Engl J Med* 319:580, 1988.

14. A. Leaf, P.C. Weber: Cardiovascular effects of n-3 fatty acids. *N Engl J Med* 318:549–557, 1988.

15. D. Rudkin, C. Felix: *The Omega-3 Phenomenon.* Rawson Associates, New York, 1987.

16. M.J. Gonzales et al.: Lipid peroxidation products are elevated in fish oil diets even in the presence of added antioxidants. *J Nutr* 122:2190–2195, 1992.

17. M.J. Wargovich, A.R. Bear, P.J. Hu, H. Sumiyoshi: Dietary factors and colorectal cancer. *Gastroenterol Clin North Am* 17:727–745, 1988.

18. C. Clifford, B. Kramer: Diet as risk and therapy for cancer. *Med Clin North Am* 77:725–744, 1993.

19. W.C. Willett et al.: Dietary fat and fiber in relation to risk of breast cancer: an 8-year follow-up. *JAMA* 268:2037–2044, 1992.

20. L.N. Kolonel, J.H. Hankin, J. Lee et al.: Nutrient intakes in relation to cancer incidence in Hawaii. *Br J Cancer* 44:332–339, 1981.

21. E. Negri, C. LaVecchia, S. Franceschi et al.: Vegetable and fruit consumption and cancer risk. *Int J Cancer* 48:350–354, 1991.

22. A. Bendich: Symposium conclusions: biological actions of carotenoids. *J Nutr* 119:135–136, 1989.

23. N.I. Krinsky: Carotenoids and cancer in animal models. *J Nutr* 119:123–126, 1989.

24. R.C. Moon: Comparative aspects of carotenoids and retinoids as chemoprotective agents for cancer. *J Nutr* 119:127–134, 1989.

25. K.A. Steinmetz, J.D. Potter: Vegetables, fruit, and cancer: I. epidemiology. *Cancer Causes and Control* 325–357, 1991.

26. K.A. Steinmetz, J.D. Potter: Vegetables, fruit, and cancer: II. mechanisms. *Cancer Causes and Control* 427–441, 1991.

27. R.E. Ziegler: A review of the epidemiologic evidence that carotenoids reduce the risk of cancer. *J Nutr* 119:116–122, 1989.

28. D. Albanes: Caloric intake, body weight and cancer: a review. *Nutr Cancer* 9:199–217, 1987.

29. D. Kritchevsky: Dietary guidelines: the rationale for intervention. *Cancer* 72:1011–1014, 1993.

30. D.A. Snowdon: Animal product consumption and mortality because of all causes combined, coronary heart disease, stroke, diabetes, and cancer in Seventh-day Adventists. *Am J Clin Nutr* 48:739–748, 1988.

31. K. Iwasaki, C.A. Gleiser, E.J. Masoro et al.: The influence of dietary protein source on longevity and age-related disease processes of Fischer rats. *J Gerontol* 43:B2–12, 1988.

32. National Center for Health Statistics: *Health, United States 1993.* Public Health Service, Hyattsville, MD, 1994.

33. J.W. Anderson, N.J. Gustafson: Hypocholesterolemic effects of oat and bean products. *Am J Clin Nutr* 48:749–753, 1988.

34. H. Kashtan et al.: Wheat-bran and oat-bran supplements effects on blood lipids and lipoproteins. *Am J Clin Nutr* 55:976–980, 1992.

35. J.W. Anderson et al.: Bakery products lower serum cholesterol concentrations in hypercholesterolemic men. *Am J Clin Nutr* 54:836–840, 1991.

36. F.L. Shinnick et al.: Oat fiber: composition versus physiologic function in rats. *J Nutr* 118:144–151, 1988.

37. J.W. Anderson et al.: Hypocholesterolemic effects of oat-bran or bean intake for hypercholesterolemic men. *Am J Clin Nutr* 40: 1146–1155, 1984.

38. N. Poulter, C.L. Chang, A. Cuff, C. Poulter et al.: Lipid profiles after the daily consumption of an oat-based cereal: a controlled crossover trial. *Am J Clin Nutr* 58:66–69, 1993.

39. J.F. Swain et al.: Comparison of the effects of oat bran and low-fiber wheat on serum lipoprotein levels and blood pressure. *N Engl J Med* 322:147–152, 1990.

40. L.R. Jacobs: Role of dietary factors in cell replication and colon cancer. *Am J Clin Nutr* 48:775–779, 1988.

41. J.R. Lupton, L.R. Jacobs: Fiber supplementation results in expanded proliferative zones in rat gastric mucosa. *Am J Clin Nutr* 46:980–984, 1987.

42. M. Hakama, E.A. Saxen: Cereal consumption and gastric cancer. *Int J Cancer* 2:265–268, 1967.

43. S.R. Williams: *Basic Nutrition and Diet Therapy,* Mosby-Year Book, St Louis, 1992.

44. National Research Council, Food and Nutrition Board: *Recommended Dietary Allowances, ed. 10.* National Academy Press, Washington, DC, 1989.

45. J.G. Chopra, A.L. Forbes, J.P. Habicht: Protein in the U.S. diet. *J Am Diet Assoc* 72:253–258, 1978.

46. B.M. Brenner, T.W. Meyer, T.H. Hostetter: Dietary protein intake and the progressive nature of kidney disease. *N Eng J Med* 307:652–659, 1982.

47. E.J. Masoro, C.A. McMahan: Nutritional influences on aging of Fischer 344 rats: I. physical, metabolic, and longevity characteristics. *J Gerontol* 40:657–670, 1985.

48. J. Yudkin: Sucrose, coronary heart disease and obesity: do hormones provide a link? *Am Heart J* 115:493–498, 1988.

49. J. Yudkin: Dietary factors in atherosclerosis. *Lipids* 13:370–372, 1978.

50. J. Yudkin: Report of the COMA panel on dietary sugar and human disease: discussion paper. *J Royal Soc Med* 83:627–628, 1990.

51. D.J.A. Jenkins et al.: Glycemic index of foods: a physiological basis for carbohydrate exchange. *Am J Clin Nutr* 34:362–366, 1981.

52. C. LaVecchia, S. Franceschi, P. Dolara et al.: Refined-sugar intake and the risk of colorectal cancer in humans. *Int J Cancer* 55:386–389, 1993.

53. G. Caderni, F. Bianchina, P. Dolara, D. Kriebel: Proliferation activity in the colon of the mouse and its modulation by dietary starch, fat and cellulose. *Cancer Res* 49:1655–1659, 1989.

54. W.H. Glinsmann, H. Irausquin, Y.K. Park: Evaluation of health aspects of sugars contained in carbohydrate sweeteners. *J Nutr* 116:S5–S216, 1986.

56. Position of the American Dietetic Association: use of nutritive and nonnutritive sweeteners. *J Am Diet Assoc* 93:816–821, 1993.

57. Report of the Panel on Dietary Sugars: *Dietary sugars and human disease.* HMSO, London, 1989.

57. H.H. Butchko, F.N. Kotsonis: Acceptable intake vs actual intake: the aspartame example. *J Am Coll Nutr* 10:258–266, 1991.

58. P.P. Stein, H.R. Black: The role of diet in the genesis and treatment of hypertension. *Med Clin North Am* 77(4):831–847, 1993.

59. M. Muntzel, T. Drueke: A comprehensive review of the salt and blood pressure relationship. *Am J Hyperten* 5:1S–42S, 1992.

60. L.J. Beilin: Dietary salt and risk factors for cardiovascular disease. *Kidney Int Suppl* 37:S90–S96, 1992.

61. E.M. Mervaala et al.: Beneficial effects of a potassium- and magnesium-enriched salt. *Hypertension* 19:535–540, 1992.

62. Anonymous: Calcium and vitamin D intakes influence the risk of bowel cancer in men. *Nutr Rev* 43:170–172, 1985.

63. M.S. Calvo: Dietary phosphorus, calcium metabolism and bone loss. *J Nutr* 123:1627–1633, 1993.

64. M.P. Harward: Nutritive therapies for osteoporosis: the role of calcium. *Med Clin North Am* 77:889–898, 1993.

65. L. Massey: Dietary factors influencing calcium and bone metabolism: introduction. *J Nutr* 123:1609–1610, 1993.

66. L.V. Avioli: Calcium supplementation and osteoporosis. In: *Nutritional Intervention in the Aging Process*, H.J. Armbrect, J.M. Prendergast, R.M. Loe, eds. Springer-Verlag, New York, 1984.

67. J. Lemann, J.A. Pleuss, R.W. Gray: Potassium causes calcium retention in healthy adults. *J Nutr* 123:1623–1626, 1993.

68. S. Calvo: Dietary phosphorus, calcium metabolism and bone loss. *J Nutr* 123:1627–1633, 1993.

69. R.P. Heaney, R.R. Recker, P.D. Saville: Menopausal changes in calcium balance performance. *J Lab Clin Med* 92:953–963, 1978.

70. L.K. Massey, S.J. Whiting: Caffeine, urinary calcium, calcium metabolism and bone. *J Nutr* 123:1611–1614, 1993.

71. C. Hasling et al.: Calcium metabolism in postmenopausal osteoporotic women is determined by dietary calcium and coffee intake. *J Nutr* 122:1119–1126, 1992.

72. B.K. Jacobsen, E. Bjelke, G. Kvale, I. Heuch: Coffee drinking, mortality, and cancer incidence: results from a Norwegian prospective study. *JNCI* 76:823–831, 1986.

73. A.A. Bak, D.E. Grobee: Caffeine, blood pressure and serum lipids. *Am J Clin Nutr* 53:971–975, 1991.

74. H.R. Superko et al.: Caffeinated and decaffeinated coffee effects on plasma lipoprotein cholesterol, apolipoproteins, and lipase activity: a controlled, randomized trial. *Am J Clin Nutr* 54:599–605, 1991.

75. D.M. Hegsted, L.M. Ausman: Diet, alcohol and coronary heart disease in men. *J Nutr* 118:1184–1189, 1988.

76. R. Jackson, R. Scragg, R. Beaglehole: Alcohol consumption and risk of coronary heart disease. *Br Med J* 303:211–216, 1991.

77. A. Klatsky, M.A. Armstrong, G.D. Friedman: Alcohol and mortality. *Ann Int Med* 117:646–654, 1992.

78. W.C. Willett, M.J. Stampfer, M.J. Colditz et al.: Moderate alcohol consumption and risk of breast cancer. *N Engl J Med* 316:1174–1180, 1987.

79. A.J. Tuyns: Epidemiology of alcohol and cancer. *Cancer Res* 39:2840–2843, 1979.

80. B.N. Ames: Dietary carcinogens and anticarcinogens. *Science* 221:1256–1264, 1983.

81. A. Nomura: Stomach. In: *Cancer Epidemiology and Prevention*, D. Schottenfeld, J.F. Fraumeni, eds. W.B. Saunders, Philadelphia, 1982.

82. J.R. Chipault et al.: Antioxidant properties of spices in oil-in-water emulsions. *Food Res* 20:443–446, 1955.

83. J. Devine, P.N. Williams: *The Chemistry and Technology of Edible Oils and Fats*. Permagon Press, New York, 1961.

FIVE.
Dietary Supplements

The question of which vitamins and other types of dietary supplements to take is probably the most contentious issue in this field. (I use the term *supplement* here to refer to vitamins, minerals, or any other substance taken as tablets, capsules, or any means other than in food.) Some people object in principle to taking supplements, believing that it is best to obtain any and all beneficial substances by eating the right foods. It is true that in general it is best to obtain nutrients in the diet rather than as separate supplements. In most cases, the evidence is best for beneficial effects from classes of foods containing certain vitamins and minerals. However, in several instances there is good evidence that substantial benefits can be derived from certain vitamins or minerals at levels far above what can be obtained from food. I don't see any reasonable objection to taking these as supplements in addition to following healthy dietary practices. You also still hear the thoughtless criticism that there is no "need" to take any supplements. Of course there is no "need" to do so, any more than there is a "need" to stop smoking, avoid fatty foods, exercise, or do most other things conducive to good health. You won't die or get sick immediately if you don't follow optimum or desirable health practices. The obvious question is not what is needed, but what is optimal. Will taking vitamin E or some other supplement significantly improve health or increase life expectancy? These are tough questions to answer: One must actually search through the extensive literature of published reports on the potential supplements. But it's foolish to evade the issue by arguing that since no actual deficiency disease will occur if you don't take a vitamin, there is no point in taking it.

There are in fact several possible reasons for taking a supplement. First, if you don't get enough of a certain vitamin (and some minerals) in your diet, you will eventually develop the so-called deficiency disease associated with the deficiency of that vitamin. Insufficient vitamin C, for example, results in the disease scurvy. Vitamin C is essential to the formation of connective tissue, so scurvy is characterized by bleeding gums, tenderness to touch, weakness, small hemorrhages in the skin, and other symptoms due to the breakdown of this tissue. The daily amount of a vitamin needed to prevent actual deficiency disease is small, below even the RDA. If you eat any kind of reasonably balanced diet in one of the developed countries, you are unlikely to develop one of the deficiency diseases. However, there are many vitamins and other essential nutrients, and some people do not eat a reasonable diet. So surveys have found marginal deficiencies of some nutrients in certain populations (the elderly, teenagers, etc.). It is probably worthwhile to take a good multivitamin containing the RDA of each of the known vitamins for this reason alone. Minerals are another matter. There is evidence that too high an intake of some minerals (iron is a good example) is harmful in the long term. So you have to be more selective in choosing which minerals to take as supplements and how much of each.

The second reason to take supplements is to help prevent disease. There is considerable evidence that certain supplements can help us avoid even serious diseases like cancer and heart disease.[1, 2] We will discuss the reasons for believing this for each supplement.

Third, and related to the second benefit of supplements, is the ability of some to prevent damage due to oxidation. Such substances are therefore called antioxidants. They inhibit the destructive chemical reactions of oxygen or "free radicals." A free radical is an atom or group of atoms with one or more unpaired electrons. This makes it highly reactive chemically; it will react with fats (lipids), DNA (the genetic material controlling how a cell functions), proteins, and many other substances. This can result in damage to essential cellular components. The products of these reactions are themselves frequently harmful. The oxidized fats that result from this type of reaction can damage DNA and are suspected of causing cancer. The lipid membrane surrounding each cell can also be damaged in this manner. Nitric oxide, superoxide (the oxygen ion with an unpaired electron), the hydroxyl (OH) radical, and similar potentially harmful substances are common in biological systems, and in fact arise during the course of normal metabolism. Free radicals are also produced by external factors, such as certain chemicals and ionizing radiation. Damage from free radical reactions has been implicated in several diseases,[1, 2] and has been theorized to be the primary cause of aging itself.[3, 4] This free radical theory of aging was developed by Denham Harman and has been popularized in recent years by Pearson and Shaw.[5] The theory is certainly plausible: Free radicals occur throughout the body and are known to produce various kinds of damage. Organisms naturally produce or utilize a number of defense mechanisms to counter this. These include several antioxidant vitamins (like vitamin E), enzymes like superoxide dismutase and catalase, which neutralize free radicals, and other biochemical systems that we will discuss shortly. Since these protective mechanisms cannot be 100 percent effective, damage could accumulate with age. Some cells and molecules, such as the proteins in connective tissue (primarily collagen and elastin), last a long time. Nerve and muscle cells must last the entire life of the animal; these cells may die, but they never divide to produce more cells. You can see how damage could accumulate in such tissues. And, in fact, we do find an increase with age in what looks like debris in such cells. Connective tissue, which contains a large portion of the total protein in the body, undergoes irreversible changes, the protein molecules becoming damaged or "cross-linked"—that is, bound to the next molecule in a nonfunctional manner.[6] This sort of cross-linking has in fact been proposed as a theory of aging itself.[7] Whole body exposure to ionizing radiation, which damages tissue primarily through production of free radicals, produces several effects similar to those that occur with age.

While the free radical theory of aging seems plausible, there is very little actual experimental evidence to support it. The crucial test is whether reducing free radical reactions over the course of an animal's life slows the rate of aging. If this were so, this type of intervention should increase not just the average, but also the maximum life span of a group of animals. Put another way, their survival curve, as we discussed in Chapter 1, should become not just more rectangular, but shifted to the right. A number of such studies have been done on the effects of antioxidants (which counter the effects of free radicals) on life span.[3, 8–10] Most of these studies have used one of the rather potent synthetic antioxidants, such as 2-mercaptoethylamine (MEA), BHT, and ethoxyquin (these last two being common commercial preservatives). Generally, antioxidants have increased average but not maximum life span. In one study,[10] the addition of BHT in the amount of 0.75 percent of the diet increased the mean life span of a fairly hardy strain of mice by up to 30 percent. What makes this even more impressive is that the mice were living in good environmental conditions, and the BHT-fed mice were generally heavier, with smoother coats and a healthier appearance. But again, if there is no increase in maximum life span, an antioxidant is not affecting the fundamental aging process. These results do not disprove the theory; it may well be that more sophisticated means than simple dietary antioxidants are necessary to counter the free radical reactions underlying aging. In particular, in order to be effective the protective substances must penetrate into the intracellular compartments where the crucial reactions are taking place, and they must be present continually in sufficient concentrations, since free radical reactions last a very short time. There *have* been a few reports of increases in both mean and maximum life span by antioxidants. In a carefully designed study by Margaret Heidrick and others,[11] a naturally long-lived hybrid strain of mice was fed the common laboratory antioxidant 2-mercaptoethanol in the amount of 0.25 percent of their food from 16 weeks of age (young maturity in a mouse) until they died a natural death. Another criticism of such studies was addressed in this experiment: It has been argued that animals refuse to eat as much food when it contains certain antioxidants, so that the effect that is seen in such experiments is due to calorie restriction, rather than to the antioxidants themselves. In this study, the researchers first determined what levels of mercaptoethanol the mice would tolerate in their food before eating less of it. Consequently, the body weights of the mice did not differ significantly from those of controls over the course of this study. The mean survival time of the mercaptoethanol-fed mice was 13.2 percent greater than controls. Their maximum life span as measured by the oldest survivor was 12.0 percent greater. The mean survival of the longest-lived 10 percent was 10.4 percent greater than controls. The antioxidant-fed mice showed other aspects of retarded aging: Certain measures of their immune function declined more slowly, their incidence of tumors was lower, and the accumulation of lipid-oxidation products (the dark material that builds up in certain cells with age) was reduced in their spleen lymphocytes.

The level of mercaptoethanol used in this experiment (0.25 percent of diet) was high, at least as compared to normal dietary intakes of antioxidants and other supplements, but was lower than the levels of antioxidants used in most other studies that did not report an increase in maximum life span. BHT, for example, has typically been fed to mice in the range of 0.5 to 1 percent of the dry weight of the diet. This would be equivalent to a human taking about 2.5 to 5 grams of BHT a day. For comparison, normal dietary intakes are in the milligram range, and even the supplements currently available are around 250mg (a quarter of a gram).

The evidence linking free radical reactions to disease is more compelling. It is well established that oxidation of various substances can give rise to carcinogens, and that this process can be blocked in many cases by antioxidants like vitamin E, vitamin C, and beta-carotene.[1, 12, 13] This protective effect has been reported for a number of carcinogens in rodents. The administration of certain known carcinogens results in a significant incidence of cancer in these animals, but when antioxidants are also given, the incidence of cancer is greatly reduced.

It is thought that this anticarcinogenic effect is related to the inhibition of chronic inflammation by antioxidants. While we normally think of free radicals as something harmful, they are actually used by our own body in fighting infection. White blood cells produce a burst of free radicals to destroy cells that they recognize as foreign: bacteria, protozoa, virus-infected cells, and possibly cancer cells. In the case of chronic infection, this causes a chronic inflammation that also damages normal tissue. This includes damage to DNA that can cause the cell to become malignant. Infection by hepatitis virus often results in later development of liver cancer. Bladder infections are common among populations that have a high incidence of bladder cancer. A bacterial infection of the stomach appears to be related to stomach cancer, ulcers, and chronic gastritis.[1] Noninfectious sources of inflammation, such as the effects of asbestos on the lung, are also thought to play a role in the development of cancer. The evidence linking cancer with free radical reactions and oxidation has become strong enough that a number of scientists in this area and in public health are speaking out on the protective effects that antioxidants could have for the general public.[12, 13]

Recent studies on the effects of supplementation with four combinations of vitamins and minerals were carried out over a five-year period on nearly 30,000 men and women in China.[14] Those people who took the combination beta-carotene, vitamin E, and selenium in the modest dose of one to two times the U.S. RDA had a 9 percent reduction in overall mortality and a 13 percent reduction in mortality due to cancer. There was also a reduction in death due to stroke, but this did not reach the level of statistical significance. The other combinations of supplements — retinol/zinc, riboflavin/niacin, and vitamin C/molybdenum — did not produce a significant reduction in mortality. Beta-carotene and vitamin E are potent, naturally occurring antioxidants; selenium is an essential component of the antioxidant and protective enzyme glutathione peroxidase and has other anticancer effects. This study could not determine definitely whether the reduction in cancer was due entirely to the antioxidant property of the supplements or to other protective effects that they probably have. Two other points about this study should be mentioned: 1) The residents of the area of China in which the study was conducted do not eat a varied diet, their staples being corn, millet, sweet potatoes, and wheat; 2) the study lasted 5.25 years, but there is usually a period of many years between the events that initiate a cancer by making a cell malignant and the clinical appearance of the disease. If a lag period was allowed between the time supplementation was begun and death rates were compiled (to allow time for the effects of supplementation to occur), an even greater reduction in mortality was observed. This may also explain why no reduction in cancer mortality was seen in groups taking the other supplements, which have been reported to have protective effects; it may just take more time for their effects to become significant.

All the vitamin and mineral antioxidants, and probably all antioxidants of any kind, can have several effects. So it is not always clear if their protection against cancer and other diseases is due just to their function as antioxidants. Some, for example, enhance immune function. Some, like vitamin C, can act as a reducing agent, combining chemically with potentially dangerous substances and thereby preventing the formation of carcinogens. It is thought that vitamin C protects against stomach cancer in this manner — preventing the formation of cancer-causing substances called nitrosamines from nitrites.[15]

Free radical reactions may be implicated in many diseases and tissue injuries, including cataracts, diabetes, atherosclerosis, inflammatory diseases such as arthritis, and damage to the liver due to alcohol, iron overload, or toxins.[16] Several antioxidant nutrients, especially vitamin E, may afford some protection against heart disease. Again, in the case of vitamin E there are a number of ways it could be doing this.

Loss of sight caused by the formation of cataracts is one of the most common problems associated with aging, and cataract removal has become an almost routine operation for people approaching old age. It is thought that oxidation is the primary pathway leading to the formation of cataracts, and there is evidence that antioxidants can prevent their occurrence.[17]

Vitamin E

Vitamin E refers to a group of related, fat-soluble compounds called tocopherols, comprising alpha-, beta-, gamma-, and delta-tocopherol. Their potency in terms of vitamin E activity has been reported to follow this order, with alpha-tocopherol being the most potent and delta-tocopherol the least.[18, 19] The amount of vitamin E is therefore usually measured in "international units" or IU, since it can be composed of one or more of the tocopherols, each with a different vitamin E activity. In the case of pure alpha-tocopherol, which is commonly used in experiments, the measurement is frequently in the usual milligrams. Vitamin E functions as an important antioxidant in the body, protecting lipid membranes and other structures from damage by free radicals. It is especially important because it is fat soluble, whereas most of the body's antioxidants are water soluble and not able to function efficiently in lipids, which are prone to damage from oxidation.

Vitamin E is itself altered to an inactive form in this reaction with free radicals, but its potency can be restored by vitamin C.

Consequently, there are theoretical reasons for thinking vitamin E plays a role in preventing cancer and other diseases, and in fact a fair amount of hard evidence exists that it helps in preventing heart disease, cancer, cataracts, and possibly other diseases that may be associated with oxidative damage. One epidemiologic study in Europe found that blood levels of vitamin E had a strong inverse correlation with heart disease, and in fact predicted it better even than the classic risk factors cholesterol and diastolic blood pressure.[20] Two large, recent epidemiologic studies examined vitamin E intake and coronary heart disease in nearly 40,000 males and 87,000 females in the United States.[21, 22] The risk of heart disease decreased in both men and women with increased intakes of vitamin E. Those who took over 100 IU/day had a roughly 40 percent decreased risk. These studies were careful to control for age and other risk factors, although the strong correlation with vitamin E does not in itself prove a causal relation or indicate how the vitamin may be protective. There is reason to believe, however, that oxidation of LDL cholesterol is a critical step in the process of atherosclerosis, so it seems reasonable — and there is some evidence — that antioxidants like vitamin E block the process.[21–23] While not every study has found this inverse correlation between vitamin E intake and heart disease, it would be fair to say that the majority have, including the largest studies.

My best estimate of the optimum level of a daily vitamin E supplement would be around 400IU for an average-size person. This is based on the dose-response observed in various studies, and the essentially benign nature of vitamin E. The data are not good enough to make this estimate with much precision, but I don't think that is really necessary, at least not in this case. There is probably a plateau on which the benefits/risk ratio does not change very much.

Selenium

Selenium is an essential trace element in human and animal nutrition.[24] There is considerable evidence that selenium can reduce spontaneous cancer incidence[25, 26] and inhibit induced and transplanted tumors. At still higher levels it can be toxic to animals. Selenium is an essential component of the widely distributed glutathione peroxidase enzyme system. This enzyme protects lipid membranes and other cellular components from damage due to oxidation, and has a role in neutralizing various toxins. Selenium and vitamin E can substitute for one another to some extent, but not completely, as essential dietary nutrients. People who consume a diet deficient in selenium develop Keshan disease, as was discovered among certain populations in China.[27, 28] The primary characteristic of this condition, which has also been found in cattle, is a degeneration of heart muscle.

Epidemiologic studies have generally found lower blood selenium levels and lower dietary intake among people who develop cancer.[26] There have also been numerous experiments in which known carcinogens were administered to mice and rats with and without supplemental selenium. In almost all cases, selenium greatly reduced the incidence of the resultant cancers.[29]

Even more remarkable, a series of experiments has shown that the administration of selenium can completely halt the growth of established cancers in mice.[30-32] In one such experiment, injection of various selenium compounds completely prevented the growth of an abdominal cancer transplanted into mice.[30] Mice not receiving selenium all developed massive tumors. A similar experiment [31] studied the growth of human breast cancer cells in a strain of mice lacking an immune system (so that even cancers from other species grow in them). Injection of selenite retarded tumor growth by 80 percent. In yet another study of selenium and cancer,[32] up to 90 percent of mice treated with selenium in the form of sodium selenite were cured of leukemia. Other selenium compounds — sodium selenate, selenocystine, and selenomethionine — were less effective in this study. The doses of selenium used in these studies were significantly greater than normal dietary levels, but not high enough to be toxic or retard growth in normal animals.

It is not understood how all of selenium's anticancer effects come about. Selenium is an essential part of the enzyme glutathione peroxidase, which protects cells from free radical damage and is thought to detoxify other potentially harmful substances.[33] This probably accounts for much of the protective effect within the range of normal dietary variations in selenium intake. But the glutathione peroxidase enzyme system is already saturated with selenium well below the levels at which direct anticancer effects have been observed. That is, adding more selenium above this level does not further increase glutathione peroxidase. Therapeutic effects against cancers in mice have been obtained with selenium doses of one part per million of diet and greater, equivalent to about 500μg a day in humans. This is well above typical dietary intakes, which are estimated to average 50 to 70μg per day, and to range up to around 200μg in the United States and the United Kingdom.[34, 35] There is some reason to believe that selenium is significantly more toxic to cancer cells than to normal cells. A number of studies have been done on the response of cells in tissue culture to selenium; these have consistently found that selenium inhibited the growth of cancer cells much more than that of normal cells.[36, 37]

There are other possible explanations. The fact that selenium is stably and consistently incorporated into specific proteins other than glutathione peroxidase in both human and mouse cells[38] suggests that it has other definite biological functions as yet unknown.

There is also evidence that selenium enhances immune function, especially that part responsible for fighting cancer. Mice maintained on a selenium-supplemented diet in one study[39] produced immune cells (lymphocytes) with greater ability to kill cancer cells than those on a diet containing normal levels of selenium; mice on a selenium-deficient diet had lymphocytes with even lower levels of this function than those on a normal diet. In another experiment on selenium and immunity, rats were given drinking water supplemented with several concentrations of selenium, and a number of measurements of their immune function were made.[40] The

"Natural Killer Cell," or NK activity, was much higher in rats receiving one of the selenium supplements. NK cells are an important part of the immune system's defense against cancer. They will recognize and destroy foreign cells, including cancer cells, even without prior exposure to such cells; other parts of the immune system need time after first exposure to foreign substances or cells to mount their defense. The levels of selenium used in this experiment were even higher than usual in such studies. The rats received 0.5, 2, and 5 parts per million (ppm) of selenium in their drinking water, which is equivalent to about 1.75, 7, and 17.5 ppm in the diet. Again very roughly, this would be equivalent to a human intake of 875µg, 3,500µg, and 8,750µg respectively. This probably explains why the highest responses were obtained at the lowest level of supplementation. At the highest dose, NK activity was about the same as in untreated animals. Other studies of this type have produced similar results in several species.[41, 42]

The chemical form in which selenium is taken can be important. The one most frequently used in experiments has been the inorganic compound sodium selenite (Na_2SeO_3). This has generally been found to be most efficiently incorporated into glutathione peroxidase, and to be the most effective common form in eliciting anticancer effects. Other selenium compounds, however, do have similar properties. These include the organic forms in which selenium is incorporated into an amino acid, such as selenomethionine (selenium incorporated into the amino acid methionine), and selenocysteine (selenium incorporated into the amino acid cysteine, as it is in glutathione peroxidase). When these organic selenium compounds are consumed, they are metabolized by the body and their selenium released as selenite.[24] The organic forms occur naturally in foods but are used less efficiently since the seleno-amino acids are to some extent incorporated randomly into proteins before their selenium can be released. It may be that selenium exerts its anticancer effects through the formation of even more potent compounds inside the cell. The so-called selenotrisulfides, such as selenodiglutathione, are being studied in this regard.[43] They are formed from the reaction of selenium with compounds having a sulfhydryl group, such as glutathione. These selenotrisulfides are quite unstable. It would be pointless to take them as dietary supplements, as I have seen suggested. It is also useless to take glutathione, which is broken down in the digestive tract and is not absorbed by cells even if placed directly in their growth medium.

Selenium is toxic in high doses, so caution is certainly advisable in taking it as a supplement. But there is a significant margin of safety between beneficial and toxic doses. Even long-term selenium intakes at the relatively high levels used in the cancer treatment studies, one part per million of diet, while not generally advisable, would amount to only about 500µg a day. This is still below that estimated to cause toxic effects in people. A supplement of 250µg a day as sodium selenite would likely provide significant benefits while still leaving a good margin of safety. It has been estimated that a chronic intake of 1,000 to 1,500µg of selenium a day is required before toxic symptoms appear in humans, and at these levels they are not severe or life threatening.[44] Studies in this regard found a number of people who consumed 1,000μg a day of selenium (as selenite) for extended periods with no observed toxic effects.[45] Even with very high doses, the toxicity manifests itself gradually and does not immediately produce dangerous conditions. One 57-year-old woman consumed daily a mislabeled supplement containing 27.3mg (27,300μg) of selenium for several weeks; toxic symptoms were noticed after 11 days and eventually included hair loss, cracked fingernails, and nausea. These toxic effects are generally reversible when selenium supplementation is discontinued.

Vitamin A

Vitamin A is a fat-soluble vitamin essential for growth, vision, and maintenance of healthy skin, mucous membranes, and similar (epithelial) tissue. A large class of related chemical compounds, called retinoids, have various degrees of vitamin A activity, retinol being the most potent. For this reason, vitamin A is measured in international units (IU), or, more recently, "retinol equivalents" (RE). One IU is equal to 0.3μg of retinol (the specific chemical form is all-*trans*-retinol), or one RE equals 3.33IU. Milk (including skim milk) and milk products are the most common dietary sources of retinol. A number of substances called carotenes, common in many fruits and vegetables, can be converted to vitamin A after ingestion. At least the human body can do this; some species, such as cats, cannot and must have preformed vitamin A in their diets. Beta-carotene, which gives many vegetables their orange color, is probably the most well known of these. It takes 6μg of beta-carotene, or 12μg of mixed carotenes, to equal about 1μg of retinol. Beta-carotene, while related to vitamin A, has other interesting properties that we will discuss in the next section.

The term *retinoids* refers to retinol, retinoic acid, and other chemically similar compounds, both natural and synthetic. Many of these have some vitamin A activity. Retinoic acid, for example, can substitute for vitamin A in maintenance of epithelial tissue and growth, but is not adequate for vision or reproduction. Animals fed retinoic acid as the sole source of vitamin A are therefore blind and sterile, but in good health otherwise.[46]

At very high levels of around 10,000 to 20,000μg of retinol, vitamin A becomes toxic. Symptoms of this toxicity include headache, nausea, pain in the bones, and abnormalities of the skin and mucous membranes. Since vitamin A is stored in the liver, injury to that organ is also common. The toxicity is not the same for forms of vitamin A other than retinol, and beta-carotene has no toxicity at all.

Retinoids strongly influence the differentiation of cells. That is, they can in many cases cause dividing, unspecialized cells to undergo differentiation to a specialized, functional cell type, such as skin cells, which no longer divide. This is in fact the common process that occurs continuously in the skin and many other tissues, in which functional cells have a limited lifetime and are continuously replaced from a pool of dividing, undifferentiated cells. What makes this even more interesting is that retinoids can suppress the transformation of normal cells to cancerous cells (which are in one sense unspecialized, dividing cells) by known chemical carcinogens and radiation.[47] Even more remarkable, retinoids can induce terminal differentiation in cancer cells;[48, 49] that is, such cells stop growing and dividing, and acquire many of the characteristics of normal, functional cells. Retinoic acid and related compounds have been more effective in this regard than vitamin A (retinol) itself. Not all cells respond in this manner; however, such findings were promising enough that a number of limited clinical trials have been done on the treatment of patients with established cancers or precancerous conditions thought to be sensitive to retinoids. These have had some success, considering the preliminary nature of the work, and remissions have been obtained in some patients.[50–52] In late 1995 the retinoid tretinoin was approved by the FDA for the treatment of a rare type of leukemia called acute promyelocytic leukemia.

It has been known for some time that animals deficient in vitamin A frequently develop cancer, especially of the gastrointestinal tract, as well as skin disorders.[51] Furthermore, several epidemiologic studies have reported a correlation between low blood levels of vitamin A and subsequent risk of cancer.[53, 54] It has become clear from all these lines of evidence that vitamin A and retinoids are linked in some ways not yet fully understood with the prevention of some types of cancer, primarily certain leukemias and epithelial cancers (carcinomas, which constitute the majority of human cancers).

Several studies have found that high dietary intakes of vitamin A or other retinoids enhance some immune functions to a significant extent, depending on the type of retinoid and the function measured. Retinol has been reported to increase the ability of mouse macrophages (a type of white blood cell) to kill tumor cells, but not to affect the NK cells.[55] Other researchers have found that retinoic acid enhanced NK activity in both mouse and human cells.[56] The levels of retinoids used in these studies were quite high, however.

Retinoids are also useful in skin disorders such as the severe acnes (cystic, rosacea) and psoriasis.[46] I should emphasize that vitamin A itself has not generally been used in these studies. Synthetic retinoids with a higher therapeutic index (ratio of effectiveness to toxicity) are available and necessary. Isotretinoin (13-*cis*-retinoic acid), an effective inhibitor of skin sebum production, is now commonly used for severe cystic acne. It has also shown promise in some of the preliminary cancer studies. Tretinoin, a close chemical relative (all-*trans*-retinoic acid, sometimes called just retinoic acid or by the brand name Retin-A), is also used to treat skin disorders and has received some attention in recent years as something of a skin rejuvenator. Applied topically, it is effective in many cases of acne. While this is the only specific FDA-approved use, it can be and is prescribed for normal skin aging and, what is closely related, aging due to exposure to sunlight. Tretinoin can reverse skin wrinkling, thickening, and sagging, and reduce the number of age spots.[57] Much of the change in skin that we associate with age comes about through exposure to sunlight. Airborne irritants can also gradually and cumulatively damage skin over a period of time. These changes, or damage, greatly increase the probability of skin cancer. In one study of the effect of tretinoin on sun-damaged skin, in all patients receiving topical tretinoin (applied as a 0.1 percent cream on one forearm), the wrinkling in treated skin was reduced, its pinkness was increased, and the number of age spots was reduced by an average of 71 percent.[58] Most people treated with tretinoin will have some initial side effects, such as dryness, peeling, and a reddening of the treated area, but these diminish after the first few weeks. The greatest susceptibility to side effects seems to follow sensitivity to sunburn and irritants, with fair-skinned, freckled, and blue-eyed people being most sensitive. Persons with dry skin or who have had previous skin disorders also have a greater than average sensitivity to topical tretinoin, while older people with advanced sun-damaged skin and darker complexioned people are less sensitive. Side effects are confined to the skin, however; there is essentially no absorption of tretinoin into the body.

While topical tretinoin is also used successfully to treat many cases of acne, severe cases of cystic acne frequently require systemic treatment with isotretinoin. This drug can usually permanently resolve such cases. Systemic treatment does have a greater potential for side effects, but these can be managed. The major danger is during pregnancy; isotretinoin can cause severe birth defects if taken then. For this reason it is not given to pregnant women and patients are advised against becoming pregnant before a course of such therapy is begun.

Tretinoin and isotretinoin are currently available only by prescription in the United States.

All this is not to say that we should take large amounts of vitamin A. It is toxic at levels around 10 to 20 times the RDA, although this toxicity is not severe at first. My own judgment is that a prudent and safe average daily intake (dietary plus supplement) of preformed vitamin A (retinol) would be around 5,000IU to 10,000IU (about 1,500 to 3,000RE), or somewhat more than the RDA. This is still well below the levels at which any toxicity would start.

Beta-Carotene

Vitamin A is a rather general term that refers to both preformed vitamin A (retinol and similar compounds) and "provitamin A"—that is, beta-carotene and other carotenes that can be converted into vitamin A in the body. A fraction of dietary beta-carotene is converted into retinol in the human intestine (6μg of beta-carotene yielding roughly 1μg of retinol at normal intakes). The fraction of beta-carotene converted decreases as the amount of dietary beta-carotene increases, so that even very large intakes of beta-carotene will not cause vitamin A toxicity (because very little of it will be converted to vitamin A). There are no known cases of toxicity of any kind due to beta-carotene, and the World Health Organization has estimated that intakes even up to 350mg a day would be harmless.[59] It does cause a yellowing of the skin at high levels, which is reversible when intake is decreased. There are many similar compounds widely distributed in plants; collectively, beta-carotene and these many relatives are called carotenoids. Over five hundred different carotenoids have been identified, only some of which can be converted to vitamin A. Overall, about 12μg of mixed, naturally occurring carotenes are considered equivalent to 1μg of retinol. Carotenes are abundant in many fruits and vegetables, giving carrots and other plant material their characteristic orange color. But they are also found in many green, leafy vegetables where their color is masked by chlorophyll. Carrots are the best-known source of beta-carotene, but substantial quantities are also present in sweet potatoes, spinach, cantaloupe, winter squash, apricots, and broccoli.

Unlike retinol, blood levels of carotene are determined directly by levels in the diet. Some dietary beta-carotene and other carotenes are absorbed unchanged from the intestine. These carotenes circulate in the bloodstream and are partially absorbed and stored in adipose (fat) tissue.

Much of the interest in beta-carotene in recent years has come about because of its properties as an antioxidant. Beta-carotene is the most efficient scavenger of the oxygen free radical (singlet oxygen) known.[60] It also traps certain organic free radicals. It can react directly with the radicals involved in lipid oxidation, thus inhibiting the oxidation of linoleic acid and other lipids and preventing the propagation of the destructive free radical reactions that would otherwise occur. Vitamin A itself is a relatively poor antioxidant and cannot quench oxygen radicals. Beta-carotene functions best as an antioxidant when there is a low concentration of oxygen, which in fact is typically the case in mammalian tissues. In a sense, it complements vitamin E, which is effective at high oxygen levels. Canthaxanthin is another common carotenoid, but it cannot be converted to vitamin A. It does have the same ability to quench oxygen and other free radicals as beta-carotene.

There have been a number of reports that beta-carotene protects animals against the induction of cancer by transplanted tumor cells or by viruses.[59] Both beta-carotene and canthaxanthin have been found to protect cells growing in tissue culture from genetic damage due to carcinogens and X-rays.[61, 62] They have also protected mice against cancer induced by ultraviolet radiation. Dietary beta-carotene has slowed the growth of cancer in laboratory animals and caused a complete regression of an induced cancer in mice when combined with X-ray therapy.[63] In this study, both vitamin A and beta-carotene, at high enough levels (and combined with radiation therapy), induced a complete remission in all mice, and the animals remained in remission as long as these dietary levels were maintained. When the supplements were removed from their diets, all the vitamin A-fed but only some of the beta-carotene-fed mice relapsed and died from the cancer.

It is possible that this anticancer effect is due, at least in part, to increased immune function. Dietary canthaxanthin has improved immune function to a similar extent as beta-carotene in laboratory animals. Such experiments have found that macrophages from animals fed these carotenoids had an increased ability to kill tumor cells.[64, 65] During the immune response, free radicals are generated by certain white blood cells to destroy foreign cells. It is thought that such radicals may be frequently overproduced in such cases, resulting in injury to white blood cells themselves as well as neighboring tissue. Beta-carotene can protect macrophages and other white blood cells from such damage, and enhance other aspects of immunity. These include an increase in the number of T and B white cells when the immune system is mobilized, the potency of cytotoxic T cells (which kill foreign cells), and NK cell function.[64, 65]

Beginning with a study at Western Electric over a decade ago,[66] beta-carotene has been associated with a reduced risk of lung cancer in epidemiologic studies.[67] Increased risk of cervical dysplasia and cervical cancer have been found in women with low dietary and/or blood levels of beta-carotene. Cervical dysplasia is an abnormal condition of tissue of the cervix that is considered precancerous. The relative risks involved here were quite significant: Women with low levels of beta-carotene had two to three times greater risk than women with the highest levels.[68] Higher consumption of carotene-rich vegetables is also associated with reduced incidence of oral cancer. The Basel study[69] followed the dietary practices, blood nutrient levels, and mortality of nearly 3,000 people over a 12-year period. Death due to cancer, and especially bronchus (lung) cancer, were up to twice as high in those with low carotene intake compared to the rates in people with high intakes. It's difficult to isolate beta-carotene as the protective factor in such dietary surveys since fruits and vegetables may well contain other protective factors; further, people who eat lots of fruits and vegetables are likely to be avoiding harmful factors in meats and high-fat products. A fair number of epidemiologic studies on carotene intake and cancer have been done. In reviewing the retrospective studies (i.e., studies in which the past dietary practices of cancer patients and controls are examined) up to 1989, Ziegler[70] noted that "all nine of the studies of diet and lung cancer showed a decreased risk with increased intake of carotenoids or green or yellow-green vegetables." Several prospective studies (relating current dietary practice with subsequent cancer incidence) were also reviewed. In three of the four prospective studies that examined "all cancers combined, risk was inversely related to vegetable and fruit or carotenoid intake."[70] Again, the strongest association was with lung cancer.

There have been a few studies that did not find any significant relation between beta-carotene and cancer. A recent study done in Finland received considerable attention because it found that beta-carotene supplements did not reduce the incidence or death rate from lung cancer in male smokers; in fact, those taking the supplement had slighter higher rates.[71] This was a fairly large study, with over 7,000 men in each experimental group, so the results are puzzling. However, while the study was large, it did have certain limitations. The duration of the study and follow-up was five to eight years. Cancers frequently take many years to develop, so that — as the authors of this report themselves point out — results may be very different in substantially longer trials. This is because for most cancers, including lung, the cancer that is diagnosed today is likely the result of actions that were taken — or not taken — 10, 20, or 30 years ago. The subjects were all male smokers aged 50 to 69 at the start. These characteristics make them a rather special group, especially since at that age men are likely to have smoked continuously for 30 to 50 years. I'm inclined to think that in such a group, damage or precancerous conditions have accumulated to the extent that it would take a very powerful agent to counter it. That's just my opinion, however; it must be admitted that this study remains largely unexplained. What there is little doubt about is that low intake of carotenoid-rich vegetables and fruits is associated with a high incidence of cancer.

There is also significant evidence that beta-carotene protects against cardiovascular disease. In one study, men who took a 50mg supplement of beta-carotene every other day for years had half the number of heart attacks or strokes as those taking a placebo. Researchers have speculated that beta-carotene inhibits the formation of oxidized LDL cholesterol critical in the formation of atherosclerotic plaques in the arteries.[72]

Although the evidence for protective effects from beta-carotene obtained in the diet is fairly consistent, it is less so for supplements. It would therefore be best to obtain most of your intake by eating fruits and vegetables. There are many that are rich in carotenes, some of which were mentioned at the beginning of this section; there are almost certainly protective factors other than beta-carotene in these foods, and this would be perfectly consistent with the dietary practices mentioned in the last chapter. Even so, a supplement of 15 to 25mg a day may well afford additional benefits, especially since we cannot always be as careful in our dietary habits as we would like. In my opinion the safest beta-carotene supplements are the dry type, usually a powder in a hard capsule. It is also included in some multivitamin tablets. Most beta-carotene supplements on the market today consist of liquid in capsules. Such products have a tendency to deteriorate over extended periods of time, so make sure that what you buy has an expiration date on the bottle and that you use it well before that date.

Vitamin C

Vitamin C, or ascorbic acid, which is the most common form, is a water-soluble vitamin essential to the maintenance of connective tissue. This includes the protein collagen and other fibrous material that form intercellular support structures in teeth, bone, cartilage, and in capillary walls. It is also thought to be involved in the synthesis of hormones, nervous system function, detoxification of ingested toxins, and cholesterol metabolism, even though its exact role in these is still unclear.[73] Vitamin C is a potent antioxidant[74] and has a major role in protecting lipids and other cellular components from free radical damage. It can restore oxidized vitamin E to its original activity. Many species can synthesize their own vitamin C and so do not require any in their diets. Primates, including humans as well as several other species, require sufficient amounts in their diets or they develop the deficiency disease known as scurvy. This is characterized by bleeding gums, tenderness to touch, weakness, widespread hemorrhages of the capillaries, and other symptoms related to the breakdown of connective tissue.

Substantial amounts of vitamin C are present in citrus fruits, including canned and frozen fruits, as well as strawberries, brussels sprouts, spinach, and tomatoes. The vitamin C in food can be easily destroyed by heat, such as prolonged cooking. It can also be degraded by oxidation, which is also increased by cooking as well as exposure to metals like iron and copper, as are found in many cooking vessels. Because it is so soluble in water, ascorbic acid is readily lost from foods cooked in water. It declines steadily in fruits and even more rapidly in vegetables stored at room temperature. Refrigeration slows this process significantly.

There is good epidemiologic evidence that vitamin C helps protect against a number of cancers.[73, 75] Several dozen such studies have been done; most have calculated vitamin C intake from its content in the foods people consume, adjusting for other possible confounding variables. About three-quarters of these studies have found a significant protective effect due to vitamin C.[73] Overall, the epidemiologic evidence is probably strongest for protection from cancer of the esophagus. While not very common in developed countries, this is an extremely deadly cancer. There is also a strong inverse correlation between vitamin C intake and cancers of the mouth, pancreas, and stomach. Again, cancers of the stomach and pancreas are not common in the United States, but are almost always fatal. There is some evidence for a protective effect against cancer of the rectum, breast, and cervix. Vitamin C has also inhibited cancer in animals in a number of experiments. This protective effect may be related to the antioxidant property of vitamin C, and to its ability to prevent the formation of carcinogens. N-nitrosamine compounds, which are known to be highly carcinogenic, are formed from chemicals called nitrates in certain foods after they are consumed. Nitrates occur naturally in some foods and are an additive in meat processing. Vitamin C prevents the chemical reaction that converts them to the carcinogenic N-nitrosamines and similar compounds in the stomach. Vitamin C enhances immune function, or at least several important aspects of it, which could also be related to this protection against cancer.[76] It has never been confirmed, however, that vitamin C can have a significant effect on the course of the common cold, or that it can aid in the treatment of cancer. Studies have found at best only weak effects in these areas.

Ascorbic acid decreases some of the risk factors for cardiovascular disease. As with other antioxidants, one way this could occur is by the prevention of oxidation of LDL cholesterol. But vitamin C can also raise HDL (the protective lipoprotein in the blood), and lower blood pressure.[77]

Again, the fruits and vegetables through which we can increase our consumption of vitamin C are desirable for other reasons that we have discussed. Vitamin C is somewhat less stable in foods, however. It is much more stable in its dry form in supplements. These can actually retain their potency for years, if kept dry and reasonably cool. There is little if any potential toxicity associated with vitamin C, but there *may* be problems with its interactions with other nutrients. For example, there have been reports that it can counter the absorption and effects of selenium, or *promote* oxidation when combined with certain forms of iron, copper, and other metals. (Ascorbic acid, in the range of 25 to 75mg or greater, increases iron absorption when ingested at the same time.) These potential detrimental effects have never been confirmed, but remain a source of concern. Basically, there is just little evidence to recommend the very high doses (in the range of grams) that some people are now taking. Most of the evidence implies that its most beneficial effects occur at lower but still substantial intakes in the range of 500 to 1,000mg a day (The RDA is 60mg.). This is best taken in divided doses, morning and evening, since vitamin C blood levels decline within a few hours of intake.

Bioflavonoids, a group of related substances that impart their coloring to many plants, fruits, and vegetables, are essential for the utilization of vitamin C. Hesperidin, found in the peel and pulp of citrus fruits, and rutin, which can be derived from buckwheat leaves but is found in many plants, are two of the most common. There are several hundred such chemically related compounds in the large class called flavonoids, but we need not go into the details of their subclassification. Bioflavonoids, especially rutin, are thought to help prevent capillary fragility. This is a condition in which the capillaries (the smallest of the blood vessels) rupture or become abnormally porous, creating small hemorrhages and/or allowing substances to leak from the bloodstream into tissue. Some flavonoids such as quercetin, from which rutin is derived, are strong antioxidants and free radical scavengers. There is also evidence that they prevent the harmful effects of excess metals (like iron) by attaching to and inactivating the metal atoms. (This is called chelating.) These last two effects may well be related since such metals promote free radical reactions.[78] Quercetin and related flavonoids have inhibited carcinogenesis in rodents and the growth of human cancer cells in culture. Citrus fruits are a common source of bioflavonoids, but actual dietary intake is from a number of vegetables, fruits, and beverages, including tea, coffee, and wine. A survey in The Netherlands, which included analysis of the amount of several flavonoids thought to have antioxidant or anticancer effects, found that tea was the major dietary source.[79] Tea consumption (which averaged two cups a day in this population) was responsible for 48 percent of total dietary flavonoid intake, followed by onions (29 percent) and apples (7 percent). This study found that quercetin was the most abundant flavonoid (of those studied) in the diet, followed in order by kaempferol, myricetin, luteolin, and apignin. Dietary deficiencies of bioflavonoids are probably uncommon, but it is unknown what amounts are optimum. Since bioflavonoids are essentially innocuous, a small to moderate supplement in the range of 250 to 500mg a day seems appropriate. I would not take this as just citrus or any other individual bioflavonoid; supplements of mixed bioflavonoids are available, or you can combine several. An unpurified mixture would be fine, since we do not know which of the dozens of such substances are most beneficial.

Calcium, Potassium, Magnesium

As we discussed in Chapter 4, magnesium, calcium, and potassium are important dietary constituents for several reasons. Adequate intake of these minerals helps in avoiding heart disease and maintaining healthy bones. Magnesium is an element, an electrolyte, and an essential mineral nutrient. It is required for proper function of the nervous system and of muscles, including the heart. The body of an average adult contains about 25 grams of magnesium, about half of that in bone and 20 to 30 percent in skeletal muscles. The heart, as well as other muscles, has a high magnesium concentration. A typical diet provides about 300mg of magnesium a day. The RDA is currently 280mg for adult females and 350mg for males. There is evidence that magnesium deficiency is a risk factor for cardiovascular disease.[78] Magnesium and potassium are interdependent nutrients because magnesium is necessary for cellular potassium storage. Magnesium deficiency can easily lead to potassium deficiency. Studies have found magnesium to afford some protection against irregular heartbeats and in cases of myocardial infarction (blockage of one of the coronary arteries). There is also some correlation between "hard" water and decreased risk of death from cardiovascular disease. Hard water contains a greater concentration of dissolved minerals than average water, or "soft" water, which has a lower concentration. Magnesium and potassium are usually especially abundant in hard water. Some epidemiologic studies have found inverse correlations between magnesium and heart disease, or between calcium and heart disease.[80] Furthermore, dietary magnesium has retarded atherosclerosis in several animal studies. It has been suggested that the beneficial effects of magnesium are due, at least in part, to its inhibition of blood clotting. By inhibiting contraction in the smooth muscles surrounding blood vessels, magnesium may also help to lower blood pressure. Large amounts (three to five grams) have a strong laxative effect.

Calcium is very important for building and maintaining bone, and may be protective against hypertension and certain cancers. Loss of bone mass with age occurs in both sexes after about age 45, but is greater in women. Their bone loss accelerates to 2 percent to 5 percent per year immediately before and for about ten years after menopause.[81] But increased calcium intake alone will not increase bone mass or prevent its decline. Weight-bearing exercise is probably a more important factor in building and maintaining strong bones. In postmenopausal women, dietary calcium alone cannot prevent osteoporosis, whereas adequate calcium plus estrogen replacement therapy can prevent loss of bone mass completely.[82]

But are there any benefits in taking supplements of these minerals, and are there possible negative effects? It is possible to create a mineral imbalance in the body in some cases by taking too much of one mineral. Furthermore, there is evidence that some minerals like calcium can promote free radical reactions and subsequent damage. While this has not been confirmed to occur in the body, it's enough of a concern, along with other factors, that we would not want to overdo calcium supplementation. Whether to take calcium supplements depends on whether you get ample amounts in the diet. It would not be desirable to have an average total daily intake much above the highest recommended level, which is about 1,200 to 1,500mg. Milk and milk products like cheese have the highest calcium content of all foods; it would take 1 to 1.3 quarts of milk a day to obtain 1200 to 1500mg, if you obtained no calcium from other sources. Studies of the dietary habits of typical

Americans have shown that, on the average, people obtain about 60 percent of their calcium from milk and milk products. If you now have a marginally adequate daily calcium intake of 800mg, you would therefore have to increase your total milk consumption to about 0.75 to 1 quart a day to obtain 1,200 to 1,500mg. Or, you could take a supplement of 400 to 700mg of calcium. It is not necessary or practicable to hit your daily intake exactly; since these figures are best estimates, amounts within a few hundred milligrams are more than accurate enough. Calcium carbonate is the cheapest form of supplementation. Other forms such as calcium gluconate, calcium citrate, and calcium lactate are equally or more effective but more expensive.

The evidence for potassium and magnesium is not strong enough to recommend substantial supplements, but moderate amounts may be beneficial, and without any downside risk. Potassium is widely distributed in foods; a number of fruits and vegetables, such as bananas, apricots, squash, and tomatoes, are good sources, as was mentioned in Chapter 4. Very high amounts, in the area of 18,000mg a day, are necessary for harmful effects. The maximum individual dose of potassium that can be sold in the United States without a prescription is 99mg, which is adequate and extremely safe as a daily supplement. Magnesium is also widely distributed in common foods; wheat bran (611mg/100g), whole wheat (130mg/100g), and spinach (80mg/100g) contain fairly high amounts. But there is enough evidence for its positive effects that 250 to 300mg would be a reasonable daily supplement.

It is not possible to take even moderate amounts of these minerals as part of a multivitamin/mineral tablet; the quantities involved would make the tablet prohibitively large. They must be taken as individual, separate supplements.

The Synthetic Antioxidants

Some of the synthetic antioxidants, BHT and BHA in particular, have been suggested and are in fact being taken by some as supplements.[5] The rationale for this lies in the findings that 1) BHT and BHA are powerful antioxidants and should inhibit damage from free radical reactions in the body, 2) BHT has increased the life span of rodents and a few other species when fed to them over their entire lives, and 3) BHT, BHA, and similar synthetic antioxidants have inhibited the development of cancer in a number of animal models. The first is almost certainly true as far as it goes: There is little doubt that BHT and BHA are potent antioxidants and would afford some protection against oxidative damage if ingested. But whether this would slow the fundamental aging process is still a debatable point.

It is also true that BHT (the most widely studied) and several other synthetic antioxidants have increased the life span of laboratory animals. We have already discussed several of these experiments earlier in this chapter.[3, 8–10] Again, there has usually been an increase in average, but not maximum, life span. Even so, some of the results have been impressive; up to a 30 percent increase in mean life span was obtained in mice fed a diet containing 0.75 percent BHT in one experiment that carefully controlled for possible confounding factors.[10] Such life span studies are in a real sense the acid test of any supplement. One can discuss the theoretical impact of a substance or its effects on various diseases at great length, but what counts most in the final analysis is whether it prolongs or shortens life, and the quality of that life.

The third point, that BHT has inhibited cancer, is true but only part of the story, and it is here that the most serious questions can be raised about the wisdom of taking such substances as supplements. BHT has inhibited the development of cancer in animals in a number of studies. One typical experiment examined the effects of the amount and type of fat (saturated or polyunsaturated) in the diet and the addition of several antioxidants on the incidence of a chemically induced mammary tumor in rats.[83] The antioxidants studied were BHT, BHA, propyl gallate (all at 0.3 percent of diet), and alpha-tocopherol (vitamin E) at 0.2 percent of diet. Animals fed high-fat diets had a higher incidence of cancer than those on a low-fat diet; animals fed polyunsaturated fat (corn oil) had more tumors than those fed saturated fat. BHT and, to a lesser extent, propyl gallate, decreased the incidence of cancer in all groups and by up to 50 percent in the high-fat groups. Neither BHA nor alpha-tocopherol inhibited the development of cancer in this study. The carcinogen used in this part of the study undergoes "metabolic activation"; that is, it is changed after entering the body by the animal's own metabolic processes into an actual cancer-causing substance. Such carcinogens do not cause cancer unless they undergo this alteration. In a second part of this study, a substance that does not need to undergo this activation process was administered with the antioxidants. In this case the same level of BHT did not reduce cancer incidence. Another study [84] found that BHT (0.7 percent of diet) and BHA (2 percent of diet) greatly increased the incidence of liver cancer caused by a carcinogen administered at the same time. A number of experiments along these lines have now been done,[85] which can be summarized as follows. BHT (and similar substances) frequently inhibit cancer, frequently have no effect, and sometimes promote the development of cancer. This is quite likely because such chemicals interact with carcinogens (and other compounds inside the body) not just as antioxidants. Depending on the carcinogen, then, this interaction may change a substance into an active carcinogen or may inactivate it. Another point that must be considered in all these studies is the amount of BHT used. Levels of 0.3 percent to 0.75 percent of the diet are typical. This would be equivalent to a human intake of about 1.5 to 3.75 grams a day. Such levels are much higher than the amount you would consume in a normal diet as part of the BHT added to foods as a preservative. It is much higher even than the amounts frequently taken as supplements, or those of the naturally occurring antioxidants such as vitamin E, vitamin C, and beta-carotene. So the first point that must be made is that these levels tell us practically nothing about the effects of BHT or BHA that we consume in cereals, oils, and so on as part of our usual food intake. This has been estimated to average about 2mg of BHT and 10 to 15mg of BHA a day in the United States and Canada,[82, 85, 86] which is over 200 times smaller than the levels used in these studies. The overwhelming evidence is that at these levels, BHT is safe and beneficial since it prevents the oxidation of fats in food, which is potentially quite harmful. How beneficial it is we just do not know. It has been suggested that the addition of even these small amounts of antioxidants is at least partly responsible for the decrease in stomach and possibly other cancers in many countries over the past century; but the evidence for this is sketchy.

But what about taking BHT or the other synthetic antioxidants as supplements? And if so, what daily dose? I don't really have a good answer for this with the data now available. The life span data certainly argue for an overall positive effect, but again, the dose involved would amount to several grams a day if extrapolated to a human diet. I would not want to take that much of something before its effect on *people* at such levels was studied, especially if that substance was known to promote cancer in some cases. My guess is that a BHT supplement at a daily level considerably less than this, but higher than normal dietary intakes, would afford significant benefits with a minimal risk. Again, my best estimate is an average daily supplement of 100mg, which is what I take myself. This amount can be averaged over a weekly period (e.g., 250mg three times a week). In my judgment, BHT is the safest of the synthetic antioxidants; it has been the most studied and is known not to damage DNA or to cause cancer by itself.[82, 87] The other chemicals in this class, including BHA, either have not been studied as thoroughly, or have produced negative results more often.

Aspirin

Aspirin has been used in one form or another for hundreds of years, originally in its naturally occurring state in the bark of the willow tree. But it is only during the past 20 years or so that the biochemical mechanisms behind its remarkable effects have been discovered. We now know that aspirin alleviates pain, reduces fever and inflammation, inhibits blood clotting, and produces its other effects through its interaction with hormonelike substances called prostaglandins. It should be considered for use as a supplement because of its demonstrated ability to reduce death from heart disease, the leading cause of death in the industrialized countries. In a number of studies involving patients who were being treated for heart disease, aspirin has greatly reduced the incidence of further cardiovascular events, such as myocardial infarction (blockage of a coronary artery), unstable angina (pain in the upper chest, frequently radiating down the arm), or ischemia (decreased blood supply and consequent pain in some portion of tissue, in this case the heart). In one study by the Veterans Administration, over a thousand hospitalized patients with unstable angina were treated with 325mg per day of aspirin (a standard-size tablet). At the end of 12 weeks, they had a 49 percent reduction in myocardial infarction and a 51 percent reduction in death rate compared to a control group.[88] Other studies have reported significant reduction of risk of subsequent heart attacks with as little as 75mg of aspirin a day.[89] It is thought that aspirin helps prevent heart disease through its effect of inhibiting blood clotting. Whether aspirin can prevent the development of cardiovascular disease among people who have not had any major symptoms is not as well established, but there is a significant amount of evidence in its favor. In the Physicians' Health Study of more than 22,000 healthy male physicians, those who took 325mg of aspirin every other day had up to a 44 percent reduction in the incidence of myocardial infarction compared to the control group.[90] Several such studies have produced similar findings,[91] so that a number of experts in this area have recommended up to 325mg of aspirin a day for people with one or more of the risk factors for coronary disease. Such risk factors include being male, cigarette smoking, high blood pressure, diabetes, and high blood cholesterol (high ratio of LDL/HDL). Others have recommended aspirin for all American men over the age of 50, and women after menopause.[91] The best dose is not known with any precision; the available data suggest from 325mg a day to 325mg every other day. The main exceptions to this recommendation would be people who have ulcers or experience significant gastrointestinal distress from aspirin. It is best taken with meals, or at least with some food, to help prevent these complications. Buffered forms of aspirin may afford some protection, although this cannot be relied upon. The effervescent soluble forms of aspirin with sodium bicarbonate (such as Alka-Seltzer) do upset the stomach much less. This was in fact the form of aspirin used in one of these studies.[88] Because of their very high sodium content and other possible problems, they cannot be recommended for prolonged, continuous use. If you already take the standard dose (two 325mg tablets) of aspirin twice a week or more for headache or other reasons, there is, of course, no reason to add even more. Aspirin may have other health benefits, although these are mainly speculative at this point. It's possible that its anti-inflammatory effects inhibit the development of cancer in certain situations. Aspirin has extended the mean life span of fruit flies by up to 40 percent; the author of this study suggested that these results may be due to aspirin's ability to stabilize cell membranes.[92]

I might mention here that, while continuous long-term use of aspirin is generally safe and probably beneficial, such use of acetaminophen, or the combination of aspirin plus acetaminophen, can result in serious kidney and/or liver damage. There is also evidence that heavy use of the nonsteroidal anti-inflammatory drugs (NSAIDS) is associated with increased risk of kidney disease.[93] At least two of these, ibuprofen and naproxen, are now available without a prescription under a number of brand names.

Fiber

I described the benefits of dietary fiber in Chapter 4. But what about taking fiber as a supplement in the form of tablets? If your diet is based on the foods we have discussed, with whole grains, vegetables, and fruits as the staples, you will automatically be getting substantial amounts of fiber. There probably will be no reason to take more. Secondly, it's difficult to take much fiber in the form of tablets. For example, wheat bran has one of the highest fiber contents of the common grains, or of any food for that matter. It consists of about 43 percent fiber (see Appendix 2). That means that a 500mg tablet (a standard and already fair-sized tablet) contains 0.2 grams of fiber. You would have to take ten such tablets a day to get just two grams of fiber. Something like 30 to 40 grams of fiber a day is considered a desirable intake, so you can see that it will be difficult for your supplement to make up an appreciable portion of that. There is nothing inherently wrong with fiber supplements, but at present they are just not a very practical means of getting significant amounts. Fiber supplements are also available as powders that can be mixed into juice or some liquid. It *is* possible to consume significant amounts in this manner, but this type of intake is more like a food; it does not have the convenience of tablets and the mixtures are not to everyone's taste. If a purified supplement of one of the desirable fibers were available, things would be different; it would be possible to add sufficient quantities of a concentrated, purified fiber as a supplement. Cellulose and lignin, for example, undergo little or no degradation by intestinal bacteria (as many fibers do), so will not give rise to the uncomfortable bloating and gas sometimes associated with high fiber intake. As insoluble fibers, they would produce a safe and natural laxative effect with possible protection against some cancers, as we discussed in Chapter 4. Unfortunately, such purified fiber supplements are not now readily available.

The B Vitamins

Several of the B vitamins have received attention as supplements. Thiamin (vitamin B1), vitamin B6 (pyridoxine), folate, B12, niacin, biotin, and pantothenic acid all have their supporters. These are all very important, water-soluble nutrients essential to normal body function. Since they are not stored in the body in significant quantities, they must be supplied fairly consistently in the diet. Generally, vitamins in this group are used in metabolic processes through which the nutrients derived from food are transformed to suit the body's needs and to release energy. Actual deficiency diseases caused by lack of one of the B vitamins are not common in the developed countries, but because they cannot be stored and are needed on a daily basis, it is probably wise to insure an adequate intake of at least the RDA.

The RDA for thiamin, frequently still referred to as vitamin B1, is 1.5mg for men and 1mg for women. The actual requirement is related to the number of calories consumed, and has been estimated at 0.5mg of thiamin per 1,000 calories. The deficiency disease associated with lack of this vitamin is beriberi, characterized by fatigue, loss of appetite, and weight loss. It became widespread in many parts of Asia when polished rice was introduced. Polishing strips the outer covering, or bran, from rice kernels. It is the rice bran that contains thiamin and that becomes crucial if a population subsists mainly on rice. Thiamin is also present in other whole grains and is now routinely added to refined (white) wheat flour.

Folacin, also called folate and folic acid, is a vitamin essential for cell division and the maturation of new cells, including red and white blood cells. There is some evidence that low dietary intakes are associated with increased risk of several cancers. The strongest association is with colorectal, which is one of the most common cancers. Some studies have also found a relation between low folate intake and cervical cancer, or cervical dysplasia, a precancerous condition. In both cases, epidemiologic studies have found that people with high levels of dietary folate had a decreased risk of developing either cancer or conditions that are known to develop into cancer.[94, 95] This inverse relation between folate intake and precancerous colorectal conditions existed even after adjusting for known risk factors, such as family history, saturated fat intake, dietary fiber, and body mass index. The evidence is sufficient to recommend a supplement equal to one to two times the RDA — 200 to 400 micrograms of folate.

Niacin is an interesting vitamin for several reasons. Like thiamin, it is essential to the body's energy processes. Nicotinic acid, nicotinamide, and niacinamide all refer to slightly different forms of this vitamin. Nicotine, the addicting substance found in cigarettes, while chemically related, has completely different properties, and cannot be converted by the body into niacin. The deficiency disease caused by lack of adequate niacin is pellagra, characterized by the "three Ds"—diarrhea, dermatitis, and dementia. Pellagra was common in many parts of the American South even until the early part of the twentieth century. Another interesting thing about niacin is that it is used as a prescription drug in the treatment of high blood cholesterol. The doses needed in this case are one to several grams a day, which is much higher than normal dietary intakes or the RDA of 15mg. While still considered an option, there are a number of newer, more potent drugs . A side effect of high doses of nicotinic acid (but generally not niacinamide) is dilation of the blood vessels and an associated pronounced flush of the skin, sometimes accompanied by itching and headache.

Vitamin B6 refers to three chemically related substances called pyridines, and is still sometimes referred to as pyridoxine, the most common of these. A deficiency frequently leads to depression and confusion. This may be an unrecognized cause in some cases of depression, the most common mental disorder. Supplementation with rather high doses of B6 has increased average life span in a few species, but there have been too few studies to make any recommendations on this. The RDA has been set at 2mg for adults. Vitamin B6 is relatively nontoxic; amounts up to 200mg have been taken for extended periods with no signs of toxicity. A supplement of one to several times the RDA would be reasonable.

Pantothenic acid is such a widely distributed vitamin that deficiencies are practically unknown. Occasionally it is called vitamin B5, but this is not standard nomenclature. The RDA is 4 to 7mg. It is essentially nontoxic up to doses of at least 1,000mg a day.[82] It is of some interest because a few experiments have found that supplemental doses in animals had several beneficial effects. In one study, a long-lived strain of mice was fed a diet supplemented with 300 micrograms of pantothenic acid a day for their entire lives, and their survival rate was compared to mice on an unsupplemented diet.[96] Mice on the supplemented diet had a mean

life span about 20 percent greater than the controls. This was a modest level of supplementation that would amount to about 30mg a day in a human diet. Because
there have been only a few such experiments with pantothenic acid, it is questionable to what extent these results can be extrapolated to humans. Since it is essentially nontoxic and may confer significant benefits, a supplement of 25 to 50mg a
day seems justified.

With the possible exception of pantothenic acid, I do not believe that supplements containing much more than the RDA of any of the B vitamins are justified.
There *is* evidence for insuring intakes of one to possibly two or three times the
RDA. This can most conveniently be done as part of a good multivitamin tablet,
which would include thiamin, riboflavin, niacin, vitamin B6, vitamin B12, folacin,
pantothenic acid, and biotin. An additional supplement of pantothenic acid could
be taken, preferably at another time of day.

Trace Minerals

Iron is essential for the production of hemoglobin, the protein that transports
oxygen in red blood cells. It is also found in muscle cells in a similar role, and is
used in various ways in a number of other cellular processes. But there is considerable evidence that too much is harmful. Iron promotes damage from the free radical reactions that we have discussed. It actually becomes toxic in doses of greater
than 100mg a day.[82] The body conserves its supply of iron very carefully; none is
excreted through normal metabolic processes. There is a slight loss due to normal
sloughing off of cells and intestinal secretions. Since something like 80 percent of
the body's iron is in the blood, iron losses are greatest when there is bleeding. This
is why the RDA for young women, who lose iron because of menstruation, is set
at 15mg, compared to 10mg for men. When you consider that average total loss of
iron has been estimated to be 1mg per day for men and 1.5mg for menstruating
women, you can see that the RDA has a more than generous safety margin. Given
the potentially negative effects of excess iron, it is doubtful whether any supplementation is justified. Even if your diet is based on vegetables, fruits, and grains,
as has been recommended, you can obtain sufficient iron through diet alone. A
number of vegetables, especially dark-green, leafy ones, contain substantial amounts
of iron. Spinach is the best known of these, with 2.7mg iron per 100 grams, but
Swiss chard (1.8mg), peas (2.1mg), lima beans (3.1mg), and kale (1.7mg) contain
comparable amounts of iron. While the so-called heme iron found in meat is
absorbed better than the iron in vegetables, there is reason to believe it is an even
greater risk factor for cardiovascular disease and cancer.[1] A number of factors can
affect your daily iron intake. Many common foods such as farina, breakfast cereals, and flour frequently have iron added to them. Vitamin C increases iron absorption from the intestine; fiber can bind to it and prevent absorption. The iron from
cooking pots and pans can contribute significant amounts. Given the multitude of
factors that can affect your net iron intake, it's essentially impossible even for an

expert to calculate how much iron you are getting with any kind of accuracy. Your body's iron status, or hemoglobin status, is measured as part of a routine blood test, which is advisable periodically in any case. If any deficiency or borderline deficiency shows up there, you can adjust your intake accordingly. It is not unreasonable to take some iron as a supplement if your diet is not adequate in this respect, but I wouldn't take more than 5 to 10mg a day without first knowing my iron status. Again, this can conveniently be done with a multivitamin/mineral supplement. Unless you are on a very unusual diet or have unusual needs, you will satisfy your iron requirement through diet or the kind of moderate supplement I have described. As I've said, you don't want to do more than that.

A number of other trace elements have been identified in human nutrition. Zinc is essential for night vision, the immune system, and other functions. An RDA of 15mg has been set. Iodine (RDA 150μg) is essential for thyroid function. Where no definite RDA has been determined, "safe and adequate" levels for adults have been recommended[97] for copper (1.5 to 3mg), manganese (2 to 5mg), fluorine (1.5 to 4mg), chromium (50 to 200μg), and molybdenum (75 to 250μg). You will probably get enough of these in a well-balanced diet, but if they are included, as most frequently are, in your multivitamin/mineral supplement, so much the better. I don't think there is evidence for taking substantially more than the levels indicated above of any of these. Zinc and chromium are sometimes mentioned in this regard, but there is little solid evidence that greater than average intakes of either are beneficial. Chromium is essential to the regulation of blood glucose, potentiating the effects of insulin and thus permitting normal function with less insulin.[98] It has improved impaired glucose metabolism in a number of studies, but not all. This is probably because such impaired metabolism can be caused by many other factors besides chromium deficiency. Chromium supplements have also improved blood lipid profiles, decreasing total and LDL cholesterol, and increasing HDL. It should be noted, however, that the supplements used in these studies were in the range of 50 to 200 micrograms of chromium a day and were of benefit only in normalizing an impaired function. However, deficiencies seem to be common, even in developed countries. The chemical form of chromium may be important (trivalent chromium seems to be the effective form). Chromium chloride ($CrCl_3$) and chromium picolinate have both been found effective; there have not been sufficient comparisons as yet to choose between them. Other chemical forms of chromium (in particular, those in which chromium has valence six) can be carcinogenic. Small amounts of chromium are included in a number of multivitamin/mineral tablets. On the basis of available data, it seems advisable to take a modest amount in this manner, or as an individual separate supplement.

Other

I have not discussed vitamin D or vitamin K because they are rarely mentioned as supplements. Vitamin D is potentially the most toxic of the vitamins; if your multivitamin contains the RDA (5 to 10µg, or 200 to 400 IU), that's fine — but it is also the upper limit that is advisable. Vitamin K (essential to blood clotting) is also usually included in multivitamin tablets. Fish oil supplements, containing semipurified DHA or EPA, the fatty acids that may be protective against heart disease, are available as capsules. First, it is questionable whether there is enough evidence that these fatty acids are beneficial. Second, in taking them as supplements you are essentially adding that much pure fat (with its associated calories) to your diet. Finally, there is reason to believe that the oil in such capsules is not protected sufficiently against oxidation, which could turn it into something actually harmful. It may be that these problems will eventually be sorted out, but based on the available data, there is more downside risk than potential benefit.

Several amino acids, especially cysteine and methionine, are sometimes suggested as supplements. Both of these contain the sulfhydryl chemical group, which can act as an antioxidant. Again, there is insufficient evidence to recommend them as regular supplements. While methionine is an important nutrient, especially for maintaining a healthy liver, in one study additional dietary methionine fed to mice over their entire lives significantly decreased average and maximum life span.[99]

A few other substances look promising as supplements, but in my opinion there is as yet too little known about their long-term effects to recommend them. Coenzyme Q10 falls into this category. Melatonin, a hormone produced by the pineal gland (which is located inside the brain) appears quite promising. It has a well-established role in promoting sleep, but there have also been claims that it extends life, acts as an antioxidant, enhances mental function, and inhibits cancer. Again, I would want to see more long-term studies before taking it as a supplement. Dehydroepiandrosone (DHEA) is a very interesting substance being studied for many reported beneficial effects. DHEA and the closely related compound DHEA sulfate (DHEAS) are hormonelike chemicals in the class of steroids. They are secreted by the adrenal glands of humans and other primates. Their concentration in the blood declines progressively with age, beginning in the teens and falling to about 10 to 20 percent of their maximum value by age 70.[100] In contrast, cortisone, another major adrenal steroid hormone, does not decrease significantly with age. There is evidence that DHEA can inhibit the development of cancer, autoimmune disease, diabetes, and atherosclerosis.[100] Its most well documented effect is the prevention of weight gain, which has been observed many times in laboratory animals. It is not an appetite suppressant, but apparently reduces caloric efficiency — that is, the processes that convert the calories in food into energy or storage as body weight. It *may* increase life span, but this has not been confirmed. Preliminary experiments with people have produced promising results. In a recent placebo-controlled crossover trial, DHEA was administered orally (50mg/day) to 30 men and women aged 40 to 70.[101] This restored blood levels of DHEA and DHEAS to those of young adults within two weeks. Improvements were noted in important biochemical growth factors that decline with age, but the most striking effect was the marked increase in the feeling of well-being reported by those receiving DHEA. While long-term treatment of laboratory animals has not produced negative side effects, there is some concern about trying this in humans, especially since DHEA can be converted into (the male hormone) testosterone and other hormones. Synthetic steroids having the same effects as DHEA but that are not so converted are being investigated as alternatives. One of these is fluorosterone. It does not affect the liver, as DHEA does, and is undergoing clinical trials as a treatment for diabetes.

One or more of the substances currently under study may well turn out to be worth taking as supplements, and it's quite likely that new substances that significantly retard aging, or at least certain aspects of it, will eventually be found. I will conclude this chapter with some advice that should be obvious: You just have to keep abreast of the work in this area, not rushing to take any new supplement on the basis of a few published positive reports, but not waiting for proof of benefits beyond any possible doubt.

References to Chapter Five

1. B.N. Ames, M.K. Shigenaga, T.M. Hagen: Oxidants, antioxidants, and the degenerative diseases of aging. *Proc Natl Acad Sci USA* 90:7915–7922, 1993.
2. A.T. Diplock: Antioxidant nutrients and disease prevention: an overview. *Am J Clin Nutr* 53:189S–193S, 1991.
3. D. Harman: Free radical theory of aging. *Mutation Res* 275:257–266, 1992.
4. D. Harman: The aging process. *Proc Natl Acad Sci USA* 78:7124–7128, 1981.
5. D. Pearson, S. Shaw: *Life Extension, A Practical Scientific Approach*. Warner, New York, 1982.
6. F.S. LaBella, G Paul: Structure of collagen from human tendon as influenced by age and sex. *J Gerontol* 20:54–59, 1965.
7. J. Bjorksten: The crosslinkage theory of aging. *J Am Geriat Soc* 16:408–427, 1968.
8. D. Harman: Free radical theory of aging: effect of free radical inhibitors on the mortality of male LAF1 mice. *J Gerontol* 23:476–482, 1968.
9. A. Comfort: Effect of ethoxyquin on the longevity of C3H mice. *Nature* 229:254–255, 1971.
10. N.K. Clapp, L.C. Satterfield, N.D. Bowles: Effects of the antioxidant butylated hydroxytoluene (BHT) on mortality in BALB/c mice. *J Gerontol* 34:497–501, 1979.
11. M.L. Heidrick, L.C. Hendricks, D.C. Cook: Effect of dietary 2-mercaptoethanol on the life span, immune system, tumor incidence and lipid peroxidation damage in spleen lymphocytes of aging BC3F$_1$ mice. *Mech Ageing Dev* 27:341–358, 1984.
12. G. Block: The data support a role for antioxidants in reducing cancer risk. *Nutr Rev* 50:207–213, 1992.
13. J.H. Weisburger: Nutritional approach to cancer prevention with emphasis on vitamins, antioxidants, and carotenoids. *Am J Clin Nutr* 53:226S–237S, 1991.
14. W.J. Blot et al.: Nutrition intervention trials in Linxian, China: supplementation with specific vitamin/mineral combinations, cancer incidence, and disease-specific mortality in the general population. *JNCI* 85:1483–1492, 1992.
15. W.A. Pryor: The antioxidant nutrients and disease prevention — what do we know and what do we need to find out? *Am J Clin Nutr* 53:391S–393S, 1991.
16. T.F. Slater: Disturbances of free radical reactions: a cause or consequence of cell injury? In: *Medical, Biochemical and Chemical Aspects of Free Radicals, Vol.1*, O Hayaishi et al., eds. Elsevier, Amsterdam, 1989.

17. A. Taylor: Role of nutrients in delaying cataracts. *Ann NY Acad Sci* 669:111–123, 1992.

18. P. Di Mascio, ME Murphy, H. Sies: Antioxidant defense systems: the role of carotenoids, tocopherols, and thiols. *Am J Clin Nutr* 53:194S–200S, 1991.

19. B.J. Weimann, H. Weiser: Functions of vitamin E in reproduction and in prostacyclin and immunoglobulin synthesis in rats. *Am J Clin Nutr* 53:1056S–1060S, 1991.

20. K.F. Gey, P Puska, P Jordan, UK Moser: Inverse correlation between plasma vitamin E and mortality from ischemic heart disease in cross-cultural epidemiology. *Am J Clin Nutr* 53:326S–334S, 1991.

21. M.J. Stampfer, C.H. Hennekens, J.E. Manson et al.: Vitamin E consumption and the risk of coronary heart disease in women. *New Engl J Med* 328:1444–1449, 1993.

22. E.B. Rimm, M.J. Stampfer, A. Ascherio et al.: Vitamin E consumption and the risk of coronary heart disease in men. *New Engl J Med* 328:1450–1456, 1993.

23. H. Esterbauer, M. Dieber-Rotheneder, G. Striegel, G. Waeg: Role of vitamin E in preventing the oxidation of low-density lipoprotein. *Am J Clin Nutr* 53:314S–321S, 1991.

24. C.F. Combs, S.B. Combs: The nutritional biochemistry of selenium. *Ann Rev Nutr* 4:257–280, 1984.

25. C. Ip: The chemopreventive role of selenium in carcinogenesis. *J Am Coll Toxicol* 5:7–20, 1988.

26. W.C. Willet, M.J. Stampfer: Selenium and cancer. *Br Med J* 297:573–574, 1988.

27. J. Neve, F. Vertongen, F. Molle: Selenium deficiency. *Clin Endocrinol Metab* 14:629–656, 1985.

28. G.Q. Yang: Research on Se-related problems in human health in China. In: *Procedings of the Third International Symposium on Selenium in Biology and Medicine*. C.F Combs, J.E. Spallholz, O.A. Levander, eds., AVI Publishing, Westport, Conn., 1986.

29. H.W. Lane, J.S. Butel, D. Medina: Selenium, lipid peroxidation, and murine mammary tumorigenesis. In: *Selenium in Biology and Medicine, Part B*. G.F. Combs et al., eds. AVI/Van Nostrand, New York, 1987.

30. G.A. Greeder, J.A. Milner: Factors influencing the inhibitory effect of selenium on mice inoculated with Ehrlich ascites tumor cells. *Science* 209:825–827, 1980.

31. A.M. Watrach, J.A. Milner, M.A. Watrach, K.A. Poirier: Inhibition of human breast cancer cells by selenium. *Cancer Lett* 25:41–47, 1984.

32. J.A. Milner, C.Y. Hsu: Inhibitory effects of selenium on the growth of L1210 leukemic cells. *Cancer Res* 41:1652–1656, 1981.

33. R.A. Sunde, W.G. Hoekstra: Structure, synthesis and function of glutathione peroxidase. *Nutr Rev* 38:265–273, 1980.

34. V.W. Bunker, B.E. Clayton: Selenium status in disease: the role of selenium as a therapeutic agent. *Br J Clin Pract* 44:401–403, 1990.

35. A.M. Fan, K.W. Kizer: Selenium. Nutritional, toxilogic, and clinical aspects. *West J Med* 153:160–167, 1990.

36. M.E. Fico, K.A. Poirier et al.: Differential effects of selenium on normal and neoplastic canine mammary cells. *Cancer Res* 46:3384–3388, 1986.

37. G. Batist et al.: Selenium-induced cytotoxicity of human leukemic cells: interaction with reduced glutathione. *Cancer Res* 46:5482–5485, 1986.

38. J.A. Golczewski, G.D. Frenkel: Cellular selenoproteins and the effects of selenite on cell proliferation. *Biol Trace Elem Res* 20:115–126, 1989.

39. M.E. Roy et al.: Selenium and immune cell functions. II. Effect on lymphocyte-mediated cytotoxicity. *Proc Soc Exp Biol Med* 193:143–148, 1990.

40. L.E. Koller et al.: Immune responses in rats supplemented with selenium. *Clin Exp Immunol* 63:570–576, 1986.

41. D.J. Blodgett, G.G. Schurig, E.T. Kornegay: Immunomodulation in weanling swine with dietary selenium. *Am J Vet Res* 47:1517–1519, 1986.

42. W.S. Swecker et al.: Influence of supplemental selenium on humoral immune responses in weaned beef calves. *Am J Vet Res* 50:1760–1763, 1989.

44. L.D. Koller, J.H. Exon: The two faces of selenium — deficiency and toxicity — are similar in animals and man. *Can J Vet Res* 50:297–306, 1986.

45. O.E. Olson: Selenium toxicity in animals with emphasis on man. *J Am Coll Toxicol* 5:45–69, 1986.

46. D.S. Goodman: Vitamin A and retinoids in health and disease. *New Eng J Med* 310:1023–1031, 1984.

47. M.B. Sporn, A.B. Roberts: The role of retinoids in differentiation and carcinogenesis. *Cancer Res* 43:3034–3040, 1983.

48. S.L. Hofman, S. Strickland, V. Mahdavi: The induction of differentiation in teratocarcinoma cells by retinoic acid. *Cell* 15:393–403, 1978.

49. T.R. Breitman, S.E. Selomick, S.J. Collins: Induction of differentiation of the human promyelocytic leukemia cell line (HL-60) by retinoic acid. *Proc Natl Acad Sci USA* 77:2936–2940, 1980.

50. S.L. Hofman: Southwestern internal medicine conference: retinoids — "differentiation agents" for cancer treatment and prevention. *Am J Med Sci* 304:202–213, 1992.

51. S.M. Lippman, J.F. Kessler, F.L. Meyskens: Retinoids as preventive and therapeutic anticancer agents (part I). *Cancer Treat Rep* 71:391–405, 1987.

52. S.M. Lippman, J.F. Kessler, F.L. Meyskens: Retinoids as preventive and therapeutic anticancer agents (part II). *Cancer Treat Rep* 71:493–515, 1987.

53. N. Wald et al.: Low serum-vitamin A and subsequent risk of cancer: preliminary results of a prospective study. *Lancet* 2:813–815, 1980.

54. J.D. Kark et al.: Serum vitamin A (retinol) and cancer incidence in Evans County, Georgia. *JNCI* 66:7–16, 1981.

55. S. Moriguchi, L. Werner, R.R. Watson: High dietary vitamin A (retinyl palmitate) and cellular immune functions in mice. *Immunology* 56:169–177, 1985.

56. R.H. Goldfarb, R.B. Herberman: Natural killer cell reactivity: regulatory interactions among phorbol ester, interferon, cholera toxin, and retinoic acid. *J Immunol* 126: 2129–2135, 1981.

57. S.W. Farnes, P.A. Setness: Retinoid therapy for aging skin and acne. *Postgrad Med* 92(6):191–200, 1992.

58. C.N. Ellis et al.: Sustained improvements with prolonged topical tretinoin (retinoic acid) for photoaged skin. *J Am Acad Dermatol* 23:629–637, 1990.

59. R. Peto et al.: Can dietary beta-carotene materially reduce human cancer rates? *Nature* 290:201–208, 1981.

60. G.W. Burton: Antioxidant action of carotenoids. *J Nutr* 119:109–111, 1989.

61. A. Peng et al.: Beta-carotene and canthaxanthin inhibit chemically- and physically-induced neoplastic transformation in 10T1/2 cells. *Carcinogenesis* 9:1533–1539, 1988.

62. N.I. Krinsky: Carotenoids and cancer in animal models. *J Nutr* 119:123–126, 1989.

63. E. Seifter et al.: Regression of C3HBA mouse tumor due to X-ray therapy combined with beta-carotene or vitamin A. *JNCI* 71:409–417, 1983.

64. A. Bendich: Carotenoids and the immune response. *J Nutr* 119:112–115, 1989.

65. Y. Tomita et al.: Augmentation of tumor immunity against syngeneic tumors in mice by beta-carotene. *JNCI* 78:679–680, 1987.

66. R.B. Shekelle et al.: Dietary vitamin A and risk of cancer in the Western Electric study. *Lancet* 2:1185–1190, 1981.

67. A.B. Miller, H.A. Risch: Diet and lung cancer. *Chest* 96:85–95, 1985.

68. V.N. Singh, S.K. Gaby: Premalignant lesions: role of antioxidant vitamins and beta-carotene in risk reduction and prevention of malignant transformation. *Am J Clin Nutr* 53:386S–390S, 1991.

69. H.B. Staehelin et al.: Beta-carotene and cancer prevention: the Basel study. *Am J Clin Nutr* 53:265S–269S, 1991.

70. R.G. Ziegler: A review of epidemiologic evidence that carotenoids reduce the risk of cancer. *J Nutr* 119:116–122, 1989.

71. Alpha-tocopherol, beta-carotene cancer prevention study group: The effect of vitamin E and beta-carotene on the incidence of lung cancer and other cancers in male smokers. *New Engl J Med* 330:1029–1035, 1994.

72. J.M. Graziano, J.E. Manson, J.E. Buring et al.: Dietary antioxidants and cardiovascular disease. *Ann NY Acad Sci* 669:249–259, 1992.

73. G. Block: Vitamin C and cancer prevention: the epidemiologic evidence. *Am J Clin Nutr* 53:270S–282S, 1991.

74. B. Frei, L. England, B.N. Ames: Ascorbate is an outstanding antioxidant in human blood plasma. *Proc Natl Acad Sci USA* 86:6377–6381, 1989.

75. A. Shibata et al.: Intake of vegetables, fruits, beta-carotene, vitamin C and vitamin supplements and cancer incidence among the elderly: a prospective study. *Br J Can* 66: 673–679, 1992.

76. A. Bendich: Vitamin C and immune responses. *Food Technol* 41:112–114, 1987.

77. D.L. Trout: Vitamin C and cardiovascular risk factors. *Am J Clin Nutr* 53:322S–325S, 1991.

78. I. Morel et al.: Antioxidant and iron-chelating activities of the flavonoids catechin, quercetin and diosmetin on iron-loaded rat hepatocyte cultures. *Biochem Pharmacol* 45(1): 13–19, 1993.

79. M.G.L. Hertog et al.: Intake of potentially anticarcinogenic flavonoids and their determinants in adults in The Netherlands. *Nutr Cancer* 20:21–29, 1993.

80. M.A. Arsenian: Magnesium and cardiovascular disease. *Prog Cardiovasc Dis* 35: 271–310, 1993.

81. R.P. Heaney: Calcium, bone health and osteoporosis. In: *Bone and Mineral Research, Annual 4.* WA Peck, ed. Elsevier, New York, 1986.

82. National Research Council: *Diet and Health.* National Academy Press, Washington, DC, 1989.

83. M.M. King, P.B. McCay: Modulation of tumor incidence and possible mechanisms of inhibition of mammary carcinogenesis by dietary antioxidants. *Cancer Res* 43:248S–2490S, 1983.

84. K. Imaida, S. Fukushima, K. Inoue et al.: Modifying effects of concomitant treatment with butylated hydroxyanisole or butylated hydroxytoluene on N,N-dibutylnitrosamine-induced liver, forestomach and urinary bladder carcinogenesis in F344 male rats. *Cancer Lett* 43:167–172, 1988.

85. H.F. Stich: The beneficial and hazardous effects of simple phenolic compounds. *Mutation Res* 259:307–324, 1991.

86. D.C. Kirkpatrick, B.H. Lauer: Intake of phenolic antioxidants from foods in Canada. *Food Chem Toxicol* 24:1035–1037, 1986.

87. E.M. Bomhard, J.N. Bremmer, B.A. Herbold: Review of the mutagenicity/genotoxicity of butylated hydroxytoluene. *Mutation Res* 277:187–200, 1992.

88. H.D. Lewis , J.D. David, D.G. Archibald et al.: Protective effects of aspirin against myocardial infarction and death in men with unstable angina. *N Engl J Med* 309:396–403, 1983.

89. I. Nyman, H. Larsson, L. Wallentin et al.: Prevention of serious cardiac events by low-dose aspirin in patients with silent myocardial ischaemia. *Lancet* 340:497–501, 1992.

90. Steering Committee of the Physicians' Health Study Research Group: Final report on the aspirin component of the ongoing Physicians' Health Study. *N Engl J Med* 321: 129–135, 1989.

91. J.E. Dalen: An apple a day or an aspirin a day? *Arch Intern Med* 151:1066–1069, 1991.

92. R. Hochschild: Effect of membrane stabilizing drugs on mortality in *Drosophilia Melanogaster. Exp Gerontol* 6:133–151, 1971.

93. T.V. Perneger, P.K. Whelton, M.J. Klag: Risk of kidney failure associated with the use of acetaminophen, aspirin, and nonsteroidal antiinflammatory drugs. *N Engl J Med* 331(25):1675–1679, 1994.

94. C.E. Butterworth et al.: Folate deficiency and cervical dysplasia. *JAMA* 267:528–533, 1992.

95. E. Giovannucci et al.: Folate, methionine, and alcohol intake and risk of colorectal adenoma. *JNCI* 85:875–884, 1993.

96. R.B. Pelton, R.J. Williams: Effect of pantothenic acid on the longevity of mice. *Proc Soc Exp Biol Med* 99:632–633, 1958.

97. National Research Council, Food and Nutrition Board: *Recommended Dietary Allowances, ed. 10.* National Academy Press, Washington, DC, 1989.

98. W. Mertz: Chromium in human nutrition: a review. *J Nutr* 123:626–633, 1993.

99. H.R. Massie, V.R. Aiello: The effect of dietary methionine on the copper content of tissues and survival of young and old mice. *Exp Gerontol* 19:393–399, 1984.

100. A.G. Schwartz et al.: Dehydroepiandrostone and structural analogs: a new class of cancer chemopreventive agents. *Adv Cancer Res* 51:391–424, 1988.

101. A.J. Morales, J.J. Nolan, J.C. Nelson, SSC Yen: Effects of replacement dose of dehydroepiandrostone in men and women of advancing age. *J Clin Endocrin Metab* 78:1360–1367, 1994.

SIX. Exercise

The health benefits of exercise are usually thought of primarily as they relate to the avoidance of heart disease, which would indeed be a major benefit in itself. But many other claims have been made for exercise in recent years. I will try to separate the facts from the hype in this chapter.

In assessing the value of exercise, there are several criteria we will be concerned with and two or three major sources of evidence. First, there have been a fair number of studies on exercise in connection with heart disease. These are mostly epidemiologic studies, but some have used human subjects in a controlled experimental setting. Some epidemiologic studies have also examined the relation of exercise to overall mortality. Second, a number of experiments have been done with laboratory animals on the effects of exercise on certain diseases and on life span. These have the advantage that the conditions can be more closely controlled and animals can (sometimes) be studied over their entire lives. In terms of the criteria for the benefits of exercise, cardiovascular effects are very important but are not the whole story. Cardiovascular disease is the number-one cause of death in the United States and most of the developed countries, and cardiovascular conditioning strongly impacts our quality of life, especially in the middle to later years. But we also want to examine the benefits of exercise in terms of other — in some cases more definite — criteria. What is its effect on overall mortality and life span? Is there evidence that exercise helps in maintaining an overall good quality of life and, if so, what type of exercise is best for this purpose?

There is considerable evidence that mild to moderate exercise helps prevent heart disease. The majority of the epidemiologic studies have found such a protective effect.[1, 2] One summary of such studies estimated that physically inactive persons have nearly 1.9 times the incidence of heart disease as the physically active. This was not far different from the relative risk associated with high blood pressure (2.1), cigarette smoking (2.5), and high blood cholesterol (2.4). Furthermore, physical inactivity seems to be a risk factor independent of its relation to body weight, blood pressure, or other risk factors. One of the large recent studies followed the habits, characteristics, and mortality of over 10,000 men (Harvard alumni) for two decades.[3] The men ranged in age from about 30 to 70 years at the beginning of the study. Those men who had begun a moderate exercise program had a 23 percent lower overall risk of death compared to those who had not. Quitting cigarette smoking and maintenance of a lean body mass were also associated with significant reductions in mortality. The death rate from coronary heart disease and reduction of this death rate were similar to these overall mortality rates.

This reported protective effect due to exercise was comparable to that of heredity, evaluated as having one or both parents live to at least age 65. The heredity factor became less important as a person aged; if he had already lived to age 60 or so, it didn't much matter anymore at what age his parents died. Translated into length of life, this study estimated that taking up moderate exercise was associated with an additional 0.72 years of life. For comparison, quitting smoking added 1.46 years and maintaining normal blood pressure 0.91 years. These figures are averages for the entire group of men; the gain in additional years of life got smaller as the lifestyle changes were made at more advanced ages. Looked at this way, the benefits do not seem very impressive. It should be noted, however, that these men were generally at least halfway through the average male life span when the lifestyle changes were made.

Most, but not all, studies of this sort have reported similar findings.[1, 4, 5] The fundamental problem in interpreting them is that it is impossible to eliminate all possible confounding factors that may have influenced the results. For example, the men who did not take up physical activity may have avoided it because they were already feeling poorly, possibly with undiagnosed heart disease. Or, the men who did begin an exercise program may well have been those with a greater regard for their health, and may have undertaken other health measures. This is a common problem with all such studies: They show correlation but cannot prove cause and effect. It seems likely that exercise did in fact cause at least some of the benefits, but it would be nice to have more definite proof. The only way to completely eliminate this problem would be to do a controlled experiment in which persons were randomly assigned to a group placed on an exercise program, another group of randomly selected persons served as a nonexercising control group, and the groups were followed for several decades (and preferably until they had all died), tabulating their mortality data and other characteristics. It is doubtful that such an experiment will ever be done; the problems of cost and compliance (assuring that everyone stayed in the study and followed the program assigned to their group) are staggering.

A few such studies have been done with laboratory animals. (Even here, the cost and logistics are daunting.) When exercise is begun shortly after weaning, so that an animal exercises for essentially its entire life, life span has almost always been reported to be increased. In a large study of male and female rats who were either not exercised or exercised ten minutes a day on a motor-driven treadmill for their whole lives, the exercised males had a 28 percent greater average (mean) life span, and the females a nearly 40 percent greater mean life span than their nonexercised counterparts.[6] Maximum life span was also longer in both exercised males and females. In another experiment, rats were forced to exercise daily for their entire lives on a motor-driven treadmill beginning at either 120, 300, 450, or 600 days of age.[7] The exercised rats had a greater average life span than unexercised controls only in the 120- and 300-day groups. When begun at 450 days, exercise shortened life span somewhat; when begun at 600 days, the decrease was quite significant. There is thus evidence for a "threshold age" somewhere between 300 and 450 days in these rats; when exercise is begun at a later age than this, it ceases to extend life span and begins to shorten it. These two ages are respectively about 40 and 60 percent of the average life span of the rat, so this threshold age is around halfway through a rat's average life (corresponding to about 37 years of age in a human). In a study by Goodrick at the National Institute on Aging,[8] male and female rats were maintained in cages either with or without exercise wheels for their entire lives beginning at 1.5 months of age. Under such conditions the animals voluntarily use these wheels to exercise as much as they want. The exercise group of female rats had an 11.5 percent greater average and a 13 percent greater maximum life span than unexercised rats. Exercised males had a 19.3 percent greater average and a 13.8 percent greater maximum life span compared to unexercised males. However, in a later study at the same laboratory, voluntary wheel exercise did not increase longevity of rats when begun at either 10.5 or 18 months of age.[9] Exercise did not shorten life span either; the exercised rats lived about as long as the nonexercised ones. This study is notable because it also examined the effects of caloric restriction, in this case by feeding the animals every other day, with and without exercise. Rats fed every other day lived considerably longer than controls whether this restriction was begun at 10.5 months or 18 months of age, but exercise did not increase this survival advantage any further. That is, rats who were both exercised and calorie restricted lived about as long as those who were just calorie restricted. The discrepancy with the study reporting that exercise begun later than 300 days of age shortens life[7] could be due to the more intense, forced exercise used in that study.

The effect of exercise on specific diseases has also been studied in animals. As might be expected, there have been reports that exercise affords some protection against cardiovascular disease. The interaction of exercise and cancer is not as clear. Overall, epidemiologic and laboratory studies generally have found that exercise decreases cancer risk or has no effect,[10–12] but several studies have reported increased risk. For example, several experiments have compared the effects of high- versus low-fat diet with or without exercise on induced mammary cancer in rats.[13] The high-fat diet increased the number of breast cancers and their rate of appearance. Moderate treadmill exercise also increased the incidence and number of cancers in rats on both high- and low-fat diets. Analysis of data from the Framingham Heart Study also found that women who were more physically active had a higher incidence of breast cancer.[14] The relative risk for the most active women was 1.6 times that of the least active. But a more recent study of over 500 women who were newly diagnosed with breast cancer and an equal number of matched controls found that women who exercised at least 3.8 hours a week had less than half the rate of breast cancer as inactive women.[15] These apparently conflicting findings remain a mystery. Breast cancer is a somewhat special case, however. It is strongly influenced by lifetime hormone levels, which are known to be altered by intense exercise. Indeed, women who exercise frequently and intensely often menstruate irregularly or stop menstruating.

In summary, it is thought that exercise does increase overall longevity, but the gain is rather modest unless the exercise program is begun early in life and continued throughout life. The epidemiologic data suggest that the gain probably amounts to several years if begun early, but less than a year if exercise is begun later than age 30.[3] This agrees fairly well with the animal studies, which indicate a cutoff age around early middle age, above which initiation of an exercise program no longer confers survival benefits, and may in fact decrease survival if the exercise is too intense.

However, longevity is just part of the story. Exercise affects quality of life quite substantially. The effects of aging on skeletal muscle* are very similar to the effects of disuse: There is loss of protein, muscle mass, and consequent strength.[16, 17] There is also a decreased capacity to utilize glucose and fatty acids for energy, and a decreased response to insulin. The percentage of lean body mass, or the percentage of the body composed of muscle, decreases considerably with age. The exact numbers depend on how the measurement is made, but all show the same trend. Typical measurements made with modern techniques indicate that, whereas muscle mass makes up nearly 30 percent of the average male body at age 25, only about 17 percent of the body of the average 75-year-old is composed of muscle.[18] There is a corresponding increase in the percentage of the body composed of fat, from around 18 percent in a 25-year-old man to over 28 percent at age 75. The muscle mass of women is about 5 percent less and body fat about 5 percent more than men, but similar changes occur with age. The percentage of body fat seems to level off around age 60 in both men and women. The rate of maximum oxygen uptake, one of the best measures of overall fitness, decreases at a rate of about 10 percent per decade (Figure 6.1). Combined with the overall loss of muscle mass, this leads to the frailty frequently associated with the elderly. Grip strength and lifting ability also decline considerably with age, and a number of changes and abnormalities appear at the cellular level. More precise studies of middle-aged to older men and women[16] have concluded that muscle mass is the major determinant of the strength remaining in an old person. It is probably the main determinant of independence in the elderly; i.e., those people who have preserved a sufficient amount of muscle mass can still care for themselves, while others of their age group are institutionalized or have lost the ability to walk. Exercise also substantially increases bone mass, helping to prevent the fractures common in the old. This loss of muscle mass probably accounts for most of the decrease in metabolic rate with age. A consequence of this is the reduced calorie needs of old people — a greater proportion of their bodies is fat, which requires far less energy and other nutrients than muscle.[19, 20] The decreased activity of the average person with age adds to this reduced energy requirement (Figure 6.2).

While it might be thought that aerobic exercise, which is most effective in cardiovascular conditioning, would also be most effective in increasing life span, the epidemiologic studies we have just discussed have found that it was weekly

The term skeletal muscle is used to refer to the muscles of the body that are attached to bone, under voluntary control, and used to move the body parts, as distinct from heart muscle or the smooth muscle surrounding the intestines, the esophagus, the uterus, and many other organs.

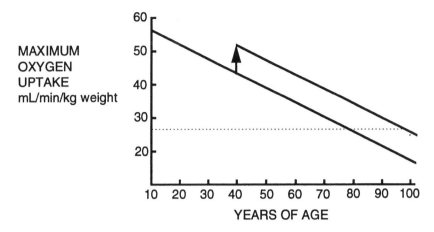

Figure 6.1 Decline in maximum oxygen uptake with age. This is a good measure of overall fitness. Exercise training increases maximum oxygen uptake typically by the amount shown by the arrow. Therefore, even if a decline still occurs with age at the same rate, the age at which the minimum level required to function will be reached is increased. If the dash line represents the minimal level needed, it would normally be reached at age 80 in the above example; exercise training delays this into the 90s.

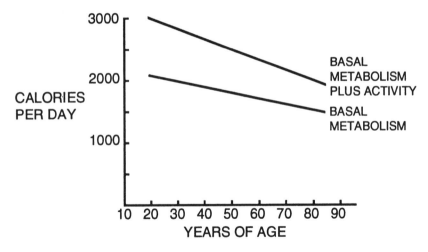

Figure 6.2 Decline in average energy expenditure with age. Most of this decline is due to the decrease in basal metabolic rate, but on average people also become less active as they age.

energy expenditure on exercise, regardless of the type, that correlated best with greater longevity. Some benefit was seen with an additional 500 calories per week of exercise; the effect seemed to peak around 2,000cal/week.

It is debatable whether exercise will slow the rate of physiologic decline (maximum oxygen uptake, muscle mass, etc.) or just provide an extra reserve capacity.

Most authorities in this field believe that exercise increases the *level* of fitness at any given age, but does not slow the overall rate of its *decline*. In this case, if an individual takes up an exercise program at age 40, as shown in Figure 6.1, his maximum oxygen uptake increases as indicated to a significant level above average, but its rate of decline, as shown by the slope of the line, does not change. However, this increased fitness capacity provides a substantial reserve in old age. If serious impairment occurs when this function has fallen to the dashed line in the figure, the age at which this occurs is delayed in this example from around 80 into the 90s. Others think that exercise slows the actual rate of decline of physical fitness. Several studies support this view. One such study examined young (age 18 to 30) and older (age 45 to 60) men who exercised a great deal — from 4 to 18 hours a week. Their percentage of body fat and maximum oxygen uptake were found to depend on the amount of time they spent exercising per week, essentially independent of age.[21] Still other studies have reported that highly conditioned athletes had less than half the rate of loss of maximum oxygen uptake over an eight-year period as did sedentary men.[17]

Exercise can certainly help preserve both muscle mass and most measures of fitness into old age. Researchers in Sweden compared many physiologic measurements in groups of men around 65 years old ranging from very sedentary to very active.[22] They found that the very active men had about 7 percent greater lean body mass, higher vital capacity, lower resting heart rate, lower systolic blood pressure, better oral glucose tolerance, and lower insulin and triglyceride levels. The men did not differ in externals: Gray hair, balding, and wrinkles were the same in exercising and nonexercising men.

The evidence that exercise benefits quality of life well into old age is impressive. It could well make the difference between being an invalid (or severely impaired) and retaining complete independence in our later years. Of course, there is also the increased feeling of well-being that comes with regular physical activity at any age.

There are a few caveats about beginning an exercise program that are mostly just common sense. The first concerns people who have never exercised, or not exercised regularly for some years. They should begin such a program slowly, say with walking, and increase their intensity level gradually. If they are already middle-aged, it is neither necessary nor desirable for them to attempt to attain a very high level of conditioning. If you have more than one serious risk factor for heart disease, it would be safest to get a physical examination before starting. High-intensity exercise is not necessary in old people; moderate walking programs have been found to substantially increase maximum oxygen uptake and overall fitness in average elderly persons. Physical fitness *can* be increased considerably even in the old by a more intense program, but it's doubtful whether the benefits of this outweigh the risks. On the other hand, there is no reason for people who have been exercising vigorously for most of their lives to significantly decrease their activity when they become old.

While a few studies have suggested that it is primarily total energy spent on exercise per week that determines its long-term benefits, it would be prudent to consider cardiovascular conditioning first, because this system is so crucial. There is no essential conflict; a good exercise program can emphasize cardiovascular conditioning while incorporating or adding muscle strength and endurance training. Flexibility — the range of motion permitted a joint — is a third important type of fitness.

First, let's review a bit about exercise physiology. Physical activity can be categorized in several ways. One is to divide all activities into dynamic or static exercise. Dynamic exercise involves the repetition of low-resistance motions, such as walking, running, swimming, and cycling. Static (isometric) exercise involves sustained contraction of muscles against a fixed resistance, without movement of the body's joints. Examples are pushing against a brick wall or pushing the palms of the hands against each other. Within each of these categories, exercise can be aerobic or anaerobic. This is determined by the rate of energy expenditure. For mild to moderate exercise, the body can continuously supply and use oxygen in the muscles. Such exercise is aerobic. If the exercise is too intense, oxygen cannot be supplied at a sufficient rate and the body reverts to other mechanisms to supply energy to the tissue. This is anaerobic exercise. Dynamic exercise is typically, but not always, aerobic, and isometric exercise is typically anaerobic. While jogging and walking are primarily aerobic, a fast sprint is anaerobic. Many activities involve a mixture of aerobic and anaerobic metabolism. As a rough rule, if the activity can be sustained continuously for more than a minute or so, it is primarily aerobic. This distinction is important because cardiovascular fitness is generally not increased by anaerobic activities. The amount of oxygen carried by and extracted from your blood determines to a large extent your ability to exercise for long periods. Aerobic training, especially that involving continuous movements of the large muscle groups, conditions the body to better distribute cardiac output and extract more oxygen from the blood. This typically results in a lower resting heart rate and blood pressure. In contrast, the response to anaerobic activities is usually highly specific — strength and muscle size in the muscles used are increased but not overall fitness.

Skeletal muscles can be exercised by contracting them against some resistance, as in weight lifting, or by repetitive contractions, as in running. Heart muscle is a bit different. Simply increasing the number of muscular contractions — the heart rate — will not improve it. The volume of blood returned to the heart by the veins and pumped by it must be increased. The heart responds to this greater volume of blood being returned to it by contracting more forcefully and gradually making itself stronger. This increase in volume can be brought about by using the large muscles of the body, especially those in the legs. When these muscles contract they squeeze the veins running through them and force blood toward the heart because of the one-way valves in the veins. This increases the amount of blood that the heart must pump with each beat, thereby inducing the conditioning that makes it stronger and more efficient. At the same time, the amount of oxygen delivered to the muscles being used is increased. The physiologic and biochemical changes resulting from cardiovascular endurance training are remarkable. The individual fibers that make up muscle increase in size in the trained muscles. Concentrations of the cellular enzymes that utilize nutrients and oxygen to generate energy become higher in such muscles so they can use the extra oxygen being delivered, and they are also able to use fat more efficiently as an energy source. The number of capillaries per volume of muscle greatly increases. (Capillaries are the smallest of the blood vessels, through which nutrients and oxygen are delivered to the individual cells and cellular wastes carried away.) As a consequence of these changes, the proportion of oxygen extracted from blood is more complete in trained muscle. These changes take place only in the muscles used, however, and are quite specific to the group of muscles used in any particular exercise. Jogging won't do much for the muscles used in swimming, even though both exercises will improve aerobic capacity and the heart. Both the size (volume) of the heart chambers that pump blood to the body and the thickness of their walls increase with appropriate endurance training. The volume of blood pumped by the heart with each beat is greater both at rest and during exercise. Together with the greater extraction of oxygen from the blood, this results in a lower resting heart rate and blood pressure in trained persons. The increase in the maximum rate at which oxygen can be delivered and utilized by the body (maximum oxygen uptake, sometimes called aerobic capacity) is one of the most important results of such fitness training. This increase also enables such individuals to utilize oxygen more efficiently even during submaximal exercise.

Weight lifting and isometric exercises are generally not effective for cardiovascular conditioning. This is because, while heart rate can be increased considerably in such exercises, blood flow to the heart is not increased. Secondly, at least with the usual routines followed in this type of exercise, the activity is not continuous enough to induce cardiovascular conditioning. There are a few weight lifting routines that may benefit cardiovascular fitness to some extent. They generally use many repetitions of light weights in a more-or-less continuous routine, such as "circuit weight training." But none of them has been proven to be consistently effective, or as effective as aerobic exercise. These types of exercise do have their place, however, which we will discuss shortly.

We can sum up the rules for cardiovascular conditioning by saying that the activity must use the large muscles of the body, be continuous, and be carried out at sufficient intensity for a sufficient length of time. Walking, jogging, running in place, bicycling, swimming, and cross-country skiing are common examples. Squash, handball, and racquetball are fine if played continuously. Studies of tennis have shown that it is usually played in too discontinuous a manner to be effective, but if you can overcome this objection it also can be used. Intensity of the exercise can be measured by how high your heart rate goes. Note that this is a *measure* of the intensity of an acceptable exercise; it is not the elevated heart rate itself that brings about the conditioning. The minimum intensity required for conditioning to occur is about 70 percent of your maximum heart rate. Maximum heart rate declines with age and also varies widely from person to person. It can be estimated by subtracting your age from 220 to find your maximum heart rate in beats per minute. Therefore, for a 40-year-old it would be 220–40=180. Seventy percent of this gives your exercise intensity threshold; so, in this example, 0.70 × 180=126 beats/min. Your heart rate can be easily determined from the pulse in your wrist; you do not, of course, have to count it for a full minute (e.g., you can count for ten seconds and multiply by six). If you don't know how to do this, it's a good thing to learn. Turn one hand palm-side up; with the middle and index fingers of the other hand feel for the pulse in the wrist. It is located on the palm side near the thumb-side edge of the wrist. If you are not familiar with your response to exercising, you may want to measure your pulse the first few times to get a rough estimate of your intensity. It is not necessary to do this every time you exercise. You will rapidly learn where your threshold is from your body's response. When your breathing becomes somewhat deeper and more labored than at rest, and you start to feel that you are exerting some effort, you are probably at your threshold. This is not as quantitative a guide as the heart rate test, but has the considerable advantages of being easier and allowing for individual variation; it becomes quite reliable once you become familiar with how your body responds to exercise.

As far as frequency goes, three days a week is the minimum required for improving cardiovascular conditioning; two days a week is the minimum needed to maintain your present level. The activity must last at least 10 to 15 minutes to obtain any conditioning benefits. At the shortest duration the benefits are minimal, but better than nothing if that's all you have time or inclination for on a particular day.

Table 6.1 gives the energy expenditure (the number of calories burned per hour) for a number of acceptable activities that emphasize cardiovascular conditioning. These figures depend on a person's weight, and are averages, of course, since for many of the activities the intensity level can vary with the individual. Some of these activities provide strength and endurance training for many muscles as well as cardiovascular conditioning.

I might also mention some common misconceptions about exercise and conditioning. Muscle conditioning will occur in those muscles used in a given exercise, but fat loss is not specific. You can't lose fat specifically in a given part of your body by exercising the muscles in that part. So, while abdominal muscle exercises are fine, they will not decrease abdominal fat any more than any other exercise.*

---

*I have occasionally been asked: Then how do you get rid of the fat in a particular part of your body? There are no exercise/diet regimens that will accomplish this. The only method is liposuction, a procedure in which an incision is made and a tubular device is inserted to suck out the fat underneath the skin. You can't get rid of very much fat by this method, but enough to make a significant reduction in the selected area. The second point to be made is that reducing your overall body fat by diet and exercise will eventually reduce the fat in the area you are concerned with; it just might take a while for the reduction to become obvious. People tend to accumulate and lose fat according to their own genetic pattern. This overall loss is, of course, what is desirable from a health perspective.

Weight: kilograms	50	59	68	77	86	95
pounds	110	130	150	170	190	210

Activity						
basketball	350	411	480	542	603	672
bicycling (10 mph)	437	519	600	681	763	844
handball	500	595	690	777	872	966
jogging (11-min. mile)	402	474	546	624	696	768
jogging (8-min. mile)	618	732	846	960	1074	1188
racquetball	523	621	720	811	910	1008
skating	234	282	324	366	408	456
skiing downhill	455	541	627	706	792	878
skiing cross country	540	644	740	843	939	1041
squash	580	690	800	902	1012	1114
swimming, crawl	420	500	580	653	733	807
tennis	330	390	450	510	576	635
volleyball	200	238	270	310	341	381
walking (2 mph)	151	183	214	239	271	296
walking (3 mph)	183	220	252	290	321	359
walking (4 mph)	265	315	365	416	466	510

Table 6.1 Energy expenditure in calories per hour during selected activities for persons of various body weights.

And the shaking machines sometimes seen at health clubs are pretty much worthless. Steam baths and saunas are also entirely useless as far as conditioning or weight loss are concerned. Any weight loss from these will just be water loss from sweat, which you will immediately regain when you next eat and drink. You can't force your body to have less water than it should; this is essentially creating the pathological condition of dehydration. There are abnormalities in which the body retains water, but these must be addressed by correcting the condition causing the abnormality. In a similar vein, exercising on a hot, humid day does no more good than on a cool, dry day. It will feel harder under such conditions, but it does nothing as far as physical conditioning is concerned. This is because the additional stress that you feel under such conditions is not due to physical activity. Your body may well adapt better to exercising in a hot, humid environment, but that is not the same as improving overall physical conditioning. An analogy may help make this clear: If you were under severe emotional stress, your heart rate could go up sharply and you may well start sweating and experiencing other signs of physical discomfort. But these physical manifestations of emotional distress would not contribute anything toward your physical fitness. It is also a misconception that it is harmful to exercise immediately before or after eating. Intense exercise after a large meal may produce nausea or discomfort, but aside from this caveat, there is no basis for such a restriction.

Since it is crucial to be regular about it, my feeling is that the activity you choose for your exercise should be something that you enjoy, or at least don't mind. Otherwise you are likely to end up skipping it. It is not necessary, as far as cardiovascular conditioning is concerned, to always do the same exercise. You can walk one day of the week, bicycle another, and play squash on a third. This is not a good way to improve your skill or the muscles used in a particular activity, of course, but unless you are training for competitive athletics, that consideration just does not apply. In my estimation, walking is a form of exercise with much to recommend it. Its only drawback, which many similar activities have, is that it does not work the upper body. It can be done almost anywhere, by almost anyone. You can do it on your lunch hour — even on your break. When the weather is bad, you can use a convenient mall, or walk through your building if it's large enough (I do both). The intensity can be decreased by slowing the pace or increased by incorporating hills or stairs on your route. You need no special equipment, just a pair of reasonable shoes. The newer high-tech athletic shoes are fine, but any well-fitting shoe will do (a cushion insole is desirable). Walking can also be used as an alternate exercise to attain an acceptable frequency if you can't engage in your favorite activity more than once or twice a week.

If you cannot or do not follow an aerobic exercise program that works the whole body, or at least the major muscle groups, you may want to add some exercises designed primarily for muscle strength and endurance. The most efficient exercises for preserving or increasing muscular ability are weight lifting and similar resistance exercises like Nautilus. The amount of weight or resistance can be adjusted to fit individual needs as they change over time. Unlike aerobic exercise, strength conditioning does not need to be performed continuously for any particular length of time; if you have only two minutes to devote to it, you will still derive benefits from whatever is done in those two minutes. Barbells are generally preferable to dumbbells, which work just one side of the body at a time. Start out gradually with light weights until you become familiar with each lift. Determine a weight at which you can do the lift about ten times continuously. This is referred to as one set of ten repetitions. This repetition number is frequently varied, however, since fewer repetitions with a heavy weight best develop strength and a high number of repetitions best develop muscular endurance. So, for example, you might do one set of bench presses with a weight you can lift 15 times, one of 10 repetitions with a heavier weight, and one set with a weight you can lift only 5 times. You gradually increase the weight lifted as the strength and endurance of your muscles increase over time. As a rule of thumb, when you can do two or three more than the prescribed number of repetitions, it is time to add more weight. Serious weight lifters have worked out many such routines, varying the number of sets, repetitions, and types of lifts. You do not have to follow a long, complicated program to derive considerable benefits, however. Even one or two sets of a lift twice a week or so is much better than nothing for maintaining muscular strength and endurance.

Most people are probably already familiar with the major types of lifts; I will briefly review a few of the most important. Curls are done by gripping the barbell with the palms up and at about shoulder width, lifting it to the level where you are standing upright with your arms extended along your body and the bar across your upper thighs, then using the muscles of the upper arm, primarily the biceps, to lift or "curl" the barbell to the shoulder by bending the arms at the elbow. One repetition of this lift is completed by lowering the weight as you "uncurl" your arms and so return the barbell to where it is resting against your upper thighs. The standard press is done by standing upright, bending at the knees and waist to grasp the barbell palms down, lifting it to shoulder height, then straight up over the head, and lowering it to shoulder height. The bench press allows heavier weights to be used but requires either a partner to hand you the barbell — while you are lying on your back on a bench — or a special support rack designed for this purpose. The barbell is gripped with the hands spaced at least shoulder width apart, lifted from the shoulders straight out, perpendicular to the body, and lowered back to the chest. It is a rather popular lift, probably because it builds the chest (pectoral) muscles fairly rapidly. The squat works a large portion of the body, especially the hips and the thigh muscles, quite strongly. One repetition is done as follows: Starting from an upright standing position with the barbell held at shoulder height, bend at the knees to lower your body into a squatting position with the thighs about parallel to the floor, then return to an upright stance by straightening your legs. The barbell can be held either across the shoulders behind the head (the more common form) or across the chest in front. You can use a heavier and more effective amount of weight in the former case, but this then requires either a partner to hand you the barbell or a rack off of which the barbell can be taken. Pullovers are done by lying on your back on a bench, grasping the barbell with the hands about a foot apart, and bringing it from a position behind and lower than your head to one straight out above you. The arms are allowed to bend at the elbow in the most common variant of this lift. A relatively light weight that can be handled alone is usually used; you can also use a dumbbell grasped with both hands together around one end. These last two lifts, the squat and bent-arm pullover, are considered by many experienced weight lifters to be among the most effective and efficient for overall conditioning

Some types of calisthenics can also be used; it's just more difficult to work much of a range of muscles and to adjust the intensity compared to weights. Generally the number of repetitions must be increased to obtain the same conditioning effect as the muscle improves. Push-ups are fine. This exercise can be modified somewhat to adjust its difficulty. Push-aways from a table or countertop about waist high are easier and can actually be part of an aerobic routine; you can vary the difficulty of this exercise by changing the height at which you place your hands, from chest height pushing against a wall to the height of a low table. Dips, which are somewhat harder than push-ups, can be done by placing two chairs about shoulder width apart, placing one hand on the edge of each, dipping your body down between the two, and pushing yourself back up. Stair stepping — stepping one step up and down repeatedly — is an effective, if monotonous, workout for the leg muscles.

There are many specialized workout machines available at health clubs permitting a wide range of motions. But it is not really critical to insure that every muscle in the body is exercised directly; there should just be enough variety to work the main groups of the upper and lower body, depending on what other type of exercise you do. Isometric exercises (pushing or pulling against a fixed resistance) can be part of a program to maintain or develop muscle strength, but they do not work a muscle over its entire range so are not considered as good as the activities we have discussed. They have the advantage of not requiring any equipment or space at all.

Flexibility is affected by several factors. The range of motion of a joint can be restricted by adjacent fat tissue, as in the well-known example of abdominal fat preventing a person from being able to bend forward to touch his toes. It can also be decreased as the tendons and muscles around a joint become less elastic. Many of the aerobic and muscle-conditioning exercises we have discussed will contribute to maintaining flexibility. You can also incorporate specific stretching exercises to this end. Stretching exercises should be fairly gentle; forceful bobbing or pushing against the limits of a joint's extensibility can do more harm than good. Simply extend the motion of the joint as far as it will go until you encounter significant resistance to further motion (e.g., reach behind your head with both arms toward the middle of your back until your hands cannot go farther down), then hold it there for about six to ten seconds. A few more such flexibility exercises are

1. Stand upright; bend at the waist to try to touch the toes.
2. Bend the neck to the front, back, and both sides.
3. Stand upright; bend your body at the waist to the left or right side.
4. Sit on the floor with legs extended; reach out with your hands to grab your feet, or as far as you can.

You can construct other stretching exercises of your own following these general principles. It may seem that it will take a lot of time and effort for a complete fitness program, but many exercises will promote more than one type of fitness. Many can be done as part of daily activity, and some at odd moments in your day. In fact, it has been suggested by a leading exercise physiologist that a good level of fitness can be attained by just 30 minutes of exercise a week.[23] The level of fitness maintained by such a program of ten minutes of exercise three days a week is rather minimal and, as we have seen, the effects of exercise on longevity and preservation of muscle into old age are proportional (within limits) to the amount of time spent exercising per week. It does illustrate that exercise is not an all-or-nothing thing; you can derive significant benefits from regularly engaging in just a few of the activities we have discussed. But you cannot store up exercise or the benefits from exercise. An exercise program must be lifelong; your overall fitness level (at least as gauged by the most common methods) will fall to nearly that of a sedentary person within months of discontinuing it.[24, 25] (There have been reports, including my own observations, that some of the gains in fitness are never completely lost. For example, several bodybuilders that I knew many years ago maintained a significant portion of their increased muscle mass decades after they had stopped weight lifting.) Generally, the longer you have maintained a good level of fitness, the longer it takes to lose it. Some measures of fitness (such as the cellular enzymes that produce energy) fall to pretraining levels in as little as ten weeks, and nearly all, including aerobic capacity (maximum oxygen uptake), have declined to that point within eight months of cessation of exercise. Note, however, that this means cessation of *all* training. If you become completely sedentary, you will lose essentially all the benefits of your training; but you can decrease the frequency and duration of exercise and still maintain most of the benefits as long as the intensity of the exercise is maintained (e.g., you jog at the same pace or lift the same amount of weight). Aerobic capacity has been maintained for up to 15 weeks when frequency and duration of exercise were reduced by up to two-thirds.[25] Similar results have been obtained with strength training exercise. However, reducing the *intensity* of exercise, even keeping frequency and duration the same, does result in a loss of fitness in both cases. To address another old myth, muscle cannot turn to fat when you stop exercising; they are completely different kinds of tissue. All that will happen if you discontinue a regular exercise program is that there will be changes in the biochemical makeup of various muscles and tissues and some loss of muscle mass. Some active people continue to consume as many calories when they become sedentary, which, since they are no longer needed for energy, can gradually accumulate on the body as fat, but this is a separate process entirely from loss of muscle.

References to Chapter Six

1. From the Centers for Disease Control and Prevention: Public health focus: physical activity and the prevention of coronary heart disease. *JAMA* 270:1529–1530, 1993.

2. K.E. Powell, P.D. Thompson, C.J. Caspersen, J.S. Kendrick: Physical activity and the incidence of coronary heart disease. *Annu Rev Public Health* 8:253–287, 1987.

3. R.S. Paffenbarger, Jr. et al.: The association of changes in physical-activity level and other lifestyle characteristics with mortality among men. *N Engl J Med* 328:538–545, 1993.

4. S.N. Blair et al.: Physical fitness and all-cause mortality: a prospective study of healthy men and women. *JAMA* 262:2395–2401, 1989.

5. J.A. Berlin, G.A. Colditz: A meta-analysis of physical activity in the prevention of coronary heart disease. *Am J Epidemiol* 132:612–628, 1990.

6. E. Retzlaff, J. Fontaine, W. Futura: Effect of daily exercise on life-span of albino rats. *Geriatrics* 21:171–177, March, 1966.

7. D. Edington, A. Cosmas, W. McCafferty: Exercise and longevity: evidence for a threshold age. *J Gerontol* 27:341–343, 1972.

8. C.L. Goodrick: Effects of long-term voluntary wheel exercise on male and female Wistar rats. *Gerontology* 26:22–33, 1980.

9. C.L. Goodrick et al.: Differential effects of intermittent feeding and voluntary wheel exercise on body weight and lifespan in adult rats. *J Gerontol* 38:36–45, 1983.

10. E.R. Eichner: Exercise, lymphokines, calories and cancer. *Physician Sportsmed* 15:109–116, 1987.

11. R.S. Paffenbarger, R.T. Hyde, A.L. Wing: Physical activity and incidence of cancer in diverse populations: a preliminary report. *Am J Clin Nutr* 45:312–317, 1987.

12. G. Wannamethee, A.G. Shaper, P.W. Macfarlane: Heart rate, physical activity, and mortality from cancer and other noncardiovascular diseases. *Am J Epidemiol* 137:735–748, 1993.

13. H.J. Thompson et al.: Effect of type and amount of dietary fat on the enhancement of rat mammary tumorigenesis by exercise. *Cancer Res* 49:1904–1908, April, 1989.

14. J.F. Dorgan, C. Brown, M. Barrett et al.: Physical activity and risk of breast cancer in the Framingham Heart Study. *Am J Epidemiol* 139:662–669, 1994.

15. L. Berstein et al.: Physical exercise and reduced risk of breast cancer in young women. *JNCI* 86:1403–1408, 1994.

16. W.J. Evans: Exercise, nutrition and aging. *J Nutr* 122:796–801, 1992.

17. J.W. Gersten: Effect of exercise on muscle function decline with aging. *West J Med* 154:579–582, 1991.

18. S.H. Cohn et al.: Changes in body chemical composition with age measured by total-body neutron activation. *Metabolism* 25:89–96, 1976.

19. E. Ravussin et al.: Determinants of 24-hour energy expenditure in man. *J Clin Invest* 78:1568–1578, 1986.

20. S.P. Tzankoff, A.H. Norris: Longitudinal changes in basal metabolic rate in man. *J Appl Physiol* 33:536–539, 1978.

21. C.N. Meredith et al.: Body composition and aerobic capacity in young and middle-aged endurance trained men. *Med Sci Sports Exercise* 19:557–563, 1987.

22. P. Bjorntorp, W.J. Evans: The effect of exercise and diet on body composition. In: *Body Composition: The Measure and Meaning of Changes With Age.* J. Watkins et al., eds. Foundation for Nutritional Advancement, Boston, 1992.

23. L.E. Morehouse: *Total Fitness in 30 Minutes a Week.* Simon and Schuster, New York, 1990.

24. R. Casaburi: Physiologic responses to training. *Clin Chest Med* 15(2):215–227, 1994.

25. American College of Sports Medicine Position Stand: The recommended quantity and quality of exercise for developing and maintaining cardiorespiratory and muscular fitness in healthy adults. *Med Sci Sports Exercise* 22:265–274, 1990.

SEVEN. Lifestyle

There are several miscellaneous factors or behaviors I will call lifestyle that can significantly affect health and longevity.

I won't bore you with another sermon on the hazards of smoking; you are probably as tired of hearing it as I am. All of this constant antismoking propaganda by the government and the American Medical Association is almost enough to make even a lifelong nonsmoker like me take up smoking. I will try to cover some points not usually mentioned.

Smoking does increase the risk of heart disease and several cancers, primarily lung, but also cancer of the larynx, mouth, esophagus, and bladder. From a health standpoint, it is certainly best to quit completely. What usually is not mentioned is that the effects of smoking, as with most things, are dose-related — the more you smoke, the greater is the risk; if you reduce the number of cigarettes smoked per day, you reduce smoking's negative effects. The incidence of lung cancer increases roughly linearly with the number of cigarettes smoked from 1 to over 40 per day. The actual constant of proportionality depends on the type of lung cancer. Approximately though, people who smoke 31 to 40 cigarettes per day have about four times the rate of lung cancer as those who smoke only 1 to 10 cigarettes per day.[1] Cancers of the mouth, larynx, esophagus, and bladder also show a dose-dependence, but the risks do not seem to be related to dose in a straight proportional manner.[1] As with many aspects of lifestyle, moderation isn't a bad policy.

Pipe and cigar smoking, by the way, are at best only weakly associated with any disease other than cancers of the upper respiratory and digestive tract — lip, mouth, pharynx, larynx, and esophagus — and not to the degree of cigarette smoking.[2] Therefore, while hardly benign, they don't carry the risk of the major killers associated with cigarette smoking — lung cancer and heart disease.

Smokers of nonfiltered cigarettes have about twice the risk of cancer as smokers of filtered cigarettes. Various studies have found relative risk ratios from around 1.6 to 2.3. This may understate the benefits of filtered cigarettes, because many smokers began smoking and continued for some years with nonfiltered cigarettes before switching to filtered. Similar reductions have been found for the other smoking-associated cancers, the relative risk of nonfiltered versus filtered cigarettes ranging from about three to seven, depending on the study and the type of cancer. There is also considerably less risk in smoking low-tar/nicotine cigarettes. A large study of smokers of low-tar/nicotine versus regular cigarettes found that lung cancer death rates were 20 percent lower in men and 40 percent lower in women who smoked low-tar/nicotine cigarettes.[3] Further analysis of these studies indicated that the increased mortality due to high-tar/nicotine cigarettes widened with the number of cigarettes smoked, as might be expected. At 10 cigarettes a day the lung cancer rate was about one-third higher in high-tar/nicotine smokers, but at 40 cigarettes per day it was about twice as high as in low-tar/nicotine smokers. While nicotine has frequently been reduced in cigarettes in parallel with tar, this may be counterproductive as smokers tend to make up for low-nicotine cigarettes by smoking more.

I don't want to minimize the health risks of smoking, but it is just one of a number of risk factors. In the study of lifestyle and longevity by Paffenbarger et al. mentioned in Chapter 6,[4] quitting smoking after age 30 was associated with an average gain in life expectancy of only 1.46 years. The Japanese smoke heavily and have done so for many years, the percentage of smokers among adult males ranging from a low of 66 percent in 1984 to a high of 84 percent in 1966.[5] Yet they have a low incidence of heart disease and the longest life span in the world for both men and women. Life expectancy at birth (1990 figures) was 76.2 years for males and 82.5 years for females.[6] Life expectancy at age 65 was also highest — 16.5 years for males and 20.6 years for females (about the same as French females). One possible explanation for this is that the effects of smoking are synergistic with other unhealthy practices, so that if you smoke heavily and drink heavily, for example, your risk of developing the related diseases, such as cancer of the mouth or larynx, is not just the added risks of smoking plus drinking, but considerably more than that. This sort of effect has also been found with smoking and exposure to asbestos, where, if smoking increased the relative risk of lung cancer to 10 times normal and asbestos increased it to 5 times, when both were present at the same levels, the relative risk was increased not to 15 but to *50* times normal. The point is that if a society generally follows healthy practices, such as a low-fat diet with ample fruits and vegetables, moderate calorie intake, and so on, the negative effects of smoking may be much less than in a society like the United States where many unhealthy practices are common. Studies have also found that smokers eat less of foods rich in vitamins A and C.[1] As we discussed in previous chapters, it is thought that these vitamins are closely related to prevention of cancer, especially the type of cancers caused by smoking. Smokers should be particularly careful to follow the dietary practices that we discussed in Chapter 4 as far as they can — particularly to insure an abundant intake of fruits and vegetables. Supplements of vitamins A and C, beta-carotene, selenium, and some of the others mentioned in Chapter 5 would also be prudent.

Sunlight and other intense sources of ultraviolet light significantly harm the skin and eyes. Such deleterious changes, whether due to natural or artificial light, are collectively referred to as photodamage or photoaging. Most of the changes in the skin that we associate with age are actually due to chronic exposure to light. In fact, it has been estimated that up to 90 percent of the deterioration of the skin with age is due to photodamage.[7, 8] It is the ultraviolet part of the spectrum that does most of the damage. Ultraviolet (UV) light has wavelengths shorter than the shortest of visible light (the violet end of the spectrum, hence the name), and is therefore, by definition, invisible to the naked eye. (See Appendix 3 for a more detailed explanation of ultraviolet light and electromagnetic radiation in general.) The portion immediately adjacent to violet is called UV-A; UV-B is adjacent to UV-A. While UV-A is far less potent in damaging the skin than UV-B, it is 10 to 100 times more intense in normal sunlight and penetrates more deeply into the skin. Some wavelengths of ultraviolet are absorbed by DNA; others by proteins and lipids. The pigment melanin, which gives tanned or naturally brown skin its color, absorbs potentially damaging ultraviolet as well as visible radiation. Lighter-skinned persons are therefore more susceptible to this damage. Coarsening, dryness, various age spots and mottling, loss of elasticity, and benign and malignant growths are due primarily to this photoaging rather than the aging process itself. Wrinkles are also due in large part to this type of damage. What's more, the skin is the site of a considerable amount of immunologic activity that is significantly suppressed by ultraviolet radiation.

The youthful, elastic texture of young skin is due largely to a protein called elastin, which is composed of long elastic fibers. In fact, it has long been a test of how badly the skin has aged to pinch up a portion on the back of the hand, hold it for a few seconds, then release it and see how long it takes to snap back into place. A young person's will do so almost immediately; an older person's skin may stay in the pinched-up condition for minutes. Sunlight gradually destroys elastin in the skin, causing this loss of elasticity. Collagen is another fibrous protein that makes up most of the total protein in the skin and, in fact, much of the total protein of the body. The collagen fibers are lined up next to each other in an orderly network, giving skin its strength and enabling it to maintain its shape. Sunlight gradually destroys this orderly arrangement; it cuts the collagen fibers into pieces that collect in a disorderly jumble. The skin responds by trying to produce more tissue to repair the damage, but repair cannot occur to any significant extent as long as photodamage continues. The result is an accumulation of thickened, tangled fibers in an amorphous mass that is never seen, even in elderly people, in nonphotodamaged skin.[7] This destruction of elastin and collagen accounts for the sagging, the pouches, and the hanging appearance common in old skin.

Photoaged skin has a variety of pigment abnormalities. There can be both the well-known darkened areas and age spots, and also areas of loss of pigmentation (whitish spots). Mottled, sometimes oddly colored areas can arise as a result of photodamage to small blood vessels. This results in internal bleeding in the skin, frequently giving rise to permanent brownish-red or similarly colored areas as the blood dries and oxidizes. Actinic keratoses, or sun-induced scaly patches, are quite common and not just a matter of cosmetic concern; a small but significant percentage of them become cancerous. The warning that there is no safe tan is worth repeating; if you have tanned through exposure to light, you have damaged your skin in the ways just discussed. There are several substances that, when ingested in sufficient quantities, will color the skin. Beta-carotene and similar substances have such an effect, although the color is not the same as a natural tan. Then there are the painted-on tans, which are essentially simply a staining of the skin. Neither of these methods, of course, has the damaging effects we have discussed. It should be noted that they do not afford any protection against photodamage.

While photoaging is sometimes used as synonymous with sunlight-induced aging, it can be caused by any intense source of light — either broad spectrum like the sun or concentrated in the ultraviolet. The most common of these are tanning salons and lamps used to induce tanning. Ordinary incandescent lightbulbs do produce a broad spectrum like the sun. In fact, they are emitting electromagnetic radiation like the surface of the sun for the same reason — their high temperature. They do not pose a danger because the intensity is so much less than sunlight, the ultraviolet component being further reduced by the glass of the bulb. Fluorescent bulbs look white but produce a completely different type of spectrum, which does contain a fair amount in the ultraviolet. Again, this is much weaker than sunlight. This will obviously vary with latitude and time of day, but in temperate latitudes sunlight is generally about 100 times as bright as average indoor lighting. It may be enough to be physiologically appreciable, though barely, in certain circumstances.[9] It's debatable whether visible light poses any significant danger. There is some evidence that the shorter (blue) wavelengths can have some effects, but overall it is far less a danger than ultraviolet.

The good news is that sun-damaged skin can repair itself to a large extent if it is protected from further photodamage. This may take a long time if the damage is extensive, and it is not known if such damage is completely reversible in old people. The other good news is that a preparation is now available that can reverse most of the effects of photodamage. As was mentioned in Chapter 5, this is a form of retinoic acid called tretinon. This chemical is probably best known to the public as Retin-A, which is actually the brand name of the topical preparation. Retin-A can reverse the damage to the skin's elastin and collagen, causing new fibers to be formed with the orderly structure of young skin. It can also greatly reduce wrinkling, repair blood vessels, fade age spots, and impart a more youthful texture and look to the skin.[10, 11] While not all the details of how Retin-A repairs photodamaged skin are known, it is most likely primarily related to the effects of retinoids on epithelial tissue that we discussed in Chapter 5. They induce cellular maturation and differentiation. These are not just cosmetic changes — the skin is actually repaired; precancerous regions become normal tissue. For this reason many dermatologists recommend Retin-A for anyone with significantly damaged skin. Its side effects are relatively minor and can be controlled. The skin will become more sensitive to ultraviolet light and to irritants, but these effects tend to decrease with continued use. There will be some increased sensitivity to sunlight for as long as Retin-A treatment is continued; people using it must have a long-term commitment to protecting their skin from overexposure by avoiding intense sunlight or using a good sunscreen. But it is not necessary to avoid the sun completely. Improvement is gradual and can take a number of months as the skin repairs itself, but ultimately Retin-A seems to work for the overwhelming majority of people.

Retin-A currently has official FDA approval only for the treatment of acne, but this is mostly a technicality. Drugs approved for one use can be and have always been prescribed for other conditions, based on accepted medical practice. Dermatologists, who are generally more familiar with the many positive effects of Retin-A, seem more enthusiastic about its use than other physicians. Such a specialist will have more experience in administering Retin-A and managing its side effects. The cosmetic effects of Retin-A may be appealing enough to many people. But considering the fact that it can reverse precancerous conditions, even many that are not readily detectable, its benefits go far beyond the cosmetic. A drawback to many has been the cost, but this is dropping now that patent protection has expired and generic equivalents are becoming available.

A number of nonprescription skin preparations are being marketed with names similar to Retin-A or vitamin A. None of these has been shown to be effective in the way Retin-A is. Many cosmetics will temporarily make the skin look more youthful. A few can rehydrate the skin; some provoke a mild inflammation that makes the skin swell slightly, smoothing out wrinkles and producing a rosy glow. There is nothing wrong with these, but the changes are purely cosmetic, unlike the effects of tretinoin.

There are of course many other treatments for aged or damaged skin. I will not discuss them in detail because these treatments must be undertaken based on individual evaluation by a dermatologist or plastic surgeon. Sclerotherapy (the removal of unsightly veins by injecting a solution into them) can be used to treat "spider veins" and frequently varicose veins. Collagen injections can be useful in smoothing out wrinkled and uneven areas. Dermabrasion can remove scarred areas. Besides this and the well-known "face-lift," chemical peel can remove many fine wrinkles over a large area. Chemical peel entails the application of a caustic solution to the skin, which becomes highly inflamed and takes a month or more to return to a presentable level.

The eye is also susceptible to damage from intense light. The lens is especially vulnerable because it cannot repair damage, which accumulates to form opaque areas called cataracts. The cornea (the clear covering at the front of the eye) and the retina (the layer of cells at the back of the eye onto which light is focused and detected) are also vulnerable.

A cataract is by definition an opaque area in the lens that impairs the normal passage of light. There are several causes of cataracts, including trauma, exposure to toxins, and nutritional deficiencies. But the overwhelming majority arise with age either as a result of the aging process itself or the cumulative damage due to light — primarily ultraviolet light. It is thought that ultraviolet rays give rise to free radicals that react with certain amino acids in the lens to produce a yellow pigment and an aggregation of proteins. It has not been determined whether longer wavelengths contribute at all to such damage. However, other factors besides exposure to ultraviolet light can generate such radicals. The proportion of damage due to ultraviolet over time is not known with any certainty; it may be that, as with the skin, the changes in the lens with age are primarily due to photodamage rather than some independent aging process. There is evidence that increased levels of dietary antioxidants retard the formation of cataracts.[12, 13] Nearly half the population will develop some form of cataract by age 65. The only treatment, surgical removal of the lens, does have a very high success rate.

The retina can be damaged by several mechanisms. Usually the lens absorbs so well in the ultraviolet that little of it reaches the retina. However, blue light can produce some damage, and this combined with some due to ultraviolet could be cumulative with age. There is evidence that macular degeneration is related to blue or other visible light. (The macula, or macula lutea, is the portion of the retina with maximum visual sensitivity.) Free radical damage may also be involved in deterioration of the retina. Vitamin E-deficient diets greatly accelerate such damage in animals.[14] One study found that patients with severe age-related macular degeneration had significantly greater lifetime exposure to blue or visible light than age-matched controls, but did not differ in exposure to ultraviolet.[15]

It is better to prevent photodamage from occurring in the first place. This means avoiding damaging light, primarily the ultraviolet in sunlight, but including some strong artificial sources, as in tanning salons. The line that some tanning salons put out — that they use just UV-A and this is relatively safe — is totally fallacious. Both UV-A and UV-B are damaging, and the tan induced by UV-A does not afford adequate protection against UV-B, so you will be even less protected from further photodamage with such a tan than by one induced by sunlight. In addition, it would be prudent to avoid too much intense visible light. To do this it is necessary to know when light is most dangerous. The shorter wavelengths of sunlight, including the ultraviolet, are scattered the most by the earth's atmosphere. This is why the sky appears blue and sunsets appear reddish. In the former case, when you are looking into the sky away from the sun, the only light that reaches the lens of your eye is light scattered from the sky into it; in the latter case, when there is a lot of atmosphere between the sun and the observer, shorter wavelengths (the blue/violet end of the spectrum) are scattered out of your line of sight before they reach you, so the red end of the spectrum is more pronounced. A similar effect occurs at other times of day, so that the only time significant amounts of ultraviolet reach the ground is when the sun is high enough in the sky that there is a minimum of atmosphere for the light to pass through. The sun rises highest in the sky at the time of the summer solstice in June (in the Northern Hemisphere); it is lowest at the winter solstice in December. The level of ultraviolet reaching the ground also increases as one moves nearer to the equator or higher in altitude. (Its intensity increases by 4 to 5 percent for every 1,000ft increase in altitude.) On a daily basis, the maximum ultraviolet occurs at true noon. During daylight saving time, the clock is moved ahead one hour, so the sun's highest elevation is at 1:00 P.M. instead of 12:00 P.M. This can also vary somewhat depending on where in your time zone you are located. The most significant levels of ultraviolet are from 10 A.M. to 2 P.M., or on daylight saving time, 11 A.M. to 3 P.M. The usual recommendation, which, as you can see from the other factors involved, is only a rough guide, is to avoid prolonged exposure to sunlight during these times. Several protective measures can also be taken. A hat with a good brim can protect the eyes and face. Tight-knit clothing will reduce exposure of other parts of the body. Open-weave summer clothing may allow substantial amounts of ultraviolet to reach the skin; when wet, all clothing becomes more permeable to ultraviolet. A sunscreen with a sun protection factor (SPF) of at least 15 is recommended when prolonged exposure is unavoidable. A number of such preparations, some waterproof and with even higher SPF, are readily available over the counter. (The SPF is the ratio of the amount of sunlight that will produce skin redness with sunscreen to the amount of sunlight needed to produce that redness without sunscreen.) Check the instructions on the bottle of sunscreen to make sure it blocks both UV-A and UV-B. Remember that it is the ultraviolet *light* that is damaging; it doesn't matter how hot or cool the day is. The heating effect of direct sunlight is due almost entirely to its infrared component, which has wavelengths longer than the red end of the visible spectrum.

Glass blocks ultraviolet light, but most plastics do not. So you are protected inside your car with the windows up or near a sunny window of your house. Clouds do not block ultraviolet completely. Shade affords some protection, but again, not complete. This is again because ultraviolet is scattered by air, so you need not be in direct line of sight to the sun for its ultraviolet to reach you. (While clouds and shade will not eliminate ultraviolet completely, they can of course reduce it to an insignificant level, depending on how intense it was to start with, and how dense the clouds and/or shade are.) Snow, sand, concrete, and other light surfaces can reflect a large amount, increasing your exposure considerably. Grass and water do not reflect significant amounts. You will therefore have little protection when sitting under a beach umbrella on a bright day at the beach; sunscreen and eyeglasses are required. Snow reflects up to 80 percent of the sunlight falling on it. You are likely to be well clothed when in a snow-covered area, but skiing on a mountain slope will hit any exposed areas of your body with the double whammy of increased ultraviolet due to altitude plus snow reflection. Sunglasses are of course valuable in such situations, protecting against both ultraviolet and high levels of visible light. But make sure that your sunglasses *are* rated as blocking ultraviolet or they can do more harm than good. Light can also strike the eye from the side to some extent; wrap-around sunglasses are therefore ideal, but not absolutely necessary.

There is a slight overlap between the output of typical fluorescent bulbs and the region of the wavelength-intensity diagram in which eye damage can occur.[9] This is a matter of some concern because little protection is usually worn indoors. Several simple protective measures are available. First, if you wear prescription glasses, make sure they have an ultraviolet-blocking coating. Such coatings are readily available at opticians for a modest price. (It would also be prudent to wear such glasses if you work at a computer screen for long periods.) Second, if you work near a bright fluorescent light you can shield yourself from its ultraviolet radiation by a piece of glass in its fixture. Third, don't have a bright fluorescent light without such a shield placed directly at the front of your desk where it will shine into your eyes. Again, the intensity of ultraviolet from fluorescent bulbs is only marginally dangerous, so any simple protective measure will suffice.

The other major lifestyle factor related to health and successful aging is psychological.[16] People who stay engaged in activities, who read, attend cultural events, or otherwise keep their minds active are generally much more alert and independent in their old age. They also tend to live longer, though whether this is correlation or cause and effect is unknown. There is no doubt that there are significant causal links between psychological health and physical health. It is thought that these effects come about through the brain-hormone-immune system links.[17] For example, stress can lead to the release of hormones and other chemicals that suppress immune function. Direct neural links to immune system organs and glands could also play a role. Interestingly, there is some evidence that a complete lack of "stress," or challenge, also leads to negative effects. The "placebo effect"—that is, the positive physical effects resulting from a person's belief that something beneficial will happen—is well documented. Norman Cousins described how significant this effect could be in his book *Anatomy of an Illness*. There are many other instances of positive psychological factors improving physical health. One study at the University of Pennsylvania found that heart attack patients who had a pet were much more likely to survive than those without pets.[18] Of 39 patients without pets, 11 had died within a year of their admission to hospital; only 3 of 53 heart attack patients with pets died in this time. Interestingly, the type of pet (dog, cat, etc.) did not seem to matter. It seems as if having something to live for, whether it is other people, a cause, or a pet, can be a powerful factor in determining disease outcome and overall longevity.

References to Chapter Seven

1. S.D. Stellman: Cigarette yield and cancer risk: evidence from case-control and prospective studies. In: *Tobacco: A Major International Health Hazard.* D.G. Zaridze, R. Peto, eds. IARC, Lyon, 1986.

2. R. Doll: Tobacco: an overview of health effects. In: *Tobacco: A Major International Health Hazard.* D.G. Zaridze, R. Peto, eds. IARC, Lyon, 1986.

3. E.C. Hammond et al.: Tar and nicotine content of cigarette smoke in relation to death rates. *Environ Res* 12:263–274, 1976.

4. R.S. Paffenbarger, Jr. et al.: The association of changes in physical-activity level and other lifestyle characteristics with mortality among men. *N Engl J Med* 328:538–545, 1993.

5. S. Tominaga: Smoking and cancer patterns and trends in Japan. In: *Tobacco: A Major International Health Hazard.* D.G. Zaridze, R. Peto, eds. IARC, Lyon, 1986.

6. National Center for Health Statistics: *Health, United States, 1993.* Public Health Service, Hyattsville, MD, 1994.

7. C. Guercio-Hauer, D.F. Macfarlane, V.A. Delea: Photodamage, photoaging, and photoprotection of the skin. *Am Fam Physician* 50:327–334, Aug. 1994.

8. B.A. Gilchrest: *Skin and Aging Processes.* CRC Press, Boca Raton, FL, 1984.

9. M. Waxler: Long-term visual health problems: optical radiation risks. In: *Optical Radiation and Visual Health.* M. Waxler, V.M. Hitchins, eds. CRC Press, Boca Raton, FL, 1986.

10. L.H. Kligman: Photoaging. Manifestations, prevention, and treatment. *Dermatol Clin* 4:517–528, 1986.

11. S.W. Farnes, P.A. Setness: Retinoid therapy for aging skin and acne. *Postgrad Med* 92(6):191–200, 1992.

12. A. Taylor: Role of nutrients in delaying cataracts. *Ann NY Acad Sci* 669:111–123, 1992.

13. R.D. Sperduto et al.: The Linxian cataract studies: two nutrition intervention trials. *Arch Ophthalmol* 111:1246–1253, 1993.

14. W.T. Ham et al.: The involvement of the retinal pigment epithelium. In: *Optical Radiation and Visual Health*, M. Waxler, V.M. Hitchins, eds., CRC Press, Boca Raton, FL, 1986.

15. H.R. Taylor et al.: The long-term effects of visible light on the eye. *Arch Ophthalmol* 110:99–104, 1992.

16. E.B. Palmore: *Social Patterns in Normal Aging: Findings from the Duke Longitudinal Study*. Duke University Press, Durham, NC, 1981.

17. R. Ader: On the clinical relevance of psychoneuroimmunology. *Clin Immunol Immunopathol* 64:6–8, 1991.

18. *Science News* 114 (No.24):408, 1978.

EIGHT.
Avoiding Disease

The death rate from heart disease has declined by over 48 percent in the United States over the past 30 years. Mortality from stroke, which is similarly related to atherosclerosis, has declined by over 66 percent during the same period (Table 8.1). Nevertheless, heart disease remains the leading cause of death in the United States and most industrialized countries. We have discussed most of the risk factors and protective factors for cardiovascular disease as part of diet, supplements, and exercise; I will not go over all the studies again but will try to summarize and tie them together here. Increased risk is associated with being male, increasing age, and a family history of such disease (Table 8.2). These are all significant factors but, of course, are beyond our control. A high ratio of total cholesterol to HDL, hypertension, dietary factors, cigarette smoking, obesity, and physical inactivity have all been associated to some extent with cardiovascular disease. Serum triglycerides and body fat distribution (upper body obesity) may also be risk factors, but their significance is not as clear.

As you can see, there are a number of factors under our control that can reduce our risk of heart disease. What's more, almost all of these have other significant health benefits. Most of these factors interact with the others so as to push the risk in the same direction. Reducing body weight to a normal level tends to lower cholesterol and blood pressure. Physical activity helps to lower cholesterol and blood pressure and to maintain proper weight. A high-fiber, low-fat diet helps lower cholesterol and maintain proper body weight, which in turn helps lower blood pressure, and so on. Ideally, of course, you would take measures to decrease all the controllable risk factors, but not everyone may be able to accomplish this and it may not be absolutely necessary. Depending on what your noncontrollable risks are, you still may be able to reduce your overall risk to a reasonable level.

As far as dietary factors go, reducing fat to a minimum, using monounsaturated fat for whatever fat you do eat, and increasing consumption of fruits and vegetables are among the most important steps that can be taken to reduce your risk. There is reason to believe that animal products in general are not heart-healthy, even aside from their higher fat content. A recent survey of diet in 40 countries found that the strongest association of coronary heart disease was with calories from animal foods and butterfat.[1] Antioxidant supplements (vitamins C and E, beta-carotene, selenium) and aspirin are simple measures that may well afford

92

	1960	1991	Percent change
Heart disease	286.2	148.2	–48.2
Stroke	79.7	26.8	–66.4
All cancer	125.8	134.5	+6.9
Respiratory cancer	19.2	41.1	+114.1
Prostate cancer	13.1	16.7	+15.7
Breast cancer (female)	22.3	22.7	+1.8
Colorectal cancer	17.7	13.3	–24.9

Table 8.1 Changes in mortality from major diseases in the United States, 1960–1991: deaths per 100,000 population, all races, age-adjusted.* Source: *Health, United States, 1993.* Hyattsville, MD; Public Health Service, 1994.

Not controllable	Subject to control
Age	Blood lipids (LDL/HDL; cholesterol/HDL ratio)
Sex (higher in males)	Obesity
Family history	Cigarette smoking
	Physical inactivity
	Diet
	Antioxidants (protective)
	Aspirin (protective)

Table 8.2 Factors related to heart disease.

significant protection.[2] As we discussed in Chapter 4, other possible protective dietary factors are magnesium, potassium, soluble fiber, alcohol, and omega-3 fatty acids. Soluble fiber, as in oat bran and beans, helps lower cholesterol, but you would need to consume large amounts of such fibers if you were to rely on this as the primary basis for improving your blood lipids. The evidence for a protective effect from fish or similar oils is not strong enough to consider it as a major determinant of a heart-protective diet. It would not hurt to include a small to moderate amount of such foods in your diet. Some people inherit a tendency for very high cholesterol levels — frequently 300 or 400mg/dL. Such disorders cannot be treated by diet or lifestyle alone, but there are several prescription medications available to control blood cholesterol.

High total cholesterol and LDL cholesterol increase the risk of developing heart disease, while HDL cholesterol has a protective effect. It has been estimated that for each 1mg/dL increase in HDL, there is a 2 to 3 percent decrease in the risk of heart disease.[3] So you want your ratio of total cholesterol (C) to HDL and

Death rates are usually age-adjusted, meaning that the figures are adjusted slightly to conform with the age distribution of some standard population. For example, it would obviously be misleading to compare disease or death rates in a population with a high proportion of old people to rates in a population with a very low proportion.

	C/HDL	LDL/HDL
Vegetarians	2.9	1.7
Boston Marathon runners	3.5	2.0
Males w/o heart disease	5.1	3.3
Males with heart disease	5.8	3.8
Females w/o heart disease	4.4	2.9
Females with heart disease	5.3	3.5
MALES		
Lowest 5 percent	2.9	1.5
Median	4.9	3.2
Highest 5 percent	8.0	5.5
FEMALES		
Lowest 5 percent	2.6	1.3
Median	4.2	2.7
Highest 5 percent	7.3	5.1

Table 8.3 Ratios of total serum cholesterol (C) to HDL and LDL/HDL in various groups. Data adapted from Framingham study.[4]

Lipid (mg/dL)	Desirable	Average	At Risk
Total cholesterol	less than 200	200–230	more than 230
LDL	less than 130	130–160	more than 160
LDL/HDL	less than 3	3–5	more than 5
HDL	more than 45	35–45	less than 35

Table 8.4 Good and bad ranges of blood lipids.

LDL/HDL to be low and your HDL to be high. Table 8.3 lists the range of such figures for the population in general and for some specific groups. I have compiled the best currently available comparative risk estimates in Table 8.4.

If you do have hypertension (usually defined as either systolic pressure persistently greater than 140 or diastolic greater than 90), you should probably be under a physician's care. The same is true for very high cholesterol levels. The medications for dealing with these can be obtained only with a prescription. Borderline cases are usually treated first with the lifestyle changes we have discussed, even by physicians. But readings well above what is considered dangerous can usually be brought under control only with medication. Also, hypertension is occasionally caused by a specific abnormality or problem; this should be ruled out first by the appropriate tests. While antihypertensive medication seems to be of benefit in the

	White male	Black male	White female	Black female
Diseases of heart	196.1	272.7	100.7	165.5
Stroke	26.9	54.9	22.8	41.0
All cancer	159.5	242.4	111.2	136.3
Respiratory	58.1	88.4	26.8	27.4
Colorectal	16.0	20.4	10.8	15.2
Prostate	15.3	35.3		
Breast			22.5	27.6

Table 8.5 Death rates for major diseases in the United States by sex and race. Figures are age-adjusted deaths per 100,000 population for 1991. Source: *Health, United States, 1993*. Hyattsville, MD; Public Health Service, 1994.

treatment of people with established heart disease, it has never been proven of value in primary prevention — that is, in preventing heart disease from occurring in hypertensive people in the first place.[5] It may be that it is overly optimistic to expect large improvements from antihypertensive therapy, which is usually begun in midlife, when atherosclerosis and cardiovascular disease are the results of processes that begin early in life. Significant plaque buildup has been found in the arteries of men as young as 20. Concerns have also been raised about the side effects of the most common antihypertensive drugs — diuretics and beta-blockers. Diuretics frequently increase total and LDL cholesterol; they can also result in electrolyte imbalance by inducing the excretion of potassium. Beta-blockers can increase triglyceride levels and reduce HDL. Both classes of drugs may contribute to insulin resistance. Some of the newer medications, like captopril, do not have these side effects, but they have not been in use long enough for all their effects to be known. Considering this, it is probably best to control hypertension to as great an extent as possible with the lifestyle changes we have discussed. Overweight can result in hypertension, and obese hypertensive people are at greater risk of disease that hypertensives of normal weight. An "enlarged heart" (left ventricular hypertrophy) is sometimes found in those with long-standing hypertension, but this condition is fundamentally different in those of normal weight and is not as much of a risk factor as it is in people who are overweight.[5]

Cancer is the second leading cause of death after cardiovascular disease in the United States and most industrialized countries. As you can see in Table 8.1, while the death rate from heart disease has dropped dramatically over the last 30 years, the cancer death rate has actually increased so that it is now a close second. The "War on Cancer" announced with much fanfare 25 years ago has essentially been a colossal failure, especially considering the amount of funding it has received. Table 8.5 breaks down the 1991 death rates in the United States by sex and race for the leading causes.

Lung cancer (which constitutes the overwhelming majority of respiratory cancer) is the leading cause of cancer death among American males, and about equal to breast cancer among women. As we discussed in Chapter 7, the major risk factors are cigarette smoking, the number of cigarettes per day smoked, and the actual amount of carcinogens inhaled. It has also been linked with exposure to airborne asbestos, radon, and several occupational and industrial chemicals like nickel, chromium, and arsenic. Protective factors include the antioxidant nutrients, vitamin A, and similar substances.

Except for skin cancer, prostate is the most common cancer in men. It ranks below lung cancer but about the same as colorectal as a cause of death. The disease occurs primarily in older men, frequently metastasizing to the bone before it is discovered. Its progression in the elderly is usually not rapid, so the patient frequently dies of other age-related problems. But for this, it would take a much greater toll. When prostate cancer does occur in middle-aged or younger men, it usually spreads rapidly, resulting in death within a year or two from diagnosis. Treatment of the disease includes hormone therapy (estrogen, which inhibits the growth of cancer cells that originated in the prostate), castration, and surgery to remove the prostate. Such surgery frequently results in impotence and sometimes incontinence because of the nerves that are cut during the procedure. The prostate is a gland whose only function is to produce part of the seminal fluid, so it is only essential to reproduction; but because of its location there is no easy way of removing it, either as a preventive measure or once disease occurs. In addition to age, risk factors for prostate cancer are thought to include family history, vasectomy, and diet.[6] Dietary fat, especially animal fat, has been most closely linked to this disease;[7] red meat and foods of animal origin in general have also been implicated.[8] Noncancerous enlargement of the prostate (benign prostatic hyperplasia) also occurs quite frequently after middle age, but no definite link has been established between this and the malignant form.

It is controversial how much screening and what tests for prostate cancer should be done on routine physical exams. The prostate can be palpated (felt) for cancer through the rectum; this is quick and inexpensive, but likely to miss early cancers. Ultrasound screening is promising, if more expensive. Blood tests for prostate cancer are at present somewhat expensive and inaccurate for routine screening.

Mortality from colorectal cancer in the United States has declined by about 25 percent over the past 30 years (Table 8.1), but it remains a leading cause of death of both men and women (Table 8.5). It is one of the cancers most closely linked to diet. Total fat, animal fat, and the protein in meat have been most clearly associated with colon cancer in the epidemiologic studies.[9] High temperatures, as frequently occur during cooking, form carcinogens from certain amino acids in meat protein. Most fats have been found to promote tumor growth or act as carcinogens under some circumstances, with two important exceptions—fish oil and monounsaturated oils like olive oil.[10, 11] Dietary fiber is an important protective factor against colon cancer. It has been long known that its incidence is much lower among vegetarians, who consume much greater quantities of fiber. Insoluble fiber, which speeds the passage of food through the digestive tract, thus exerting a natural laxative effect, is thought to be most effective. But it is still unclear whether it is cereal or vegetable and fruit fiber that is most effective in this regard. The trend in recommendations from the National Cancer Institute has been to shift the emphasis from cereal fibers to vegetable and fruit consumption in recent years. Almost all the case-control studies have found a significant protective effect from at least one measure of fruit or vegetable consumption.[9]

Calcium may afford some protection against colon cancer; a dietary intake of 1,500 to 2,000mg of calcium a day is thought to significantly reduce the risk of developing this disease. Some clinical trials have already been done using calcium carbonate supplements in the range of 1,200 to 2,000mg/day, with encouraging results. This level of dietary calcium reduced the tendency for colon cells to change to a precancerous condition.

Other possible protective factors now being investigated include vegetables in the broccoli family, garlic and onions, spices, and citrus fruits. All these are suspected of possessing inherent anticancer factors (aside from fiber), operating by still-unknown mechanisms. Aspirin and similar drugs (the nonsteroidal anti-inflammatory drugs like ibuprofen) also seem to have a protective effect.

In areas where the incidence of colorectal cancer is high, such as the United States, colon cancer occurs about twice as often as rectal cancer. Family history and chronic inflammatory bowel disease and polyps are also significant risk factors, as is residence in an urban area.

While the five-year survival rate is 80 to 90 percent for cases in which the cancer is localized to the colon or rectum, this disease is advanced at diagnosis in about 65 percent of patients. In the latter case the five-year survival is at best 50 percent. Screening is therefore especially important for this cancer. Many, possibly most, early stage colorectal cancers can be detected with a rectal exam, occult blood testing, and the sigmoidoscope — a flexible fiberoptic tube through which the physician can examine the interior of the colon.

Cancer of the breast is the most common cancer among American women, with mortality about equal to that from lung cancer. The incidence of breast cancer is also high in most industrialized countries, but not in Japan or the rest of Asia. It is clear that there are important environmental factors involved. Its incidence among women born in countries with a low incidence increases when they move to the United States, and their daughters have the same risk as the rest of the population. Risk increases with age, as with most diseases. Family history is significant; a woman's risk is doubled if her mother or a sister have had breast cancer, and increased six times if both have had it. Women who have had cancer in one breast have four to five times the average risk of developing it in the second breast. Women who have their first child after age 30, or who have never had children, have a greater than average incidence. The incidence of breast cancer is related to lifetime exposure to the female hormone estrogen — the younger the age at which a woman began menstruating, the greater is her risk; similarly, risk increases with increasing age at menopause. The role of diet in breast cancer is controversial because studies of this have obtained conflicting results. Some epidemiologic studies have found an association with high fat intake; others have not. Almost all the animal studies have found breast cancer increased by dietary fat. It may be that the connection is only apparent when there are large differences between two diets, as is the case between the United States and Japan. Saturated fat is known to induce estrogen production, and elevated levels of estrogen are associated with an increased risk of breast cancer, providing a plausible causal link. It has been suggested that exercise decreases the risk of breast cancer in a similar manner — by decreasing the cumulative number of menstrual cycles and therefore lifetime exposure to certain female hormones. Whether exercise does have a protective effect is far from proven, however, as we discussed in Chapter 6. The risk of *dying* among women diagnosed with breast cancer was significantly associated with prediagnosis saturated fat intake in a recent Canadian report.[12] For every 5 percent increase in calories from saturated fat, the risk of dying from breast cancer increased by 50 percent, so that women who ate the most saturated fat had nearly double the mortality of those who ate the least. Vitamin C and beta-carotene had a significant protective effect; women with the highest intakes had less than half the risk of dying as those with the lowest intake, the death rate decreasing in a dose-dependent manner.

Five-year survival rates (and cures) vary widely depending on the stage of the disease at diagnosis, ranging from greater than 95 percent for tumors completely localized to the breast, to 10 percent when distant metastases are present. Usually, of course, it is somewhere between these two extremes; the prognosis then depends largely on the extent of involvement of the regional lymph nodes as well as the size of the tumor. Frequent self-examination of the breasts and mammography (X-rays of the breast) are extremely important, especially for women at high risk. Women should begin having yearly mammograms between the age of 40 and 50, depending on their risk factors; even younger for those at high risk.

As we discussed in Chapter 7, exposure to ultraviolet light, primarily through sunlight, greatly increases the risk of skin cancer. The most common of these, basal and squamous cell carcinoma, are usually curable because they grow slowly and rarely metastasize. They can be quite invasive, however, leading to considerable disfigurement. Malignant melanoma is not as common but much more deadly. It arises from the skin cells that produce the dark pigment called melanin. Primarily a disease of Caucasians, a genetic predisposition as well as ultraviolet exposure are risk factors. There is evidence that melanoma risk is related more to severe sunburn, including and possibly especially those suffered when young, rather than the cumulative photodamage related to the more common skin cancers. Changes in a pigmented area should be watched closely for signs of melanoma; it is highly curable if caught early, but almost always fatal once it has spread. The most dangerous moles are the smooth, slightly raised, dark brown ones. A minority of malignant melanomas arise from a previously unpigmented area. The classic warning signs are

- Irregular borders of the mole or pigmented area
- Variation in color within the area
- Bleeding or scaliness

- Changes in size or the way a mole feels, especially if hard or lumpy
- Diameter greater than about that of a pencil eraser (0.6cm)

The 1991 rate of ovarian cancer was about 15 per 100,000 women; while not extremely common, it is the cause of a significant number of deaths because prognosis is usually poor. Median age at diagnosis is 63. Ovarian cancer has the highest mortality rate of all the gynecologic cancers and is the fourth leading cause of cancer death among American women. The five-year survival of about one-third has not changed much in the last 30 years. As with breast cancer, the risk of ovarian cancer seems related to hormonal factors, but they are not quite the same as for breast. There is some evidence that dietary saturated fat increases risk.[13] Childbearing or the use of birth control pills (which creates a similar hormonal balance) reduces the risk by 10 to 50 percent. Women with breast cancer have an increased risk of developing ovarian cancer, and vice-versa. There are no reliable means of screening for the disease, so it is frequently well advanced at diagnosis.

Stomach cancer was a major cause of death in the United States in the early part of the twentieth century, but its incidence has fallen steadily over the past 60 years. Mortality from stomach cancer is about one-fourth what it was in 1930. It remains a source of concern because it is essentially always fatal. This disease may be related to pickled, salted, and smoked food, since it is highest in countries where consumption of such foods is high. There is strong evidence that vitamin C is a significant protective factor. Epidemiologic studies support this association, and vitamin C is known to prevent the formation of cancer-causing chemicals called nitrosamines. Such substances are the product of a chemical reaction involving nitrates, a class of chemicals common in a number of foods such as cured meats and some cheeses. It has also been suggested that the introduction of refrigeration or certain preservatives like BHT over the past century has produced a protective effect, either by increasing year-round access to fruits and vegetables in the former case, or preventing the formation of carcinogens in food in the latter.

Japan, Chile, Singapore, and Iceland have high rates of stomach cancer. It is by far the leading cause of cancer death in Japan. There are clearly environmental factors at work, since studies of Japanese who have moved to the United States have found that their rate of stomach cancer declines to the typical American rate within a couple of generations.

Cancer of the bladder is most common among white males, who had an incidence of 31.6 per 100,000 in 1991. This was double or more the rate of blacks and women. Risk factors include cigarette smoking and industrial chemicals, particularly those used in making dyes and in the rubber and leather industries. Other occupations with a suspected link to bladder cancer include metal workers, hairdressers, and chemical workers. Persistent infections of the bladder, particularly parasitic infections, are associated with bladder cancer worldwide, but this is not common in the United States. Earlier reports of a link with coffee have been completely discredited. Reports that the artificial sweeteners cyclamate and saccharin caused bladder cancer in rats caused concern some years ago; in fact, the FDA tried to ban saccharin but was prevented by Congressional action. A number of more recent and thorough epidemiologic studies found no relation between saccharin or cyclamates and bladder cancer, or at most a very weak link.[14]

Bladder cancer has a survival rate somewhat better than most cancers, but is still usually fatal if the cancer has already spread when discovered. Symptoms include blood in the urine, pain during urination, and frequent urination.

Cancer of the uterine cervix has declined significantly over the past 20 years; its incidence in 1991 was about 8 cases per 100,000 women. This cancer may remain localized for years before spreading. A change to an abnormal cell type (dysplasia) can often be detected well before it becomes actually malignant. Such changes are seen in cells scraped from the cervix and examined in the Pap smear test. At these early stages, uterine cancer is curable about 95 percent of the time. Major risk factors are multiple sex partners, early age at first intercourse, and possibly venereal disease. The carotenoids and retinoids, which tend to maintain healthy epithelial tissue, as well as vitamin C, may have a protective effect.

Cancer of the uterus is frequently called endometrial cancer, but this is actually just the most common form. The endometrium is the inner layer of cells that is shed during menstruation. Incidence is about twice as high as cervical cancer among American women. Most cases of uterine cancer occur in later life; the average age is around 60. Risk factors are similar to those for breast cancer. Obesity and hormonal imbalances (excess estrogen) are especially significant. Obese women have twice the risk of endometrial cancer as women of normal weight. Estrogen replacement therapy, which we will discuss shortly, may be associated with endometrial cancer, while use of birth control pills seems to decrease the risk. There is also some evidence that physical activity reduces the risk.[15]

Osteoporosis is the loss of bone mass. It has been estimated that it causes well over a million fractures a year in the United States. The major sites are the backbone (half a million) and the hip (250,000). In the backbone, these are usually crushing-type fractures of the vertebrae that frequently go unnoticed or unreported. Hip fractures have a particularly large impact. In the six months following such a fracture, there is a 12 to 20 percent decrease in expected survival rate.[16] Up to 35 percent of such victims of hip fracture will need to enter a long-term care facility such as a nursing home soon after the fracture; about half of them never regain their former level of function.[17]

The major risk factors for osteoporosis are sex (it occurs in women four times as often as in men), age, low bone mass, early menopause, race (greater in Caucasians and Asians), lack of calcium, physical inactivity, and heredity. Dietary phosphorus, sodium, alcohol, and caffeine *may* increase risk, but only at very high levels.

Bone is not fixed, inert matter; it contains living cells that form and control its structure. A matrix of the fibrous protein collagen and similar substances supports the calcium-containing mineral phase, which makes up about 65 percent of the total. It is constantly being remodeled throughout a person's life, even in the absence of growth or fractures. Specialized cells break down small portions of the bone mineral and matrix; other cells in the bone, called osteoblasts, then form new bone. The breakdown phase is relatively rapid, as short as a week or two; but formation of new bone may take several months. Parathyroid hormone, vitamin D, and several other growth factors and hormones interact in this process. While overall growth in the length of bone is usually complete by age 20, peak bone mass is not attained until sometime in the 30s. The overall structure of bone is genetically determined, but large variations can arise from environmental influences. Bone adapts to the strain placed on it. Thus disuse or physical inactivity leads to a loss of strength and actual bone mass; weight-bearing activity that places a strain on bone gives rise to processes that strengthen it.

A slow decrease in bone mass begins in both sexes around age 40. This appears to be due to the overall aging process, but it varies somewhat depending on individual differences. At least two other processes or diseases are known that can greatly accelerate bone loss. One, which is thought to affect only a minority of people, is related to poorly understood interactions between bone cell growth factors and overall metabolism. In this condition, bone cannot be formed as fast as needed because of impairment of the cells that produce new bone (the osteoblasts).

Secondly, accelerated bone loss due to the cessation of estrogen production is seen in postmenopausal women. This is greatest in the first five years or so following menopause, but can continue for up to 20 years. This loss of estrogen increases bone remodeling, with breakdown exceeding buildup. Typically, a woman with osteoporosis will lose 35 to 50 percent of her peak bone mass. There is no doubt that estrogen helps build healthy bones, although not all of the details of its interactions in this regard are known. The fact that bone cells have specialized receptors for estrogen on their surface is one indication of how fundamental it is to the process. There is also no doubt that the loss of this hormone, as at menopause, greatly increases the rate of bone resorption or breakdown. Administration of estrogen beginning at menopause greatly reduces bone loss and subsequent fractures. Such estrogen replacement therapy also greatly reduces the risk of heart disease, and possibly stroke, in postmenopausal women. The positive effects of estrogen can be seen in essentially all bones in the body; its effects last for as long as it is administered. Epidemiologic studies have confirmed that women on estrogen replacement therapy have a greatly reduced incidence of fractures, with up to 90 percent reduction of fractures of the vertebrae.[17] If estrogen replacement is stopped, bone loss begins at a rate about equal to that immediately after menopause. The fact that estrogen also greatly lowers the risk of heart disease and possibly strokes in postmenopausal women may be brought about by its effect on blood lipids, since it is known that estrogen lowers LDL and raises HDL in such women.

Unfortunately, there may be negative effects associated with estrogen replacement. These are an increased risk of endometrial cancer and, possibly, an increased risk of breast cancer. The increase in incidence of endometrial cancer can be significant; one review of the studies in this area concluded that the yearly rate of endometrial cancer for women on estrogen was four to five times the rate of women not taking estrogen.[18] Since estrogen is typically administered for a decade or more, this increase in yearly rate would amount to a significant cumulative risk. The numbers involved are relatively small, because the incidence of endometrial cancer is not high, and most women survive estrogen-related endometrial cancer.[19] Administration of the other class of female hormone, progestin,* as part of estrogen replacement therapy, reduces or eliminates this increased risk of endometrial cancer.[16] It also eliminates the incidence of irregular bleeding sometimes associated with estrogen. However, progestin tends to raise LDL and lower HDL, thereby counteracting, although probably only slightly, estrogen's positive effects with respect to the risk from heart disease.

To what extent estrogen replacement increases the risk of breast cancer remains controversial. A number of epidemiologic studies have been done on this question, with conflicting results. Some have found no increase, some a small increase, and some a small to moderate increase in breast cancer among women receiving estrogen.[20, 21] Even a small to moderate effect would be a matter of concern because of the relatively high rate of breast cancer to begin with. A large, recent study found that women who had taken estrogen or estrogen and progestin for five or more years after menopause, and were still taking it, had a significantly higher incidence of breast cancer.[21] After accounting for other risk factors such as age at menopause and family history, such postmenopausal women had about a 50 to 70 percent greater risk of breast cancer than postmenopausal women who had never taken the hormones. But women who had formerly taken estrogen but had stopped did not have a significantly greater risk of breast cancer, even if they had taken estrogen for five or more years. It is generally thought that whatever effect exists is dose-related, so small amounts of estrogen would increase risk little, if at all. Progestin does not seem to counteract the estrogen-related increase in breast cancer, as it does for endometrial cancer; in some studies it actually increased risk further.[20, 21]

Dietary calcium deficiency *can* lead to osteoporosis. Other dietary factors, such as excess phosphorus, sodium, caffeine, and alcohol, or deficiencies of vitamin D or magnesium, could also have a role in engendering a negative calcium balance and subsequent bone loss,[16, 22] but none of these factors is the usual cause of osteoporosis. It is certainly prudent to insure an adequate intake of calcium, magnesium, and vitamin D; as we discussed in Chapter 5, a daily total calcium intake (including dietary and supplements) of 1,200 to 1,500mg is advisable. A magnesium supplement of 250 to 300mg a day may be helpful in several respects. But these minerals alone, or even large quantities of them, cannot prevent osteoporosis.

Bone responds to the loads placed on it in much the same manner as muscle. Weight-bearing exercise helps build and maintain strong, healthy bones.[23] It is unknown whether osteoporosis can be completely prevented through exercise and good diet, at least in women, but there is no doubt that exercise can help substantially in preventing bone loss.[24] There is also no doubt that physical inactivity at

---

The terms estrogen and progestin refer to classes of several closely related hormones rather than to specific chemicals.

any age will result in weaker bones. The type, frequency, and duration of exercise most effective in strengthening bone have not been worked out. One would suspect that actual weight-lifting exercises would be most effective. There is good reason to believe that bones become stronger with the same sort of specificity as muscles, so jogging may not help your arm bones very much. But any exercise in which the body is supporting itself and moving its large bones will place some strain on and therefore strengthen the major bones, including the vertebrae, hips, and legs. Ordinary activities such as jogging, walking, tennis, and the like, should be effective to at least some extent. The associated increase in muscle strength from such exercise also aids significantly in preventing falls, and thus the most serious consequences of any osteoporosis that does occur. Even postmenopausal women in their 50s and 60s can increase bone density through exercise; one study reported a 6.1 percent increase.[16] In another recent report, 40 postmenopausal women from 50 to 70 years of age underwent high-intensity strength training using resistance machines (similar to weight lifting) two days a week for a year.[25] Their bone density as measured by X-ray increased in several important bones, including the spine. Total bone mass stabilized in these exercising women, whereas it was found to decrease significantly in a control group of nonexercising women. Muscle mass, strength, and balance also increased in the exercising women and decreased in controls.

Young women who exercise vigorously and frequently, such as those training for competitive athletics, sometimes stop menstruating or menstruate irregularly.[26] This has negative implications for the maintenance of bone mass. It has been suggested that in such cases the women reduce the intensity and/or frequency of their regimen, or consider estrogen replacement.[26] However, as we have discussed, a reduced number of menstrual cycles probably decreases the risk of breast cancer. This situation is very unlikely in any usual kind of exercise program.

It is much easier to build and maintain a strong skeleton than to treat bone loss once it has occurred. Exercise and adequate intakes of calcium, magnesium, and vitamin D are advisable for both premenopausal and postmenopausal women as overall health measures, in addition to conserving bone. The decision to begin estrogen replacement at menopause, as well as the type and dose, must of course be made by each woman on an individual basis in consultation with her physician, since estrogen is only available by prescription. There is no certain way to predict which persons will develop osteoporosis, and no simple means to precisely measure bone mass. Your risk factors for this disease and the other major estrogen-related diseases, breast cancer and heart disease, can guide your decision. Estrogen can reduce the incidence of heart disease by up to 50 percent in postmenopausal women. The general feeling today is that some estrogen therapy is advisable, even if low-dose, if there is any significant risk of the diseases associated with estrogen loss. But there is no way at present of maintaining all the benefits of hormone replacement therapy while avoiding the risks. You can, however, minimize your risk for the diseases associated with loss of estrogen by exercise, diet, and supplements, as we have discussed. This would minimize your need for postmenopausal estrogen and, as I mentioned, the potential negative effects can be minimized by using as low a dose of estrogen as possible, in combination with progestin, for as short a time as possible.

There are several newer drugs such as calcitonin that are thought to prevent bone loss without the negative effects of estrogen. Calcitonin is now available (by prescription), but most of these drugs are currently (1996) in the development or approval stage. They have their own adverse side effects and, because these drugs have not been used extensively, all their potential adverse effects may not be known. Hopefully, in the near future one or more of the newer drugs will eliminate the need for estrogen replacement therapy for osteoporosis, or at least allow the dose to be reduced to a very low level. Some estrogen may still be advisable in certain cases for the other benefits that we have discussed.

Men also suffer a loss of bone with age. Though it is not usually to the same extent as women, it is not uncommon for it to become significant. There is a second kind of osteoporosis, not dependent on estrogen loss, that occurs in both men and women after the age of 70.[16] This type of osteoporosis is due to a decreased rate of bone buildup rather than an increased rate of breakdown. Men can also build a strong skeleton by the exercise and dietary practices we have discussed, which, again, are advisable as overall health measures and in the prevention of several diseases.

References to Chapter Eight

1. S.M. Artand-Wild et al.: Differences in coronary mortality can be explained by differences in cholesterol and saturated fat intakes in 40 countries but not in France and Finland. A paradox. *Circulation* 88:2771–2779, 1993.

2. P. Knekt et al.: Antioxidant vitamin intake and coronary mortality in a longitudinal population study. *Am J Epidemiol* 139:1180–1189, 1994.

3. D.L. Tribble, R.M. Krauss: HDL and coronary artery disease. *Adv Intern Med* 38: 1–29, 1993.

4. W.P. Castelli et al.: Summary estimate of cholesterol used to predict coronary artery disease. *Circulation* 67:730–734, 1983.

5. N.K. Hollenberg: Management of hypertension and cardiovascular risk. *Am J Med* 90(2A):2S–6S, 1991.

6. K.J. Pienta, P.S. Esper: Risk factors for prostate cancer. *Ann Intern Med* 118: 793–803, 1993.

7. E. Giovannucci et al.: A prospective study of dietary fat and risk of prostate cancer. *JNCI* 85:1571–1579, 1993.

8. R. Talamini et al.: Diet and prostate: a case-control study in northern Italy. *Nutr Cancer* 18:277–286, 1992.

9. M.J. Wargovich, A.J. Mastromarino: Dietary factors in the etiology and prevention of colon cancer. *Cancer Bull* 46:303–308, 1994.

10. B.S. Reddy: Dietary fat and colon cancer: animal models. *Prev Med* 16:460–467, 1987.

11. B.S. Reddy, C. Burrill, J. Rigotty: Effects of diets high in omega-3 and omega-6 fatty acids on initiation and postinitiation stages of colon carcinogenesis. *Cancer Res* 51:487–491, 1991.

12. M. Jain, A.B. Miller, T. To: Premorbid diet and the prognosis of women with breast cancer. *JNCI* 86:1390–1397, 1994.

13. H.A. Risch et al.: Dietary fat intake and risk of epithelial ovarian cancer. *JNCI* 86:1409–1415, 1994.

14. Artificial Sweeteners. On-line gopher.nih.gov Health & Clinical Information/CancerNet Information/Fact Sheets from the NCI/Risk Factors & Possible Causes.

15. F. Levi: Selected physical activity and the risk of endometrial cancer. *Br J Med* 67: 846–851, 1993.

16. U.S. Department of Health and Human Services: *Osteoporosis Research, Education, and Health Promotion.* Public Health Service, Bethesda, MD, 1991.

17. R. Lindsay: The pathogenesis, prevention and treatment of osteoporosis. In: *New Techniques in Metabolic Bone Disease.* J.C. Stevenson, ed. Wright, London, 1990.

18. H.B. Peterson, N.C. Lee, G.L. Rubin: Genital neoplasia. In: *Menopause; Physiology and Pharmacology*, D.R. Mishell, ed. Year Book Medical Publishers, Chicago, 1986.

19. J. Chu, A. Schweid, N.S. Weiss: Survival among women with endometrial cancer; a comparison of estrogen users and non-users. *Am J Obstet Gynecol* 143:569–575, 1982.

20. K.F. Ganger, M. Cust, M.I. Whitehead: Controversies in the use of hormone replacement therapy. In: *New Techniques in Metabolic Bone Disease.* J.C. Stevenson, ed., Wright, London, 1990.

21. G.A. Colditz, et al.: The use of estrogen and progestins and the risk of breast cancer in postmenopausal women. *N Engl J Med* 332:1589–1593, 1995.

22. M.S. Seelig: Interrelationship of magnesium and estrogen in cardiovascular and bone disorders, eclampsia, migraine and premenstrual syndrome. *J Am Coll Nutr* 12:442–458, 1993.

23. P.H. Fentem: Exercise in prevention of disease. *Br Med Bull* 48:630–650,1992.

24. C.H. Chesnut: Bone mass and exercise. *Am J Med* 95(5A):34S–36S, 1993.

25. M.E. Nelson et al.: Effects of high-intensity strength training on multiple risk factors for osteoporotic fractures. A randomized control trial. *JAMA* 272:1909–1914, 1994.

26. C.M. Snow-Harter: Bone health and prevention of osteoporosis in active and athletic women. *Clin Sports Med* 13:389–404, 1994.

NINE. Recommendations

We have discussed a great many things that may lead to disease and early death, as well as factors that may enhance health and extend life span. You may well be wondering which of them are most important, for which of them the evidence is strongest, and how these many factors may interact with each other. I will try to answer these questions in this chapter. In most cases no definite answer is available, but there is substantial evidence one way or another. My recommendations are, of course, my own opinions, based on the many studies that we have discussed plus many more that I have not cited. I have in all cases followed the weight of the evidence in making these determinations. (You can almost always find one or two studies that seem to contradict the majority, even when the evidence is overwhelming.) As I indicated in Chapter 2, in the real world we usually do have to come to a decision when the evidence is not as good as we would like. You can't avoid the issue by doing nothing, or making no changes in diet, lifestyle, and so on. In not deciding, you have decided. In making no changes, you would continue with your present diet, your present intake of vitamins, and so on. In many cases, these are probably not optimal for health and longevity. The questions then become: How strong is the evidence? Are you willing to change your diet, lifestyle, etc.? Are the benefits worth the change? I will use the imperative often in this chapter since it is difficult to make recommendations otherwise, but only you can answer the last two questions for yourself. I can tell you that for the most part, the potential benefits are substantial. In this chapter, and mainly in the next, I will let you in on many helpful tips that I have accumulated in making such changes.

Of all the life-extension strategies, caloric restriction is probably the one best supported by evidence. It has extended both average and maximum life span in many widely different species. It is the *only* method that has been proven to consistently increase maximum life span. While it is true that caloric restriction has not been tried on humans, at least not in a long-term controlled experiment,* it is difficult to see why its effects would be any different in people than in the many species in which it has extended life. It will almost certainly work if you apply it properly. Nevertheless, it has several disadvantages.

First, it is the most difficult to apply. Restricting caloric intake by a significant amount over the remaining course of your life is probably not something most people

---

*Caloric restriction has been undertaken by many people on an individual basis, and there have been a few short-term trials with people in a controlled, experimental setting. Results from these efforts have been encouraging, but do not constitute proof in the way that a controlled life-span study would.

are willing to undertake, or be successful at if they do. And on-and-off calorie restriction may be worse than none at all.

Second, there is evidence that caloric restriction cannot be combined with some other life-extension measures to give an additive effect. There have not been a sufficient number of experiments examining the addition of other life-extension techniques to caloric restriction for us to reach definite conclusions. Until there are, we can only go by what evidence we have. Attempts to combine caloric restriction with exercise or with antioxidant supplementation have at best resulted in no increase in life span over caloric restriction alone.[1, 2] In one of the few studies of this type, mice fed a calorie-restricted diet supplemented with the antioxidants ethoxyquin or 2-mercaptoethylamine had about the same life span as nonrestricted mice (with or without antioxidants). Mice on a calorie-restricted diet without the antioxidants had a 22 percent greater average life span and a 14 percent greater maximum life span than nonrestricted mice.[2] In other words, adding antioxidants negated the increase in life span due to calorie restriction. It should be noted, however, that the levels of antioxidants used in this study, while comparable to levels previously found to extend life in mice, were much greater than the amounts most people, even those enthusiastic about supplements, would generally take. They would amount to about 1.25 to 5 grams in a human diet.

Also, while it is possible to double an animal's life span by severe caloric restriction begun at weaning and continued throughout life, the gain is not that great when caloric restriction is begun in midlife. Even with fairly severe restriction, increases have been around 10 to 28 percent, as in Walford's original experiment in which the restricted mice consumed 44 percent fewer calories than controls.[3] Translated into human terms, this would be about 7 to 20 years added to average life expectancy.

This is not to argue against significant caloric restriction; just be aware of the associated considerations. Undertake it gradually, cutting back on calories over a year or more; life expectancy can be decreased if the change is too rapid. Take a multivitamin and some extra minerals. Eat a varied diet with plenty of vegetables, fruit, and whole grains. The evidence is against adding very large amounts of antioxidants to such a diet. It is also against anything but mild exercise on a calorie-restricted diet.

However, caloric restriction is not an all-or-nothing strategy; benefits (decreased disease incidence and increased life span) are roughly proportional to the degree of restriction, from small amounts up to something like a 60 percent reduction in calories. So you will still derive some benefit from even small reductions in your caloric intake, and this probably *can* be combined with other life-extension techniques.

As we discussed in Chapter 5, there is reason to believe that a number of vitamins and other supplements will help prevent disease and increase life expectancy. I do not believe, however, that there is anything like sufficient evidence to rely on large amounts of antioxidant supplements as the primary means of avoiding disease and retarding aging. It is true that some antioxidants have significantly increased average and, in a few cases, maximum life span in animal experiments (see Chapter 5 for details and references). But some studies did not find any increase or a very small one. The levels of antioxidants used in such experiments were quite high, generally from around 0.3 to 1 percent of the diet. This would be roughly equivalent to a human intake of 1.5 to several grams a day. There have been no long-term studies of such high levels in humans. Anecdotal reports that such levels are not harmful and have been beneficial in some cases do exist, but that's not hard evidence. Also note that almost all such experiments studied the effect of administering just one antioxidant at a time, and not in combination with other factors that might affect life span (exercise, vitamin/mineral intake, etc.). So we don't know what the effect of large amounts of, say, BHT and vitamin E, or BHT and exercise, might be. It may seem reasonable that two substances or strategies, both beneficial in themselves, would give some kind of additional benefit when taken together, but nature frequently just doesn't work that way. Things sometimes do produce a simple additive effect when combined, but sometimes the combined effect is greater or less than the sum of individual effects, and sometimes things counteract each other in such a way that the combined effect is zero or negative. As we just discussed, there is some evidence that the combination of significant dietary restriction and antioxidants produces no increase in life span. There have been some studies that examined the effect of more than one antioxidant or other dietary supplement at a time, but these have almost always used much lower doses than the 0.3 to 1 percent of diet we are talking about here. If you did decide to use a high dose of antioxidants, I would recommend one that has been studied most thoroughly. While the natural antioxidants like vitamin E would seem a logical choice, almost all the studies that reported significant extension of life span in laboratory animals used one of the synthetic antioxidants like BHT. (Some scientists have speculated that the body might respond to high intakes of natural antioxidants by decreasing its own production of antioxidants.) High intakes of a well-studied substance like BHT are *probably* safe, but there is an element of risk involved in taking them over a very long term. If you did choose this strategy, I would not combine it with more than moderate amounts of anything else. Again, we don't know that such combinations would be harmful, but there is just too much downside risk involved in such a strategy. I also don't think that monitoring your physical condition via blood tests and other physiologic exams is sufficient protection against such harm. Some such readings (like liver enzymes) may be elevated without any significance, while others may not change much until an actual pathologic condition has developed.

While I can see the rationale for the strategies of caloric restriction and high antioxidant supplementation, my preference is for a broader-based program of dietary modification, moderate supplementation, and exercise. This would still include mild caloric restriction. If you eat anything like the typical high-fat American or Western diet, dietary modification is probably the most important change that you can make to ensure a long and healthy life. Dietary fat has been linked to heart disease, stroke, prostate cancer, and colorectal cancer, and may well be associated with several other cancers and diseases. It should be reduced to as low a level as possible, and monounsaturated fats like olive oil should be used whenever possible. Monounsaturated fats are the safest in all respects and olive oil is the safest of these, mainly because it has been in use for so long and is the most purely monounsaturated of all. Indeed, there may be no risks associated with olive oil itself, as there are for saturated and polyunsaturated fats.* But it still has the high calorie content of all fats; intake must therefore be limited to help keep total calories (and body weight) within acceptable levels. There is overwhelming evidence for the health and longevity benefits of reducing consumption of meat and other animal products, of reducing total dietary fat, and of making vegetables, fruits, and grains the staples of your diet. There is *no* risk in this strategy. Almost all the evidence is in favor of some benefits; it's just a question of how great they will be. At worse, the causal links between some cancers and the high-fat Western diet have not been proved. For example, there is some debate over whether breast cancer is linked to dietary fat. My own opinion is that the association between diet and cancer will eventually be more firmly established in almost all cases; it's just a question of how strong the causal links are. As we have discussed in previous chapters, there is also substantial evidence for the health benefits of increasing the fiber in your diet and minimizing consumption of animal products. Fortunately, all of these goals can be achieved by essentially the same dietary modifications. Replacing foods like meat, eggs, and other high-fat dairy products and high-fat processed foods with vegetables, fruits, and grains will substantially decrease the fat in your diet and increase the fiber. Legumes (beans, peas, lentils, soybeans) and some fish (including shellfish) are also acceptable. These need not always be fresh; plain canned and frozen foods are fine. Such a diet also almost automatically decreases total calories consumed, since fats are the most calorie-dense foods. Fruits and vegetables are almost all remarkably low in calories. Dried fruits, however, including raisins, prunes, and the like, are much more calorie dense just because they have had most of their moisture removed. Grain products tend to be low to moderate in calories, depending not only on what they are but how they are prepared. Cooked grains like spaghetti and hot cereals are relatively low in calories. All oils are pure fat and should be used sparingly. The same goes for butter and margarine, which are composed of about 80 percent fat on average and derive all their calories from fat. You therefore must be careful of the sauces and other coatings on otherwise acceptable foods; they are frequently prepared with large amounts of butter, margarine, or oil. This is not to say that no fat can be used in their preparation, but it should be kept to a minimum. This sort of diet is not really very restrictive, and in fact I don't think it's a good idea to approach dietary modifications as so many restrictions. There are several dozen common vegetables and fruits, and half a dozen common grains, and

---

*In Crete, 40 percent of calories are derived from fat, mainly in the form of olive oil, but there is still a very low incidence of heart disease. Also, in contrast to nearly all other fats, olive oil does not promote cancer. In fact, several studies have reported significant inverse relations between olive oil consumption and the incidence of various cancers.

many ways of preparing each of them. With a little trial and error, everyone can find dishes that are both healthy and appealing. It is also not necessary to avoid higher-fat foods and treats completely. A piece of cake or candy once a week or so will not add significantly to your fat intake. A cupcake or a comparable-sized piece of coffee cake has about six grams of fat, which amounts to less than 3 percent of your average total daily calorie intake and less than half a percent of weekly intake. There are also a fair number of nonfat cakes, candies, and other treats that can be eaten more often than this.

A low-fat diet emphasizing vegetables, fruits, and grains makes it easier to avoid excess body fat. Fat has over twice the calorie content of carbohydrate or protein, and calories from dietary fat are incorporated into body fat more easily than calories from carbohydrate or protein. Excess body fat is thought to contribute to a number of diseases, including endometrial cancer, breast cancer, cancer of the gallbladder, colorectal cancer, heart disease, hypertension, and diabetes.[4–6] It is, of course, difficult to separate the effects of excess fat and calories in the diet from the effects of body fat alone. However, in a number of studies which have done so, an independent risk was associated with excess body fat even when calories, fat intake, and other risk factors were accounted for.[4] Of the cancers, the evidence for a relation to body fat is strongest for endometrial; the causal link is thought to be through increased production of estrogen, as we discussed in other contexts.

Obesity is associated with increased overall mortality. The incidence of hypertension is three to five times higher in obese people than in those of normal weight. The rate of diabetes is three to four times higher in the obese. Lowest mortality is found among people of average weight and those 10 to 20 percent below average. Mortality among those 30 percent to 40 percent above average weight is nearly 50 percent higher than in people of average weight. Among people more than 40 percent above average weight, mortality is nearly 90 percent higher.[6]

It is more accurate to speak about the dangers of excess body fat, or obesity, than the dangers of being overweight, even though the two are correlated. There is no reason for thinking, and no evidence, that additional muscle contributes to any disease. Weight alone, or weight at a given height, is not a really good measure of leanness or obesity in a person. Accurate determinations of body fat can only be made using a number of more sophisticated techniques. One of these, based on the lower density of fat compared to lean tissue, is the measurement of body weight while the subject is completely submerged in water. Others include measures of certain elements (like total body potassium) that correlate with lean tissue using radioactive isotopes. These techniques are, of course, far beyond what is available to the average person or physician. However, a fairly straightforward calculation based on height and weight has been found to correlate well with the measurements of body fat made by the more sophisticated techniques. This is the body mass index, or BMI. It is defined as body weight in kilograms divided by the square of the height in meters:

$$BMI = weight(kg) / [height(m)]^2$$

This is still cumbersome for the average person to use. Since the BMIs corresponding to normal, below-average, and above-average weights/heights are known, the values of height and weight corresponding to these can be calculated. This is sometimes done on a nomogram of height, BMI, and weight. I have simplified this by calculating weights versus height from the established BMIs for 20 percent underweight, low "normal," high "normal," and 20 percent overweight. These data are given in Appendix 4.

While the correlation of BMI with body fat is good, the values in Appendix 4 might not be accurate for very muscular persons, since much of their weight would be composed of muscle, not fat. A somewhat better measure of body fat, but more difficult to make and to quantify, is skinfold thickness. The skin is pinched up between thumb and index fingers on various parts of the body — abdomen, hips, thighs, and arms are good regions. This skinfold thus includes two thicknesses of skin and two of subcutaneous (below the skin) fat, which can be measured with an ordinary caliper. Skinfold calipers are used in laboratories to make this measurement, but they are much more expensive and difficult to obtain, and not much more accurate. An ordinary inexpensive shop caliper is good enough for the job. Any skinfold that measures more than one inch (2.54cm) indicates excess fat. Do not include any muscle in the skinfold; usually this is obvious, but the muscle in the area can be contracted and relaxed to distinguish it if there is any doubt. Make the measurement several times and compute an average, applying the jaws of the caliper about a half inch from the fingers and one-half to one inch from the top of the skinfold. It is possible to translate this measurement into percent body fat by taking it at various places on the body and using tables and formulas to make the conversion, but this is rather complicated and not something most people need do.

There is some evidence that the distribution of body fat is an important determinant of the consequences to health. Excess abdominal fat, which is more common in men, is correlated with greater risk of disease than fat accumulation below the waist (typically on the hips and thighs), which is more common in women. It has not been well established whether this is just a correlation, or if there is some causal relation.

Assuming average proportions of muscle and fat, in terms of longevity it is best to be at or even somewhat below the normal weight for your height. Even if you are of normal weight you can still increase your chances for a longer life by losing weight. This is a subtle point that sometimes creates confusion. Compilation of weight versus life span for a population as a whole shows only what happens to people under normal — or typical — conditions. (Such data alone do not even prove a causal relation, although further analysis has in fact done so in this case.) So, for example, some people might be thin because they eat less; but many, possibly most, are thin because they have a genetic predisposition to it. (Additional reasons, such as illness, are possible.) If they now impose caloric restriction on themselves and lose more weight, the evidence from the studies of caloric restriction is that they increase their longevity further, at least up to a point. People who are normal weight to overweight will probably benefit most from such restriction, however. As we discussed in Chapter 3, while it is somewhat easier to gauge your caloric intake from watching your weight, which is easily measured, body weight may not always accurately reflect calorie intake. It's more difficult to calculate the actual calories in the food you eat and relate it to your amount of activity, or number of calories expended each day, but you can make a fair estimate.

Again, these considerations may not apply if, in making a weight change, a person adds a significant amount of muscle. There is no reason to believe that gaining weight by increasing muscle mass would do any harm. Similarly, maintaining a given weight by losing fat while gaining muscle is probably as beneficial as just losing fat, but no one has done actual life span experiments on this. As we have discussed, there are other health reasons for providing yourself with a good reserve of muscle.

I can only touch on the subject of weight control here; it would take another book to do it justice. The considerations we have discussed can be applied by everyone, and will be sufficient to control weight for the great majority of people. Those who are significantly overweight (that is, obese), who have tried unsuccessfully to lose weight permanently, and who find that they cannot do so even with the program described here, should seek help at one of the centers or clinics that specialize in this problem. Weight control is frequently a complex problem that goes far beyond the simple notions of will power and just eating less.

Alcohol can be consumed in moderation; it may even be beneficial. By moderation, I mean an average of one to two drinks a day for men, and up to one drink a day for women. Above these amounts, it starts to increase the risk of several serious diseases and overall mortality. Alcoholic beverages are not especially high in calories. An average, standard-size 12-fluid-ounce bottle of beer has about 145 calories; an equal amount of lite beer has about 100 calories. This is equivalent to 41 and 27 calories per 100 grams, respectively, which is less than whole milk (65 calories/100g) and about the same as skim milk (36 calories/100g). Wine averages around 70 calories per wineglass (100mL). But like anything else, the calories from alcohol can add up to a significant amount if it is overdone.

The evidence is that caffeine, at least up to the amount in about four or five cups of coffee daily, is harmless. Coffee and tea themselves are also fine in such moderate amounts. The caffeine content of a cup of coffee or tea can vary widely, depending on how they are brewed. Typical values per cup (237mL) are 237mg for drip coffee, 164mg for percolated coffee, 145 to 166mg for instant coffee, and 35 to 85mg for tea.[7] The amounts in soft drinks (usually colas) are in the range of 30 to 65mg per 12 oz (360mL) can, or 21 to 43mg per cup. By comparison, a stay-awake pill like NoDoz has 100mg. But again, unless you are really overdoing such beverages, or are particularly sensitive to caffeine, it's not something to worry about.

Sugar and salt are minor evils. As I mentioned in Chapter 4, some people are salt-sensitive; they must restrict their salt intake to avoid hypertension and possibly heart disease and stroke. Salt may be weakly connected to one or two diseases, so it's best not to overdo it, but I don't believe that it's a major hazard for most people. There is even less evidence that moderate amounts of sugar are harmful. Avoid it as a source of empty calories if possible. Choose a diet soft drink instead of one with sugar. Choose a breakfast cereal with no or small amounts of added sugar; use fruit preserves instead of jellies and jams. In the latter two cases, as often happens, sugar replaces some of the actual beneficial ingredients (the whole grain in cereal and the fruit in preserves).

Exercise should be an important part of your program for the many reasons we have discussed. It has a small but positive effect on overall longevity; it helps in avoiding a number of serious diseases, including heart disease, stroke, and osteoporosis; it will enable you to extend your independent, active years and possibly avoid an infirm old age; it helps in maintaining proper body weight; it generally has a positive psychological effect. How much exercise and what kind are things that must be determined largely on an individual basis. I would avoid the extremes. Mild exercise totaling less than 30 to 40 minutes a week is not likely to do you a significant amount of good. An hour or more of daily, high-intensity exercise may be associated with increased risk of injury, several diseases, and shortened life expectancy. As we discussed in Chapter 6, aerobic exercises, which promote cardiovascular conditioning, are the most prudent, but weight lifting and other non-aerobic activities are also beneficial. It is far more important to pick an activity that you will be consistent about doing — whether jogging, walking, tennis, skiing, and so on — than it is to pick some "best" exercise. You do not have to limit yourself to one type of exercise; you can, if you prefer, engage in different activities on different days of the week. You can also devise a short but effective minimal general routine that can be done in your home. This sort of ten minute routine is better than nothing for days when you cannot do more. You might start out, for example, with some stretching; then do push-aways for a couple of minutes. As mentioned in Chapter 6, this is like a push-up but done with the hands on a support waist to chest high (such as the edge of a table, or against the wall) instead of the floor. You could finish with an aerobic activity like running in place or stair-stepping for about eight minutes.

Some people prefer to make a major commitment to exercise. That's fine; you will derive increased benefits from increased activity, as I indicated, up to a point. A more thorough exercise program could include an aerobic activity two or three times a week, plus weight lifting or a similar resistance exercise like Nautilus or some calisthenics that works both the upper and lower body. More of the flexibility exercises of the type mentioned in Chapter 6 could be added.

The main caution in beginning an exercise program is for people who have never exercised, or have not exercised in many years. The former case is probably rare. Many people fall into the latter category. They may have engaged in a significant amount of activity when young, but they became inactive as they became involved with jobs and families in early maturity. Some of the animal longevity experiments indicate that animals who have been inactive (simply kept in cages) from birth up to midlife do not benefit from beginning to exercise then, and may even have their lives shortened.[8, 9] But again, it would be unusual for a person to be completely inactive when young. In the more usual case, in which a person has simply not exercised significantly for some years, we just don't know what's best for overall longevity. No one has performed specific experiments to determine the effects on longevity when exercise is reinstituted after such a gap. The epidemiologic studies suggest that there is a gain, although a small one, from taking up a physical activity in midlife for people in general.[10, 11] Some sort of exercise program would then be beneficial just for the other positive effects mentioned earlier. What type of program (type of exercise, intensity, etc.) may be optimal in this case is debatable. It's not obvious that a high-intensity program would result in the best long-term benefits, although the human body is capable of responding to intense exercise and increasing its fitness level considerably, even well into middle age. But a very intense program would probably not appeal to most people anyway. My own best judgment for such cases is that a program consisting of something like two to five hours per week of moderate exercise would provide significant gains in cardiovascular fitness, muscle and bone strength, and other measures of fitness with a minimum of risk.

The other pitfall that some people seem to drift into is relying primarily on exercise for overall health. Exercise, no matter what kind or how intense, cannot negate the effects of poor diet or the other health and longevity factors we have discussed.

I will review my own program, as I promised in the Preface, not because there is anything special about it, but it can serve as an example of how the various elements of a healthy lifestyle can be put into practice. My diet is largely vegetarian. I rather like whole grains, so I will have one of the hot or cold cereals for breakfast and sometimes for other meals; this is sometimes varied with added fruit such as raisins or chopped apples or dates. These cereals include oatmeal and oat bran; I like the taste of these even plain, but if you find them too bland, a number of spices like cinnamon, nutmeg, allspice, cloves, or ginger can easily be added. I have weeded out the high-fat and otherwise objectionable cereals in compiling the list in Appendix 2; if you are considering one not included there (new products and revised formulations are common), check out its ingredients and nutrient breakdown on the required package labeling. Some of the worst breakfast cereals are the granola types and those labeled "natural." Heartland Natural Cereal, for example, contains 15 percent fat, with 32 percent of its calories from fat; 100 percent Natural Cereal is 22 percent fat, with a whopping 42 percent calories from fat.

Lunch is usually a sandwich of bread and fruit preserves, bread and salad, or muffins that I make with the low-fat, no-cholesterol recipes in Chapter 10; in addition, a piece or two of fruit and/or a nonfat snack. For dinner, one of the vegetables or vegetable and bean recipes from Chapter 10 might be prepared, served with Italian bread. Sometimes spaghetti or other pasta is made with vegetables (primavera). Sometimes I'll have a light dinner of hot cereal, cereal and fruit, or toast. Occasionally it is a nonfat or low-fat soup or canned soup. There are a few acceptable canned soups, though one has to search for them; most have too much unnecessary fat.

I do include some acceptable nonfat or low-fat snacks such as pretzels, non-fat cakes, gumdrops, and so on. (I might even splurge on a donut or crumb bun once a week or so.) Beverages are quite commonplace: coffee in the morning, diet cola at lunch, and tea at dinner. Alcohol intake — beer, wine, and some cordials — averages a drink a day at most.

Walking constitutes most of my exercise; I average about three hours a week at a moderate pace. In addition I do a few of the weight lifts (curls and press) that I discussed, and some stretching or calisthenics. I've found that the racquet games can provide a very good workout and are quite enjoyable, but eventually any exercise that involves scheduling with other people runs into problems. If you can overcome this problem, fine; but you can always walk at some time of almost any day.

I take supplements at the levels that I recommended in Chapter 5. These include a multivitamin three days a week (the equivalent of something like Theragran brand multivitamin tablets) and a multivitamin/mineral combination (the equivalent of Centrum) four days a week. These have the following composition (The RDA or "safe and adequate" of each for adult males and females is listed as a reference):

Supplement	multivit./mineral	multivitamin	RDA(male/female)
vitamin A	5,000IU	5,000IU	5,000/4,000IU
thiamin (B1)	1.5mg	3mg	1.5/1.1mg
riboflavin (B2)	1.7mg	3.4mg	1.7/1.3mg
niacin	20mg	20mg	19/15mg
vitamin B6	2mg	3mg	2.0/1.6mg
vitamin B12	6µg	9µg	2.0µg
folacin	0.4mg	0.4mg	200/180µg
pantothenic acid	10mg	10mg	4 to 7mg
vitamin C	60mg	90mg	60mg
vitamin D	400IU	400IU	400IU
vitamin E	30IU	30IU	30/24IU
biotin	30µg	30µg	30 to 100µg
magnesium	100mg		350/280mg
calcium	162mg		800 to 1200mg
phosphorus	125mg		800 to 1200mg
iodine	150µg		150µg
iron	18mg		10/15mg
copper	2mg		1.5 to 3mg
zinc	15mg		15/12mg
manganese	2.5mg		2 to 5mg
potassium	40mg		

Supplement	multivit./mineral	multivitamin	RDA(male/female)
chromium	25µg		50 to 200µg
molybdenum	25µg		75 to 250µg
selenium	25µg		70/55µg
vitamin K	25µg		75/65µg
nickel	5µg		
silicon	2mg		
vanadium	10µg		
boron	150µg		

Most individual supplements are taken at another time of day and a few not every day; I've listed the doses of those taken separately and the averaged daily dose when the contribution of the multivitamin and multivitamin/mineral are factored in, as well as any nondaily dosing.

Supplement	individual dose	averaged daily dose
vitamin E	400IU	430IU
vitamin C	500mg	575mg
beta-carotene	15mg	19mg
selenium (as selenite)	250µg	265µg
magnesium	250mg	300mg
potassium	99mg	125mg
bioflavonoids	450mg	450mg
BHT (3 days/week)	250mg	100mg
pantothenic acid (4d/w)	100mg	67mg
chromium picolinate (3d/w)	200µg	100µg

The vitamin C, E, pantothenic acid, and chromium are taken in the morning; magnesium, selenium, and BHT during the day; and the multivitamin or multivitamin/mineral, bioflavonoids, and beta-carotene with dinner. In addition I average at least one 325mg aspirin a day.

I do not think there is any significant risk in supplements at these levels, and the potential benefits are substantial. This may seem like a lot of supplements, but the overwhelming majority are in the multivitamin or multivitamin/mineral at levels around the RDA, which is about what you would get in a good diet. It's true that we don't know for certain the effects of a lifetime of this combination of supplements, but the epidemiologic and laboratory evidence that we do have suggests that the benefits from moderate levels of combinations of nutrients are usually additive.[12–14] (I do not mean that the benefits add in an exact mathematical sense; in some cases the benefit of a combination may be less than the sum of individual ones, while in other cases combination of nutrients produces a benefit greater than the sum of the individual benefits.) I have recommended significantly greater than average doses only in cases where the supplement has been shown to have substantial benefits at these levels, and for which the risk of a negative interaction is minimal. These have been my best judgments; I cannot prove that these are the optimal intakes, but again, we have to make some judgments based on the evidence we now have. I indicated in Chapter 5 that there are a few cases where you might want to be careful of possible interactions among supplements, and I will repeat them here. Ascorbic acid (vitamin C), in addition to its many essential roles in the body's metabolism, is normally an antioxidant. However, in the presence of metals like iron and copper it can become pro-oxidant, generating destructive free radicals like the hydroxyl radical.[15] This has in fact been known to occur when ascorbic acid was given to patients suffering from iron overload. There is normally such a low concentration of such metals in the body that ascorbic acid almost always functions as an antioxidant. But it is one more reason for avoiding too high an iron intake and for not taking a substantial vitamin C and iron (or copper or similar metal) supplement at the same time. It's true that vitamin C and iron are both present in the multivitamin/mineral, but both at fairly low levels, so I don't think there is any significant danger. I've had a tendency to be slightly anemic since childhood, and I eat no meat, but I've found that I can maintain an adequate iron supply (as measured on blood tests) with this average daily supplement of 10mg (18mg four days a week). There is also some evidence that high levels of vitamin C might counter the anticancer effects of selenium. One study that reported this also found that vitamin E *added* to the anticarcinogenic effect when administered with selenium.[16] In my judgment there is more risk than potential benefit in vitamin C supplements of greater than 1,000mg a day, at least on a continuous, long-term basis. The evidence is probably best for selenium, vitamin E, vitamin C, and vitamin A, but there is good reason for thinking that insuring at least minimum levels of a number of vitamins and minerals, as with the multivitamin and multimineral supplements, will have a significant positive effect. In the other cases, my feeling is that the potential benefits at the levels recommended at least outweigh any risk. I think that selenium is underappreciated; a substantial body of evidence has accumulated on its anticancer and other beneficial effects. Note that I recommend the inorganic form, sodium selenite. This has been the most studied selenium compound and is used more efficiently by the body than the organic forms. Not all suppliers carry selenium as sodium selenite. Twinlabs makes it in the dose I recommend, and Puritan's Pride, which sells by mail order, has also begun offering it.

To what extent you alter the aspects of your lifestyle based on the considerations we discussed in Chapter 7 is largely an individual decision; you have to weigh how important each of them is to you against their potential health effects. You can in almost every case at least reduce the associated dangers by following the tips described there. Some are so simple that it's hard to see why anyone would not follow them; an ultraviolet-block coating on my eyeglasses cost me $20, for example, and is no more trouble than ordinary glasses. Again, it is not absolutely necessary to adopt all the recommendations regarding diet, supplements, exercise, and so on discussed in this book in order to obtain some benefits in health and longevity. Diet is probably most important, but you will benefit to some degree depending on the extent to which you follow the recommendations.

References to Chapter Nine

1. C.L. Goodrick et al.: Differential effects of intermittent feeding and voluntary wheel exercise on body weight and lifespan in adult rats. *J Gerontol* 38:36–45, 1983.

2. S.B. Harris, R. Weindruch, G.S. Smith, M.R. Mickey, R.L. Walford: Dietary restriction alone and in combination with oral ethoxyquin/2-mercaptoethylamine in mice. *J Gerontol* 45:B141–147, 1990.

3. R. Weidruch, R.L. Walford: Dietary restriction in mice beginning at 1 year of age. *Science* 215:1415–1418, 1982.

4. A.B. Miller: Cancer and obesity. In: *Obesity and Weight Control.* R.T. Frankle, M. Yang, eds. Aspen Publishers, Rockville, MD, 1988.

5. G.A. Barkan et al.: Body weight and coronary disease risk: patterns of risk factor change associated with long-term weight change. *Am J Epidemiol* 124:410–419, 1986.

6. M.R.C. Greenwood, V.A. Pittman-Waller: Weight control: a complex, various, and controversial problem. In: *Obesity and Weight Control.* R.T. Frankle, M. Yang, eds. Aspen Publishers, Rockville, MD, 1988.

7. M.L. Bunker, M. McWilliams: Caffeine content of common beverages. *J Am Diet Assoc* 74:28–32, 1979.

8. D. Edington, A. Cosmas, W. McCafferty: Exercise and longevity: evidence for a threshold age. *J Gerontol* 27:341–343, 1972.

9. C.L. Goodrick et al.: Differential effects of intermittent feeding and voluntary wheel exercise on body weight and lifespan in adult rats. *J Gerontol* 38:36–45, 1983.

10. R.S. Paffenbarger, Jr. et al.: The association of changes in physical-activity level and other lifestyle characteristics with mortality among men. *N Engl J Med* 328:538–545, 1993.

11. S.N. Blair et al.: Physical fitness and all-cause mortality: a prospective study of healthy men and women. *JAMA* 262:2395–2401, 1989.

12. P. Palozza, N.I. Krinsky: Beta-carotene and alpha-tocopherol are synergistic antioxidants. *Arch Biochem Biophys* 297:184–187, 1992.

13. W.J. Blot et al.: Nutrition intervention trials in Linxian, China: supplementation with specific vitamin/mineral combinations, cancer incidence, and disease-specific mortality in the general population. *JNCI* 85:1483–1492, 1992.

14. B. Leibovitz, M. Hu, A.L. Tappel: Dietary supplements of vitamin E, beta-carotene, coenzyme Q10 and selenium protect tissues against lipid peroxidation in rat tissue slices. *J Nutr* 120:97–104, 1990.

15. B. Halliwell: Free radicals and antioxidants: a personal view. *Nutr Rev* 52:253–265, 1994.

16. C. Ip: Susceptibility of mammary carcinogenesis in response to dietary selenium levels: modification by fat and vitamin intake. In: *Selenium in Biology and Medicine*, G.F. Combs et al., eds. Van Nostrand, New York, 1987.

TEN. Recipes and Tips

In this chapter I will discuss some of the practical considerations you will encounter and some tips I have found that make it easier to stick to a healthy lifestyle. To a large extent, however, these are things that must be determined according to individual preferences. Changing your diet is probably the most difficult adjustment for most people. Don't approach this as restricting what you can eat, but as finding the healthy dishes that really appeal to you. There are several dozen common vegetables and fruits, and a fair number of common grains and legumes listed in Appendix 2. There are scores of ways of preparing each one, not to mention the many combinations. I will list a few of my favorite recipes here, as well as some other typical low-fat acceptable ones. Many more are available in low-fat and vegetarian cookbooks and the Internet resources that I have listed in the Further Resources section.

Eliminating the major sources of dietary fat immediately poses the problem of what to use in place of butter or margarine on bread and other baked goods and what to use in recipes that require oil or shortening. Healthy alternatives for bread are fruit butter (like apple butter) or fruit preserves. The same can also be used on toasted bread, English muffins, and bagels. Olive oil is also good on toasted items; this doesn't save you any calories over butter, but at least you are getting the most acceptable fat. Preserves, while containing a lot of sugar, are mostly fruit and have little or no fat. They are preferred over jams, which contain more sugar, and jellies, which are mostly sugar. Fruit butters have the fewest calories of all. Apple butter is readily available in supermarkets and prune butter is fairly common; some more unusual types can be found in specialty stores. Marmalade is another good alternative; again, while orange is the most common, a number of other flavors can be found with a little searching. I have found that olive oil works fine in recipes for most baked goods. So does canola oil, based on my own limited experience with it plus others' recipes; I normally use olive oil. You can omit eggs entirely from many if not most recipes; it's frequently just from tradition that they have been included. Both eggs and fat can be omitted from pancake and waffle batters, for example, with little or no detectable difference in taste. Or, one of the following substitutes can be used for one egg: one-half small mashed banana; one-quarter cup applesauce; one tablespoon of flaxseed pureed in a blender with one-quarter cup water; two tablespoons of cornstarch. An egg replacement consisting of a mixture of potato starch, flour, and leavening is available at some health food stores. Which works best depends on the type of recipe; I've found that a small amount of applesauce is most convenient to use, but again, I rarely find it necessary. The finished product without eggs may or may not taste exactly the same, but it is in any case quite good even when different. A few baked items do depend on eggs or egg whites (angel food cake, for example) for their basic structure. The amount of oil in many recipes can be reduced with little or no reduction in flavor, but there is frequently a loss in texture if it is omitted entirely. In terms of taste and texture, olive oil is fine for baking muffins, many cakes, and dinner rolls; it is probably *better* than anything else in cooking vegetables. You can even make a good pie crust with it, but you still need a fair amount to get a flaky texture. It can be used in the recipes for some cookies, although some kinds do not stick together properly with olive oil as the sole shortening. For some bakery items, applesauce can be substituted for the shortening.

In selecting low-fat or nonfat foods, you can be guided by the tables in Appendix 2 or other tables of the composition of foods, or the required labeling on packaged foods.* Much can be learned about a product by simply reading the ingredients list on the label. This is required on essentially all packaged foods and lists the ingredients in their order of abundance. Thus the ingredients list on strawberry preserves might typically be: strawberries, sugar, pectin, and citric acid, meaning that strawberries are the major ingredient, sugar is the second most abundant, pectin is third, and citric acid the least. This can get confusing if there are many ingredients with strange-sounding names. Even in this example you would have to know that pectin is a fiber found in many fruits and commonly used in fruit preserves, and citric acid is the common acid from citrus fruits. But it's a good starting point; if the first listed ingredient is not what you think it should be, or if you see that some kind of fat has been added where it shouldn't be, it can alert you that something is wrong.†   Pasta, for example, should be composed essentially of flour, or a combination of flours (like semolina); if eggs or some kind of fat are listed in the ingredients, avoid it.

The same is true with breakfast cereals; the amount of fat added to some

---

*According to the provisions of the new FDA regulations that went into effect in 1994, food container labels must specify serving size and number of servings per container as well as calories, calories from fat, total fat, saturated fat, cholesterol, sodium, total carbohydrates, dietary fiber, sugars, protein, vitamins A and C, calcium, and iron per serving. If a serving of this food contains essentially none of one or more of these nutrients, the label can simply state that fact (e.g., "not a significant source of protein, vitamin A..."). This information applies to the product before any consumer preparation such as cooking. There are several classes of foods that are exempt from these labeling requirements, including food items like tea and coffee, which do not contain significant amounts of any of the listed ingredients. The new regulations did not really address the problem of serving size. There are no standard serving sizes for classes of food, so, to give an example that I actually found, one breakfast cereal may list a serving size of 30 grams while another may list one of 59 grams. To make a claim of "reduced," "less," or "fewer" with regard to calories, sugar, fat, and so on, the labeled food must have at least 25 percent less of whatever the claim is made for, compared to the reference food. A food can be labeled "fat-free" if a serving contains less than 0.5 grams of fat, "saturated fat-free" if it contains less than 0.5g of saturated fat, "sugar-free" if it contains less than 0.5g of sugar, "sodium-free" if it contains less than 5mg of sodium, and "calorie-free" if the serving contains less than 5 calories.

†Some people have voiced concern over the inclusion of monoglycerides and diglycerides in various products, and whether these should be counted as fat. Theoretically, yes, they are components of the fat molecule (triglyceride) and are included in the total fat determination; in practice, no, they are added in such trivial quantities that they are not worth worrying about.

breakfast cereals may or may not be large, but it has no business being there at all. There are many good cereals; pick another brand. Shredded Wheat & Bran is just whole wheat and wheat bran with no added sugar or salt; Fiber One is almost all bran (sweetened with aspartame) with a very high fiber content.

There are several good hot cereals: Oatmeal, oat bran, Wheatena, and Ralston are fine; farina is OK (it lacks the fiber of the others). Some commercial varieties of oat bran (like Quaker and some of the store brands) cook into a creamy, pleasant-tasting cereal; others are so coarse as to be almost inedible. Frequently the instant cereals have replaced much of the grain with sugar (which makes them too sweet for my taste anyway), but a few, which I have listed in Appendix 2, are acceptable. They are occasionally a convenience, but can't compare in taste with the regular hot cereals, which only take a minute to prepare. One objection that I do have for many hot cereals is the lack of sealable packaging. It is quite important, especially for the whole grains, to protect them from oxidation. Ideally, they should have a small amount of antioxidant included as well as a reclosable package. If they do not, after opening them I simply transfer the contents to a container that can be closed completely, such as an oatmeal canister.

While we are on the subject of storage, let me add that while all foods should be stored properly, it is more important for some than others. All foods should at least be kept in closed containers to prevent contamination by insects, airborne bacteria or fungi spores; this applies even to dry products, which are not likely to spoil this way. Whole grains and whole grain products are more subject to degradation by oxidation than those based on white flour. This is because whole grains contain a small amount of oil, whereas white flour has practically none. The oil is primarily in the "germ," as in wheat germ oil, but there is also some in the outer coating of most grains. The germ actually contains the plant embryo that would grow into a new wheat plant; it is removed, along with the outer covering, or bran, when whole wheat is milled into white flour. Such foods, or products that contain them, should be stored in a container that can be more or less tightly closed, depending on how long it takes you to use up the product after opening its package. For hot breakfast cereals, as I've said, the cylindrical oatmeal containers are fine unless it takes you more than a few months. Cold breakfast cereals usually have an inner plastic bag that can be rolled shut. If you do keep foods for extended periods after opening (not a good idea to begin with), you might consider putting them into glass jars with screw-top lids. Small amounts of antioxidants like BHT are added to a few packaged cereals, or sometimes to their packaging (as with Shredded Wheat & Bran); some people add a small amount themselves, but it is not as effective as when incorporated by the manufacturer and can impart an odd taste if overdone. Soybean oil and corn oil frequently do have BHT or some other antioxidant included because these polyunsaturated oils are quite prone to oxidation. Antioxidants are usually not added to olive oil, presumably because it is less vulnerable. Olive, canola, or any other oil can still be degraded by oxidation, so I think it's wise to add some after opening the container; it must, of course, be an oil-soluble antioxidant like BHT or BHA. BHT can be added at the rate of 170mg per quart (or liter) of oil, which is equal to about one 250mg capsule per 1.5 quarts. The exact concentration is not critical. Oils especially should be kept in tightly closed containers.

The storage of bread varies slightly depending on the type. Breads produced by the major bakeries and sold in supermarkets packaged in plastic bags should and usually do contain preservatives. (Calcium propionate is a widely used mold inhibitor.) Avoid those that do not; such products may be sold and consumed a week or more after they are baked, and the molds that can grow on unprotected bread are potentially harmful. If you are going to use it within a week, it may be stored at room temperature. Bread can be kept frozen for longer periods if tightly wrapped. This can be the original plastic bag, but half the loaf, or whatever portion you want to save, can be placed in a separate plastic bag or wrapping. The plastic zip-closure bags sold as "freezer bags" leave too much air space around most foods, which allows them to dry out or develop "freezer burn." Foods are especially prone to this in frost-free freezers. I double bag everything that I freeze using ordinary plastic food bags of a decent thickness closed with twist ties and eliminating as much space as possible between the food and the bag. Bread should not be stored in the refrigerator; oddly enough, the process of becoming stale proceeds faster at lower temperatures (above freezing) than at room temperature.[1] This is because staling is not just a drying out, but involves physical-chemical changes in the structure of the bread. Stale bread is not *necessarily* spoiled or any worse nutritionally; it's just unpalatable. Fresh bread from a bakery does not have preservatives because it is intended to be eaten fresh, when it is at its best. That's fine, but it can also be frozen with good results if you follow the procedures just discussed. These are not just nutritional considerations but will help maintain a good taste and texture. (Of course, you generally can't beat a fresh-baked bread for taste, texture, *or* nutrition.) You can use whatever particular kind of bread you prefer as a staple, but you can also give yourself some variety with the many kinds of good breads available—whole wheat, Italian, multigrain, and sourdough, to name a few. These considerations apply to similar products like English muffins, rolls, and bagels. English muffins, which are generally only available packaged, contain a small but usually insignificant amount of oil. Packaged frozen bagels cannot usually compare in taste and texture with fresh ones, which are also available in a variety of flavors (oatmeal, rye, garlic, etc.) and freeze quite well.

Olive oil has, of course, always been used in salad dressings. That's OK, but if you want to save on calories, some of the newer nonfat dressings are good. These usually use gums (a form of fiber) as thickening agents. You have to read the ingredients label even for dressings calling themselves low fat or nonfat; some do have added oil. If you see this anywhere on the ingredients list, choose another brand.

Almost all fast food is terrible. It ranges from high to very high in fat and, because of the way the food is prepared, the fat is likely to be oxidized to a significant extent, giving you the worst of both worlds. Hot dogs, hamburgers, and french fries are among the worst. But even foods like fish or chicken breast, which start out with a low fat content, are loaded with so much fat during preparation at fast food vendors that they are not much different from hamburgers and hot dogs. The one acceptable fast food is pizza — at least some pizzas. The fat content of pizza is about 5 percent to 7.5 percent on average for plain cheese pizza according to the USDA database; this amounts to 20.6 percent to 28 percent of calories from fat, and it is otherwise good nutritionally. But this can vary depending on how the pizza is made — on whether part skim or full-fat cheese is used, if fat is added to the dough, and how much oil is added. I suspect the fat content of most pizzas is now somewhat above this figure. Pizza Hut plain cheese pizzas average around 9 percent fat, according to other sources;[2] frozen pizzas range from 6 percent to about 13.5 percent fat, with an average around 9 percent. It's impossible to say what the product from your local family pizzeria will be. But it's almost certain to be much better than other fast foods like hot dogs (15 percent fat with over 54 percent calories from fat), hamburgers (13.1 percent fat and 38.7 percent calories from fat) and french fries (16 percent fat with 46.6 percent calories from fat). You spoil it, of course, if you add a high-fat topping like sausage or pepperoni. On the other hand, it can be made even more acceptable, in fact downright healthy, by adding such vegetable toppings like peppers, mushrooms, broccoli, and onions. Pizza dough itself is *usually* fine, consisting of flour, water, yeast, and salt, but this can vary; occasionally some type of fat or oil is added (which is totally unnecessary for taste or texture, by the way). This is another case of checking the ingredients first if you buy it separately; they are listed now even on such items in a supermarket's deli section. If you want to go even farther, you can make your own pizza with very low fat content by using nonfat mozzarella cheese (which works quite well) or no cheese with vegetable toppings. As I mentioned in the last chapter, it's not necessary to completely avoid treats, desserts, and fast food (what is sometimes called "junk food"); some such products are not that bad, and even the really high-fat ones can be enjoyed occasionally. But be aware of approximately how much fat a particular food contains so you don't overdo the really bad ones. Appendix 5 lists three categories of this type of food in the order of increasing fat content.

For canned items, check that you are getting just the canned food specified on the label without objectionable additives. Canned vegetables frequently have added salt; that's OK as long as you're not salt-sensitive. But avoid anything with fat or oil. Canned fruits frequently have a lot of sugar added. While not as bad as fat, it does add unnecessary calories. Unless you really prefer fruit this sweet, look for the cans that have only fruit juice or small amounts of added sugar. These are not necessarily the ones labeled "lite." The regulations governing the application of this term to relatively low-fat, low-calorie foods like fruits are rather complicated.*

A food can be labeled "light" or "lite" if 1) its fat content is 50 percent lower than ordinary or "reference" foods of the same type, if the reference food derives more than half its calories from fat, or 2) its calorie content has been reduced by at least one-third or its fat content reduced by at least one-half in the case where the reference food derives less than half of its calories from fat. A "lite" claim cannot be made if the reference food is both low fat and low calorie. Other rules govern the term when applied to sodium or other attributes like texture.

You have to be especially vigilant in reading the labels of processed and prepared foods. I include in this category frozen dinners, canned and dried soups, and other products that have undergone significant processing and are intended for consumption with minimal preparation. There are some acceptable ones if you look for them. Health Valley Fat-Free soups are good, and there are one or two varieties among other brands (Campbell's Vegetarian Vegetable Soup is one). In soups especially, you can avoid added fat and calories with little or no loss in taste appeal. Frozen dinners, even the ones I've seen labeled reduced calorie, "lite," or something similar, all have too much fat to be recommended.

A fairly large selection of nonfat and low-fat baked goods and desserts is now available as a number of producers have attempted to capitalize on this market. Quality is uneven tastewise; you just have to try a few to see which appeals to you. Many have a high sugar content, but this is far preferable to the regular products, which are high in both fat and sugar. Entenmann's has an especially good and varied line of nonfat cakes and snacks (apple coffee cake, carrot cake, oatmeal cookies, etc.); some are excellent.

Prices of vitamins and other supplements can vary by more than fourfold. There is no reason to believe that the highest-priced ones are any better than the lowest; surveys that have analyzed lots from different manufacturers and distributors have found some (usually small) differences among brands, but they were not related to price. These surveys also found that most products do have the potency stated on the label. There is also no reason to think that "natural" vitamins are any better than synthetic ones. In most cases they are chemically identical; in some cases the evidence actually favors the synthetic form of the supplement; in other cases vitamins advertised as "natural" are composed almost entirely of the synthetic form. The terms *sugar-free* and *starch-free* frequently encountered on bottle labels or advertisements are another annoying marketing gimmick. The inclusion of sugar or starch (which would be present in truly trivial amounts) in tablets is a good means of ensuring that they dissolve readily after ingestion. This had been a serious problem in the past, with many tablets passing through the entire digestive tract intact, but nearly all manufacturers seem to have worked it out in the past few years. (It is not a problem for soft-gels or the two-piece hard gel capsules, by the way; the covering of these dissolves rapidly in the stomach, releasing the contents to be absorbed.)

Check for an expiration date on any bottle of vitamins that you buy. Some manufacturers will also be following standards set for vitamins and minerals by the U.S. Pharmacopoeia (USP), intended to assure both potency and adequate tablet dissolution. This will entitle them to note as much on their labels. The USP is an independent organization that sets such standards for pharmaceutical products.

You can save a fair amount of money by buying vitamins and supplements from some of the mail order vitamin/health products dealers. A few that I've used and that have been reliable are Nutrition Headquarters, Puritan's Pride, and Arizona Health Foods; I cannot, of course, vouch for all of their products or future service. Some of the store brands (like Shop-Rite) are OK — they are sealed well and the bottle is dated, but only the most common vitamins and minerals are available.

As far as storing vitamins goes, the dry ones are really quite stable. Keep them away from excessive heat as a precaution, of course, but it's not necessary to store them in a refrigerator. Vitamin E and beta-carotene supplements are usually in liquid form (in a sealed capsule); these especially I keep in a cool place since vitamins are usually much less stable when in a liquid. Dry vitamin C, for example, will retain its potency for years under reasonable storage conditions, but starts to deteriorate within a few days when in solution. I suspect that vitamins are in more danger of deterioration after you start using them than sitting on a shelf beforehand. They are now exposed to fresh oxygen each time you open the bottle. This is not a problem if you use them within a reasonable time — the usual 100-count bottles would generally be used up within a few months. If you buy larger-sized bottles, you can simply transfer about a hundred to a smaller bottle for daily use, keeping the larger one tightly closed until you need to transfer more. Minerals are not as much of a problem in this regard; they are generally stable inorganic chemical compounds.

I've compiled below a selection of recipes to suit a variety of tastes. They are almost all low-fat to nonfat. I tend to favor the simple vegetable and bean dishes, which are simple enough to prepare even on weekdays. I also make a lot of muffins and similar baked goods, most of which freeze well and can be thawed to take for lunch.

—RECIPES—

Vegetables and Legumes

ESCAROLE AND BEANS

Escarole, about 1 lb.
2 cups beans; kidney beans (can-
   nellini), small white, or navy
   beans may be used
4 cloves garlic
2 tablespoons olive oil
⅛ teaspoon salt
Water sufficient to cover escarole

Canned beans can be used, or dried beans can be separately soaked in water and simmered for about an hour, or until tender. They will expand about fourfold in volume. Wash and trim escarole. Cut bunches about in half, into pieces about 3–4 in. long. Place into large cooking pot. Add salt, then water sufficient to cover the escarole. Bring to a boil, then turn down heat and simmer for about 10 min. Chop and add garlic along with oil and beans and simmer for 5 min. longer. Best served with a firm Italian bread to soak up juice.

SPINACH AND BEANS

About 1 lb. fresh spinach

Follow same recipe as for escarole.

ZUCCHINI AND BEANS

Zucchini, about 1 lb. or 4 medium-
   size squash, washed and cut
   across into circular sections

Follow same recipe as for escarole.

BROCCOLI AND BEANS

Broccoli, about 1 lb.
2 cups beans, kidney beans (can-
nellini), small white, or navy
beans
4 cloves garlic
2 tablespoons olive oil
⅛ teaspoon salt
Water sufficient to cover broccoli

Wash and trim broccoli and cut into
sections several inches on a side. Place
into large cooking pot. Add salt, and
water sufficient to cover broccoli. Bring
to a boil, then turn down heat and simmer for about 15 min. Chop garlic and
add along with oil and beans and simmer for 5 min. longer. The cooking time
can be varied to suit your individual
taste of how firm you like broccoli. Best
served with a firm Italian bread.

CALZONE WITH BROCCOLI
OR SPINACH

Pizza dough, about 1 lb.
Broccoli, 1 medium head (about ¾
lb.), chopped into 1- to 2-inch
pieces, or Spinach, about ¾ lb.
Small can mushrooms (about 8 oz.)
2 cloves garlic
Shredded nonfat mozzarella cheese,
about ⅔ cup
Salt, ⅛ teaspoon
Olive oil, 1 tablespoon

Roll and stretch out pizza dough on
floured board to about 1/4-inch thickness. Cut into strips about 4 inches by 8
inches. Mix other ingredients in a bowl
and place onto dough. Roll up dough,
narrow end to narrow end, thus layering
the ingredients inside. Pinch the ends
closed, patting a small amount of water
on opposite sides of the dough to make
it stick. Alternately, the dough can be

simply stretched out and cut into pieces
about 6 inches square onto which the
mix is placed. The dough is then folded
over the mix, trimmed, and pinched
closed like a tart. Place on cookie sheet
or aluminum foil sprayed with cooking
spray. Bake at 400 degrees for 25 minutes, or until dough turns a golden
brown. The amounts of garlic, salt, and
oil can be adjusted to your taste, and
others of your favorite vegetables can be
substituted.

LENTIL SOUP

Dry lentils, ¾ cup
One large sliced tomato, or ⅓ cup
(an 8-ounce can) of canned
tomatoes
2 carrots, sliced, or one 8-ounce can
1 medium onion, coarsely chopped
3 cloves garlic, chopped
1 teaspoon thyme
2 bay leaves
Approximately 4 cups water

Place lentils into pot and cover with
several times their volume of water.
Bring to a boil, then reduce heat and
simmer for an hour or until lentils
begin to soften. Add enough water to
cover ingredients by about 1 inch. If
you find that lentils produce too much
intestinal gas, this can be reduced by
pouring off the water they were cooked
in and replacing it with fresh water
before adding the other ingredients.
Simmer another 30 min. Remove bay
leaves and serve. Alternatively, lentils
can be soaked overnight to reduce their
initial cooking time.

BAKED TOMATO

4 large tomatoes, cored, each cut
into 3 thick slices

4 large leaves fresh basil
1 stem fresh Italian parsley
1 teaspoon fresh thyme leaves
1 teaspoon fresh oregano leaves
1 clove garlic
1 cup coarse bread crumbs made
  from 4 slices dried Italian bread
1 teaspoon olive oil
Salt
Freshly ground pepper

Place tomato slices in single layer on lightly sprayed or oiled pan. Finely chop all the leaf herbs and garlic. Combine bread crumbs, olive oil, and half of the herbs and garlic mixture in a bowl. Add salt and pepper to taste and toss to blend. Sprinkle tops of tomatoes with crumb mixture, distributing evenly. Bake at 375 degrees until crumbs are lightly browned, about 25 minutes. Sprinkle with remaining herbs and garlic and serve warm.

RIGATONI COMBINATION

⅓ pound rigatoni or other pasta
1 onion, chopped
1 clove garlic, minced
½ green pepper, chopped
1 teaspoon olive oil
1 small can tomato sauce
1-pound can kidney beans, drained
1 teaspoon soy sauce (optional)
¼ teaspoon salt (optional)
½ teaspoon chili powder
Black pepper to taste

Cook pasta to the firmness that you prefer. Sauté onions, garlic, and green pepper in oil 4–5 minutes. Stir in tomato sauce, kidney beans, soy sauce, salt, chili powder, and black pepper. Simmer several minutes. Drain pasta when done and stir into sauce. You can sauté in white wine instead of oil if you really want to save calories. Serves 4.

SPICY POTATOES, CABBAGE, AND PEAS OVER RICE

2 cups rice
4 cups water
5 medium potatoes, peeled and
  thinly sliced
2 cups water
½ green cabbage
10-oz. box of frozen peas (or equivalent fresh)
2 teaspoons curry powder
1 teaspoon turmeric
½ teaspoon ginger
½ teaspoon garlic powder
⅛ teaspoon cayenne pepper
Salt to taste (optional)

Cook rice in 4 cups water in a covered pot over medium-high heat until done. In a separate pan, add sliced potatoes to 2 cups of water and heat over medium-high heat. Shred cabbage and add to potatoes. Add peas and spices. Cover pan. Continue heating, stirring occasionally, until potatoes are tender. Serve over rice. Serves 6.

SWEET SAUTÉED RED CABBAGE

½ red cabbage, shredded
1 apple, chopped
Small onion, chopped
½ cup water
½ cup raisins
½ teaspoon cinnamon

Put all ingredients into a nonstick pan and place on stove burner, stirring occasionally, over medium-high heat for 10 minutes. Serves 4.

MUSHROOMS WITH WILD RICE

1 cup wild rice
2½ cups water

1 tablespoon soy sauce or mushroom
  soy sauce
¼ cup minced scallions
1 medium yellow onion, chopped
2 stalks celery, chopped
½ cup water
½-lb. white button mushrooms,
  sliced
8 fresh shiitake mushrooms (discard
  the stems)
⅔ cup chopped oyster or morel
  mushrooms
¼ cup trimmed enoki mushrooms
Snow peas, to taste (optional)
½ red bell pepper, diced
2 tablespoons soy sauce
½ teaspoon dried sage
¼ teaspoon salt
Freshly ground black pepper to taste

Place rice, water, soy sauce, and scallions
in a saucepan with a tight-fitting lid.
Bring to a boil, reduce heat, cover and
cook over medium heat until liquid has
evaporated and rice is tender, about 1
hour. Set aside. Place onion, celery and
water in a large pan. Cook and stir for
several minutes, until vegetables soften
slightly. Add button, shiitake, and oyster mushrooms. Cook, stirring occasionally, for 10 minutes. Gently stir in cooked
rice, enoki mushrooms, snow peas, red
pepper, and seasonings. Cook over low
heat for another 10 minutes. Serves 4.

BEAN BURGER

2 cups dry kidney beans
1 teaspoon curry
4 tablespoons cornstarch
4 tablespoons cornmeal
1 onion, minced
4 cloves garlic, minced
1 teaspoon black pepper
2 carrots, grated

Cook the beans (or use canned beans),
then mash. Add the spices. Form into

thin patties and fry in a nonstick pan.
Add condiments to taste and serve on
bun of your choice.

CREAMY CUCUMBER
DRESSING

1 cup plain nonfat yogurt
½ medium cucumber, chopped fine
1 teaspoon fresh-squeezed lemon
  juice
1 clove garlic, minced very fine
½ teaspoon salt
½ teaspoon ground white pepper

Blend ingredients together in a jar and
store in the refrigerator. Use generously
with falafel as well as with fresh green
salads. Makes about 2 cups.

ROASTED RED BELL
PEPPER

Place 4 or 5 red bell peppers, whole, into
a shallow baking pan or cookie sheet.
Place into broiler and broil for about
15 minutes until skin is very browned
or blackened. Remove from oven, and
place into brown paper bag for about 10
min. Remove from bag and peel off
skin. You can use other techniques than
placing into a bag to remove the skin,
such as doing it under running water.
Slice peppers into sections; clean out
seeds. Place into a glass jar with a little
salt and 4 or 5 whole peeled cloves of
garlic. Store in refrigerator and remove
pepper as needed; usually served on a
firm Italian bread, or you can make a
sandwich of them.

ROASTED EGGPLANT AND
RED PEPPER SANDWICH

Bread of your choice, toasted or not
1 clove garlic (optional)

1 unpeeled eggplant, cut into circular slices about ½-inch thick
Slices of roasted red bell pepper, to taste
Onion, to taste
Basil, to taste
Sliced fat-free cheese of your choice (optional)
Sliced tomato

Place eggplant slices in a single layer on a baking sheet coated with vegetable cooking spray. Lightly coat the eggplant (and onion) with olive oil. Broil for 5 minutes; turn eggplant (and onion) over and broil an additional 5 minutes or until lightly browned. Arrange eggplant, pepper, onion, herbs, tomato, etc. on bread. A slice of your favorite nonfat cheese can be placed on top and heated slightly to partially melt it.

EGGPLANT PARMIGIANA

1 eggplant, about 1 pound, peeled and sliced
1 16-oz. can of tomato sauce
1 tablespoon oregano
1 teaspoon chopped basil
2 cloves garlic, minced
¼ cup fine bread crumbs or flour
Pinch of salt
2 teaspoons olive oil
About ½ cup nonfat mozzarella cheese, sliced

Spray a (coverable) casserole baking pan or bowl with baking spray. Peel and slice eggplant into circular sections, no more than ¼-inch thick. Place the eggplant sections into the baking pan to form one layer covering the bottom. Place a slice of mozzarella on each section of eggplant. Mix flour or bread crumbs, garlic, oregano, basil, and salt in shallow bowl, then mix in tomato sauce and olive oil. Pour some of this mixture over each eggplant section sufficient to cover it. Continue adding eggplant slices in layers in this manner; cheese can be added to each layer or alternate layers, according to taste, but should be on topmost layer. When you are finished stacking eggplant (about four layers, or not so many that the cover will not go on), pour remaining tomato sauce over tops. As an option, some sliced mushrooms and a few sliced olives can be added. Cover and bake at 400 degrees for 40 min.

STUFFED PEPPERS

4 green bell peppers
2 cups bread crumbs
1 small can mushrooms
2 cloves garlic, minced
1 teaspoon oregano
1 16-oz. can of tomato sauce
½ cup chopped celery (optional)
½ teaspoon salt

Cut off the tops and scoop out the insides of the peppers. Place the peppers into a sprayed or lightly oil-coated casserole baking dish. Mix the bread crumbs, mushrooms, garlic, oregano, salt, and celery, and fill each pepper with it. Pour tomato sauce over each pepper. Cover and bake at 400 degrees about 25 minutes. You can make bread crumbs by toasting and dicing Italian bread, or use a lowfat packaged variety. A variant of this recipe uses rice in place of bread crumbs; you can use whatever type (regular, brown, wild) that you prefer, cooked to near completion before stuffing the peppers.

ITALIAN PEPPERS AND ONIONS

4–5 Italian peppers (the long, light green peppers sometimes called frying peppers)

½ *medium white onion*
2 *cloves garlic, minced*
1 *tablespoon olive oil*
1 *15-oz. can tomato sauce*
1 *cup water*

Cut off stems, slice peppers lengthwise, and clean out seeds. Cut into pieces about 2 inches long. Cut onion into about 1-inch pieces. Place all ingredients into cooking pot. Simmer for about 10 to 20 minutes. Serve with firm Italian bread.

BAKED CAULIFLOWER

1 *large head of cauliflower*
1 *onion, diced*
2 *stalks celery, sliced into cross-sections*
2 *cups chopped tomatoes*
1 *tablespoon chopped parsley*
1 *clove garlic, minced*
½ *teaspoon paprika*
¼ *teaspoon pepper*

Wash cauliflower and break into individual sections. Mix onion, celery, tomatoes, parsley, and garlic. Add cauliflower and mix well. Sprinkle the paprika and pepper over mixture. Place into a casserole baking dish and cover. Bake at 350 degrees for 30 min.

MARINATED MUSHROOMS

½ *lb. fresh mushrooms*
1 *small red onion*
Romaine lettuce, small bunch

For dressing:
4 *tablespoons olive oil*
1 *tablespoon Dijon mustard*
2 *tablespoons white wine vinegar*
¼ *teaspoon black pepper*
¼ *teaspoon salt*

Mix dressing well in a bowl or place into a jar with a screw-top and shake well.

Clean and trim ends of mushrooms; place in a bowl with sliced onion and lettuce. Pour dressing over all and toss. Cover and marinate in refrigerator 2 hours.

CARROTS AND GREEN BEANS

4 *carrots, scraped and sliced*
½ *lb. green beans, cleaned and trimmed*
2 *tablespoons finely chopped onion*
½ *cup tomato juice or ½ cup tomato sauce plus 3 tablespoons water*
¼ *teaspoon dried rosemary*
½ *teaspoon chopped fresh parsley*

Place carrots and beans into a saucepan; add onion, tomato juice, rosemary, and parsley. Cover and cook over low heat until carrots are just tender. Serves 4.

Several Mideast dishes are quite good — low fat and tasty. Pita bread is now available in whole wheat or regular white and is usually very low in fat.

Hummus is traditionally made with tahin, or tahini paste, the main ingredients of this being ground sesame seeds and sesame oil. This adds a substantial fat content. These low-fat alternatives are quite similar.

HUMMUS-1

1 *can chickpeas (about 1 pound)*
2 *tablespoons lemon juice*
1 *large clove garlic*
⅛ *teaspoon of salt*
1 *teaspoon olive oil, optional*
Coriander to taste

Drain most of the water from the chickpeas. Place everything into a food processor and puree (you can also mash the chickpeas with a potato masher and mix by hand) until you get a paste with the consistency of a thick dip — it should not be fluid but just firm enough to hold its shape; you can add more water if necessary to achieve this. Usually served scooped into pita bread or as a dip.

HUMMUS-2

1 lb. chickpeas (canned or
rehydrated dry)
2 cloves garlic, chopped
¼ cup lemon juice
¼ cup chopped parsley
⅛ teaspoon salt

Cayenne pepper can be added to taste Place everything into a food processor and puree or mash by hand and mix until you get the consistency of a thick dip; you can add some water if necessary. Usually served scooped into pita bread or as a dip.

BABA GHANOUJ

1 pound eggplant
¼ cup hummus (see above)
2 cloves garlic, chopped
3 tablespoons lemon juice
¼ teaspoon ground cumin

Bake eggplant whole at 400 degrees for about 40 minutes. Let cool, peel, and cut into pieces small enough to fit into blender. Place all ingredients into blender and puree. Serve in pita bread.

FALAFEL

4 cups cooked chickpeas
(equivalent to about 2 cans
of 14–16oz. each)
4 medium cloves garlic, minced
2 teaspoons cumin
1 teaspoon turmeric

1 teaspoon salt
½ cup finely minced onion or
6 minced scallions
¼ cup (packed) minced parsley
¼ cup water
1 tablespoon lemon juice
Dash of cayenne
⅓ cup flour

Drain the chickpeas. Combine all ingredients (except flour) in a food processor or a medium-sized bowl and process or mash until batter is uniform. Add flour and stir/process until thoroughly combined. The batter can be stored in the refrigerator in a tightly covered container for days. Preheat oven to 400 degrees. Spray a baking pan, cookie sheet, or pie tin with nonstick spray. Form the batter with a spoon into a flattened ball. It should not be much bigger than your spoon. For a falafel in a small pita bread, make 2–3 falafel patties; for a larger one, 4–5 will do. Bake them for about 20–25 minutes, or until they are golden brown. Serve in pita bread with sliced bell peppers, onions, tomatoes.

TOMATO AND BASIL SANDWICH

Firm whole wheat or Italian bread. Per sandwich:

1 small tomato
1–2 basil leaves
1–2 slices red onion

Slice tomato and place on bread. Coarsely chop red onion; add shredded basil leaves and balsamic vinegar and/ or splash of olive oil. Oregano and/or crushed garlic can be added, to taste. You can also chop the tomato first and mix it in with the onion and basil before placing on bread.

CARROT SALAD SANDWICH

½ small banana, peeled
1 cup shredded carrots
2 teaspoons lemon juice
¼ teaspoon grated lemon zest
2 lettuce leaves
1 slice whole grain pumpernickel
*   bread*
2 thin, unpeeled apple slices

Mash the banana in a small bowl. Add the carrots, lemon juice and lemon zest, and stir to combine. Place the lettuce on the bread; top with the carrot salad and apple slices.

SCALLOPED POTATOES

1 cup corn, fresh or frozen
1 cup water
2 sticks celery, chopped
1 onion, chopped
2 small bell peppers
3 medium potatoes, peeled and
*   sliced ¼-inch thick*
1 large carrot, sliced ¼-inch thick
Minced parsley

Preheat oven to 350 degrees. Make a thin sauce of the corn and water in your blender. Then place vegetables, potatoes, and parsley in the pan in layers, alternating vegetables. The total depth of food in the pan should be about 1¾ inches (not more than 2 inches). Bring the corn sauce to a boil, stirring to prevent burning. Pour it evenly over the vegetables. Cover the pan and bake 1¼ hours. Remove cover. Broil to lightly brown top.

POTATO BURGERS

½ to 1 raw onion, grated
4 large potatoes, grated (peeling
*   is optional)*

½ cup of whole wheat flour
¼ cup of water

Mix all ingredients in a bowl. Using a nonstick pan on medium heat, or a griddle at 325 degrees, ladle the mixture on pan and mash down until flat, about burger thickness. Cook for 8–10 minutes. Turn over and cook 5–8 minutes. Hints: Use a food processor to grate the potato and onion. These freeze well. One potato is about one serving. The usual condiments like catsup or mustard can be added.

BAKED POTATO

Bake potato as usual. Slice thinly one onion for each baked potato. Mince 1–2 cloves of garlic per potato, to taste. Sauté garlic and onion for a few minutes in wine or balsamic vinegar. Jalapeños can be added if you like. Slice open hot baked potato and pour in.

PASTA

Pasta is nutritious in itself, and can be easily combined with various vegetables and vegetable sauces into appetizing and even healthier meals.

ANGEL HAIR PASTA AND STEWED TOMATOES

½ lb. angel hair pasta
8-oz. can stewed tomatoes
Juice from one small lemon
1 cup chopped broccoli
3 cloves garlic, chopped up fine
2 teaspoons fresh oregano
1 teaspoon basil
1 teaspoon thyme

Cook pasta. Cook broccoli by steam or boiling for about 10 minutes. Mix pasta, broccoli, and rest of ingredients.

PASTA PRIMAVERA

⅓ lb. pasta (fusilli is traditional, but any pasta can be used)
1 small onion
¼ lb. mushrooms or one 4-oz. can
4 cloves garlic
2 tablespoons olive oil
⅓ cup white wine or dry sherry
1 green pepper
⅛ to ¼ teaspoon salt, to taste
Black pepper, to taste

Put the pasta water on to boil. Put the oil into a pan. Chop the onion, garlic, pepper, and mushrooms and add to the pan with the wine. Sauté for about five minutes. Reduce the heat and simmer while the pasta cooks. Add salt and black pepper to taste. Drain the pasta, pour the sauce over it, and serve. Many other vegetables can be added or substituted in this recipe, according to your taste. Sun-dried tomatoes are very good; broccoli, green beans, zucchini, carrots, and fresh tomatoes are common variations. The frozen packages of mixed vegetables can be fairly good, if not quite up to the fresh.

Grains

OATBURGERS

4 cups water
½ cup soy sauce
½ cup nutritional yeast
1 large onion, diced
½ tablespoon garlic powder
½ tablespoon Italian seasoning

4½ cups rolled oats (old-fashioned or quick oatmeal)

Bring to a boil all ingredients except the oats. Turn heat to low and stir in 4½ cups rolled oats. Cook for about 5–10 minutes until the water is absorbed. Do not overcook. If still too thin, add more oats and cook for a few more minutes. Place into a rectangular non-stick baking pan 9 × 18 inches or larger, depending on how thick you prefer them; ½-inch is usual. Bake at 350 degrees for 25 minutes. Then use a utensil that won't scratch your pan to cut the giant burger into little burgers, and flip them over. Cook another 20 minutes. Can be eaten hot or cold. Makes around 12 burgers.

BISCUITS AND GRAVY

4 tablespoons flour
¾ cup water
2 cups skim milk or milk substitute
1 teaspoon sage
⅛ teaspoon cayenne pepper
½ teaspoon Tabasco sauce
¼ teaspoon salt
½ teaspoon fresh ground black pepper

Mix flour and water until smooth with no lumps. Put into medium saucepan and heat over medium-high heat until the mixture boils. Reduce heat, stirring constantly, and boil for 4–5 minutes. Mixture should be very thick. Add milk and stir until the mixture is smooth again. Add spices and return to boil, cooking until it has the consistency of thick gravy. Serve over baking powder biscuits, beans, rice, etc. Makes a good accompaniment to fruit (whole-berry cranberry sauce, etc.). Makes about 4 biscuits.

Baked Foods

In baking, it is usually advisable to spray the bakeware with a light coating of one of the cooking sprays to prevent sticking. This adds next to no calories.

DINNER ROLLS

2 cups flour
4 teaspoons baking powder
¼ teaspoon salt
4 tablespoons olive oil
¾ cup skim milk

Mix the flour, baking powder, and salt in a bowl. Add the milk and oil and mix until it is just absorbed. Mold into portions about 2 inches across by hand. Place on a sprayed baking sheet and bake at 400 degrees for 20 minutes.

PIES

The problem with pies is that the crust is almost always loaded with shortening, i.e., fat; even worse, it's usually hydrogenated oil or lard in commercial crusts. But the filling of fruit pies is usually OK, consisting of fruit, sugar, and a thickener like flour or cornstarch. You can make a pie crust without fat, but it won't have a texture anything like a regular crust. The pie crust recipe below is a reasonable compromise; you can reduce the fat and calories even further by using a strip upper crust (or none at all).

PIE CRUST

I have yet to find a good low-fat pie crust, but this recipe contains only a moderate amount of acceptable olive (or canola) oil and has the taste and texture that a crust should have. To make two 9-inch crusts:

2½ cups flour
1¼ tablespoons sugar
Pinch of salt
½ cup oil
8 tablespoons skim milk

Mix the flour and sugar. Add oil while mixing and continue mixing until it has a lumpy, pebblelike texture with some flour left. Add milk gradually and mix a little more. Place half on floured wax paper and press it into a ball with your hands. Place a little more flour on top and cover with another piece of wax paper. Press down to flatten and roll out with a rolling pin until it is about ⅛-inch thick. Remove top sheet of wax paper, invert into a sprayed pie pan, and peal off the wax paper. Do the same for top crust after adding pie filling. As with any pie crust or pastry, handle the dough just enough to get it into the shape you want; if you work it too much it will become tough.

STRAWBERRY-RHUBARB PIE

A tasty and nutritional pie that you don't see too much anymore.

1½ cups strawberries
1½ cups rhubarb
¼ cup sugar
3 tablespoons flour or cornstarch

Clean and trim the strawberries, or you can use frozen strawberries. Trim and chop the rhubarb stalks into ¾-inch sections; you can use frozen rhubarb, which usually comes already cut into sections, but thaw it completely first. Mix strawberries, rhubarb, sugar, and flour in a bowl, then pour into the bottom 9-inch crust described above. Add top crust as desired. Bake at 400 degrees for 40 to 45 minutes.

APPLE-RAISIN SQUARES

For crust:

1¾ cups flour
6 tablespoons water
2 tablespoons sugar
5 tablespoons applesauce
4 tablespoons olive oil

Mix and roll out half on floured board or wax paper to about ¼-inch thickness. Cut out about a 6 × 9-inch rectangle for the bottom crust and place in the bottom of a sprayed baking pan of the same size. You can also do this in sections using a spatula, if you like; simply press the sections together.

For filling:

1 cup sliced apples (canned are acceptable)
1 cup raisins
3 tablespoons brown sugar
4 tablespoons flour
1 tablespoon cinnamon
1 teaspoon vanilla
1 tablespoon water

Mix and place evenly over bottom crust. Cut out top crust of same size and place over filling, pressing down slightly to make it even. Bake at 400 degrees for 35 minutes. Sprinkle with powered sugar when done and cut into squares about 2 inches on a side.

CINNAMON-RAISIN ROLLS

2 cups flour (½ cup of oat bran can be substituted for ½ cup of flour)
⅛ teaspoon salt
2 tablespoons sugar
3 tablespoons applesauce

4 tablespoons olive oil
⅔ cup water
1 teaspoon vanilla
5 teaspoons baking powder

Combine ingredients in mixing bowl, then place on well-floured board. Sprinkle some flour over top and press down on it with hands to flatten out to about ¼-inch thickness. Sprinkle cinnamon generously over entire surface. Place about ½ cup white raisins evenly on dough. Place about ¾ cup brown sugar evenly over dough. Press down lightly with hands to press toppings into dough. Starting from end farthest from you, roll the dough toward you, thus layering the ingredients inside. When you have rolled it all the way to its opposite end, pinch dough closed, adding a little water to the end if necessary. Wet a sharp, broad-blade knife and slice the roll into circular sections about ¾-inch thick. Place these on a sprayed baking sheet. You can use the knife to do this as you cut the sections, or use a spatula; don't worry if some of the ingredients fall off. Bake at 400 degrees for 20 minutes. Especially great when eaten warm from the oven.

APPLE-CHERRY CRISP

6 or 7 apples, peeled, cored, and cut into chunks
1 cup sour cherries
1 cup sugar
¾ cup oatmeal
½ cup whole wheat flour
⅓ cup apple butter

Mix apples, cherries and ½ cup sugar and place into baking pan. Mix remaining ingredients and sprinkle on top. Bake 45–50 minutes at 350 degrees.

MUFFINS

Muffins are a favorite. Many different fruits, berries, and even vegetables can be included in them. Most are at their best when fresh-baked and warm, but they freeze well if tightly wrapped in aluminum foil. They are thus convenient to take for lunch, either left out to thaw the preceding night or thawed in a microwave. I've found that olive oil works fine in all of them, but you can substitute canola oil if you prefer. You *can* substitute applesauce for the oil in most muffins, but they tend to dry out and I don't think it's worth it. The egg-free, low-fat recipes given here have all been tested and are among my favorites, but feel free to improvise; muffin recipes are generally quite forgiving about the quantities added. The dry ingredients should always be mixed well first. Once the liquids are added, the batter should be mixed just enough to blend in all the ingredients; do not mix too long and do not use an electric mixer. Vigorous or extended mixing tends to cause the protein gluten in wheat flour to develop into the elastic texture that is desirable in making bread, but not muffins.

BLUEBERRY MUFFINS

2 cups flour
1½ tablespoons baking powder
¼ cup sugar
1½ cups blueberries
1 cup water
5 tablespoons olive or
*   canola oil*
2 teaspoons vanilla

Mix the flour, baking powder, and sugar in a bowl; mix in the blueberries; add the water, oil, and vanilla and mix just until all the liquid is absorbed. Spoon batter into sprayed muffin tin and bake at 400 degrees for 20 to 25 minutes. Makes 10 muffins.

OAT BRAN MUFFINS

1 cup flour
1 cup oat bran
2 tablespoons baking powder
1 teaspoon cinnamon
½ cup raisins
1 cup water
2 tablespoons applesauce
2 tablespoons olive or canola oil
1 teaspoon vanilla

Mix the flour, oat bran, baking powder, raisins, and cinnamon. Add and mix in the applesauce, water, oil, and vanilla. Do not over mix. Place batter into sprayed muffin tin and bake at 400 degrees for 20 to 25 minutes.

BRAN MUFFINS

1 cup flour
2 cups wheat bran
3 teaspoons baking powder
⅛ teaspoon baking soda
¼ teaspoon salt
2 tablespoons brown sugar
1 cup raisins
2 tablespoons corn syrup or
*   molasses*
2 tablespoons olive oil
2 tablespoons applesauce
1 cup water

Mix together the flour, bran, baking powder, soda, salt, sugar, and raisins. Add the applesauce, water, oil, and syrup and mix in. Place batter into muffin tin and bake at 400 degrees for 20–25 minutes. Makes about 9 muffins.

APPLESAUCE MUFFINS

1 cup whole wheat flour
1 cup oatmeal
3 teaspoons baking powder
1 teaspoon baking soda
1 teaspoon cinnamon
1 cup applesauce
3 tablespoons olive or canola oil
⅓ cup honey
½ cup water
½ cup raisins, optional

Mix together dry ingredients in bowl. Add water, oil and honey and mix. Place into sprayed muffin tin and bake at 400 degrees for 20–25 minutes.

PUMPKIN MUFFINS

These have a rather unique texture, somewhere between muffins and pumpkin pie.

2 cups flour
3 teaspoons baking powder
½ teaspoon salt
½ teaspoon cinnamon
½ teaspoon nutmeg
¼ teaspoon ginger
½ cup brown sugar
¾ cup canned pumpkin puree
½ cup raisins
¾ cup skim milk
4 tablespoons (¼ cup) olive or
  canola oil

Mix together dry ingredients in bowl. Add pumpkin, milk, and oil and mix in. Place into sprayed muffin tins and bake at 400 degrees for 20–25 minutes. Let cool on rack. Makes 8 muffins.

PINEAPPLE-DATE MUFFINS

1 8-oz. can crushed pineapple
1⅔ cups flour
3 teaspoons baking powder
½ cup sugar
⅔ cup water
3 tablespoons olive or canola oil
⅓ cup chopped dates

Mix together dry ingredients in bowl. Add pineapple, water, and oil and mix in. Place into sprayed muffin tin and bake at 400 degrees for 20–25 minutes.

FLAX SEED MUFFINS

1 cup flour
⅔ cup flax seeds
4 tablespoons brown sugar
1 teaspoon ginger
1 tablespoon oatmeal
1 tablespoon baking powder
5 tablespoons applesauce
2 tablespoons olive oil

Mix together dry ingredients in bowl. Add applesauce, water, and oil and mix. Place into sprayed muffin tin and bake at 400 degrees for 20–25 minutes.

CARROT MUFFINS

1½ cups flour
1½ cups shredded carrot
½ cup raisins
½ cup brown sugar
1½ teaspoons baking powder
1 teaspoon cinnamon
½ teaspoon nutmeg
1 teaspoon vanilla
¼ cup skim milk
3 tablespoons olive oil
3 tablespoons applesauce

Mix the flour, raisins, sugar, baking powder, cinnamon, and nutmeg in a bowl. Add the shredded carrot and mix in. Mix in the milk, oil, vanilla, and applesauce. Place into sprayed muffin tin and bake at 400 degrees for 20–25 minutes. Makes 6 muffins.

Snacks And Desserts

PUMPKIN COOKIES

2 cups flour
1 cup oatmeal
1 teaspoon baking soda
1 teaspoon cinnamon
½ teaspoon salt
1 cup brown sugar
1 cup canned pumpkin or puree
1 teaspoon vanilla
1 cup raisins
¾ cup oil
3 tablespoons applesauce

Mix the flour, oatmeal, baking soda, cinnamon, raisins, sugar, and salt. Add the applesauce, oil, and vanilla and mix in. For each cookie, place about 3 tablespoons onto a lightly sprayed cookie sheet. Bake at 350 degrees for 20 to 25 minutes.

OATMEAL-BRAN COOKIES

1 cup whole wheat flour
2 cups rolled oats
¼ cup oat bran
¼ cup wheat bran
¼ cup soy flour
1 tablespoon baking powder
1 teaspoon baking soda
2 teaspoons ground cinnamon
¾ cup honey
½ cup frozen apple juice concentrate, thawed
½ cup unsweetened pineapple juice
½ cup raisins
½ cup chopped dates
2 teaspoons vanilla extract

Mix the dry ingredients together, then mix in the liquid ingredients. Drop tablespoon-size portions onto nonstick or lightly sprayed baking sheet. Bake at 350 degrees for 15 to 20 minutes, or until golden brown.

POACHED PEARS

4 pears, preferably Bosc;
    Bartlett also good
2 teaspoons fresh lemon juice
1 cup cranapple juice

Halve, peel, and core the pears. Sprinkle freshly cut pears with lemon juice to prevent browning. Place in bowl or dish suitable for microwave and cover with cranapple juice. Cover and microwave on high 6–8 minutes, or until pears are fork-tender. (Check the pears after 6 minutes; the fresher the pears, the longer they'll take to cook. You can also cook in a conventional oven at around 375 degrees; check whether the pears are tender after about 15–20 minutes in this case.) Spoon juice in bowl over pears, cover, and refrigerate at least 30 minutes.

NO-BAKE FRUIT CRISP SQUARES

½ cup lightly packed brown sugar
¼ cup corn syrup
2 cups crisp rice cereal
¾ cup chopped mixed dried fruits
½ cup rolled oats

In small saucepan, heat brown sugar and syrup on low, stirring to dissolve sugar. In large bowl, combine remaining ingredients. Add syrup mixture. Mix well, until all ingredients are moistened. Press firmly into 8-inch square pan sprayed with cooking spray. Let cool but do not chill. Cut into squares.

Salads

ITALIAN POTATO SALAD

1 lb. new red potatoes
¼ cup water

1 small red onion, thinly sliced
Several sliced black olives
(optional)
1 small cucumber, chopped
1 tomato, chopped
½ cup fat-free Italian dressing
2 tablespoons fresh parsley

Scrub potatoes; cut crosswise into ¼-inch slices. Place in 1½ qt. microwave-safe casserole. Add water. Cover with lid. Microwave on high for 9–10 minutes or until potatoes are tender; stirring once. Drain and cool. You can bake them in oven if you prefer, instead of microwaving. Add onions, olives, cucumber, tomato, dressing, and parsley. Mix lightly to coat evenly. Refrigerate until chilled. Stir before serving.

POTATO SALAD

---

2 lbs. (about 6 large) potatoes,
peeled and quartered

2 stalks celery, chopped
1 small onion, finely chopped
4 green onions, sliced
¼-inch thick
1 large carrot, shredded
¼ cup sweet pickle relish
¼ cup chopped red onion
½ teaspoon mustard seeds
1 teaspoon dry parsley
Salt/pepper to taste
Balsamic vinegar or wine
vinegar to taste
Add nonfat mayonnaise or
yogurt to taste (optional)

Cook potatoes in boiling water for about 15 minutes or until just barely tender (check every minute or so after the first 10 minutes). Cut into smaller pieces. Let cool. Mix together all other ingredients in a large bowl. Add cooled potatoes. Mix well. Chill (stir once or twice while it is chilling).

References to Chapter Ten

1. H. McGee: *On Food and Cooking,* Macmillan, New York, 1984.
2. J.A.T. Pennington: *Bowes and Church's Food Values of Portions Commonly Used,* 16th ed. Lippincott, Philadelphia, 1994.

Appendix 1:
Fatty Acids

A molecule of fat, or triglyceride, can be thought of as a molecule of glycerol plus three fatty acids, which can be diagrammed as below. Glycerol is represented by the rectangle G. The fatty acids F1, F2, and F3 consist of chains of carbon atoms with hydrogen bound to them and may be saturated, unsaturated, or polyunsaturated, depending on whether they contain no, one, or more than one carbon-carbon double bond.

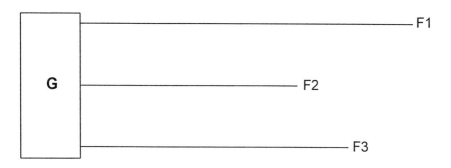

Tables of the nutritive values of food and scientific papers frequently list the fatty acid composition using the following standard nomenclature. This is to first list the length of the fatty acid as measured by the number of carbon atoms (sometimes prefixed by a C), followed by a colon and the number of unsaturated bonds; the position of the first unsaturated bond from the omega end of the fatty acid (the end not bound to glycerol) sometimes follows this. Thus EPA is C20:5omega3, meaning there are 20 carbon atoms and 5 unsaturated carbon-carbon bonds, the first being third from the omega end. The letter n is occasionally used instead of the Greek letter *omega*, so one sometimes sees C20:5n-3. A more complete description of the fatty acid can be given by including the positions of all the unsaturated bonds; C20:5n-3,n-6,n-9,n-12,n-15 for EPA.

The following figure diagrams the vicinity of the omega end of an omega-3 and an omega-6 fatty acid to illustrate the meaning of these terms; the fatty acid chains continue in the direction of the dots.

The fatty acids in most naturally occurring fats are the so-called *cis* form, which means that the fatty acid chain changes direction at the double bond, as in

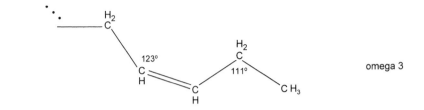

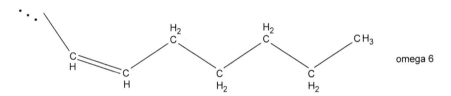

the above illustration. In hydrogenated fats, as are found in margarine, some of the fatty acids have been converted to the *trans* form, where the chain is stretched out (like a saturated fatty acid, which doesn't have any double bonds) instead of having a kink at the double bond.

The most common fatty acids and some dietary sources are listed below.

butyric	4:0	butter
caproic	6:0	butter, coconut oil
caprylic	8:0	butter, coconut oil
capric	10:0	butter, coconut oil
lauric	12:0	coconut oil, palm kernel oil
myristic	14:0	coconut oil, butter
palmitic	16:0	palm oil, beef, cocoa butter
stearic	18:0	cocoa butter, beef
oleic	18:1n–9	olive oil
linoleic (LA)	18:2n–6	soy, corn, many vegetable oils
alpha-linolenic (LNA)	18:3n–3	linseed oil
gamma-linolenic (GLA)	18:3n–6	evening primrose oil
arachidonic	20:4n–6	eggs
eicosapentaenoic (EPA)	20:5n–3	salmon, herring, other fish oils
docosahexaenoic (DHA)	22:6n–3	salmon, herring, other fish oils

In speaking about the effects of dietary fats on blood lipids, you really must be careful of how the comparison is made; that is, is the fat raising or lowering blood lipids compared to what? For example, if you replace dietary saturated fat with an equal amount of olive oil, total blood cholesterol will be significantly lowered. But if you replace dietary carbohydrate with an amount of olive oil that supplies an equal number of calories, blood cholesterol will fall only slightly.

Palmitic acid is usually the most abundant saturated fatty acid in human diets, followed by stearic, myristic, and lauric acids. Both palmitic and myristic acid strongly raise total cholesterol and LDL cholesterol. (All these comparisons are to an amount of carbohydrate equal in calories.) Lauric acid has a similar but somewhat smaller effect. Stearic acid, even though a saturated fatty acid, does not increase total cholesterol or LDL. Oleic acid, overwhelmingly the most prominent fatty acid in olive oil, slightly lowers total and LDL cholesterol. Linoleic acid has a similar, slightly greater, effect. All of these fatty acids increase HDL (Remember, this is when replacing carbohydrate). *Trans* fatty acids, even the *trans* form of oleic acid, raise total cholesterol and LDL, and generally *decrease* HDL. Fortunately, you are unlikely to consume a large amount of *trans* fatty acids unless you eat a lot of hydrogenated margarine. The brands of margarine listing a *liquid* vegetable oil as the first ingredient are the safest in this regard.

References to Appendix 1

1. M.T. Katan, and P.L. Zock, RP Mensink: Dietary oils, serum lipoproteins, and coronary heart disease. *Am J Clin Nutr* 61(Suppl):1368S–1373S, 1995.

Appendix 2:
Nutritive Values of
Recommended Foods

Data were adapted and calculated from the U.S. Department of Agriculture Nutrient Database, except where noted, rounded to the nearest tenth or whole number. This is not an exhaustive list, but covers most of the common foods and some not so common. The snack food category is included since it is generally understood that such foods should be consumed only in moderation, and it is instructive to see that, even in this category, a fair number of nonfat or low-fat items are available.

Grams of protein (PRO), fat (FAT), carbohydrate (CARB), water, and dietary fiber in 100 grams of an edible portion are listed. This value therefore also equals the percentage of each item in the food. This allows for a more direct comparison of foods than the current trend of listing amounts in a serving size, which varies widely. The number of calories (CAL) in 100 grams is also listed, as well as the percentage of calories from fat (FAT%CAL). A blank space indicates that data is not available.

In a few cases, the USDA database was out of date or did not list the item or a particular datum. This was primarily for packaged cereals; in such cases the values were calculated from the required package labeling or other producer data. This is not as precise as the USDA data, but is accurate enough for most purposes. Such items are marked with a star (*).

Unless indicated otherwise, data are for raw foods. I have included values for both raw (or dry) and cooked in a number of cases, especially when there was a significant difference between them. It is, of course, the dry foods such as oatmeal, dried beans, and spaghetti that change the most in this regard.

There are two other caveats. First, the percentage of calories from fat may be higher in some foods because they contain very few calories; in such cases this percentage is not a good measure of how acceptable the food is. Second, the carbohydrate content of foods includes nondigestible carbohydrates — that is, fiber. This may not be the best way to list content, but it's the way nutritive data have been compiled. As a result, the total grams of everything in the table in 100 grams of a food may add up to more than 100 grams, because carbohydrate fiber, which is most fiber, will be counted twice. For such items, the sum of the calories calculated from protein, fat, and carbohydrate may be quite different from the actual number of

144

calories, which is what is listed in the CAL column. This is usually only significant in foods with lots of fiber, like the brans.

The food groups generally follow the usual culinary classifications, which are also those of the USDA database; thus tomatoes, squash, peppers and such — botanically fruits — are classified with the vegetables.

Food : Vegetables	Pro	Fat	Carb	Cal	Water	Fiber	Fat %Cal
artichoke, raw	3.3	0.2	10.5	47	84.9	5.4	2.9
artichoke, boiled	3.5	0.2	11.1	50	84.0	5.4	3.6
asparagus, raw	2.3	0.2	4.5	23	92.4	2.1	7.8
asparagus, boiled	2.6	0.3	4.2	24	92.2	2.1	11.6
bean, lima, raw	6.8	0.9	20.2	113	70.2	4.9	6.8
bean, snap, green, raw	1.8	0.1	7.1	31	90.3	3.4	3.5
beets, raw	1.6	0.2	9.6	43	87.6	2.8	3.6
broccoli, boiled	3.0	0.4	5.2	28	90.7	3.0	11.3
broccoli, raw	3.0	0.4	5.1	28	90.7	2.9	11.3
brussels sprouts, raw	3.4	0.3	9.0	43	86.0	4.2	6.3
cabbage, raw	1.4	0.3	5.4	25	92.2	2.3	9.7
carrots, raw	1.0	0.2	10.1	43	87.8	3.0	4.0
cauliflower, raw	2.0	0.2	5.2	25	91.9	2.5	7.6
celery, raw	0.8	0.1	3.7	16	94.6	1.7	7.9
chard, swiss, raw	1.8	0.2	3.7	19	92.7	1.6	9.5
chicory greens, raw	1.7	0.3	4.7	23	92.0	4.0	11.7
chives, raw	3.3	0.7	4.4	30	90.7	2.5	21.9
collards, raw	1.6	0.2	7.1	31	90.6	3.7	6.4
corn, sweet, yellow, raw	3.2	1.2	19.0	86	76.0	2.7	12.3
cucumber, raw	0.7	0.1	2.8	13	96.0	0.8	9.0
dandelion greens, raw	2.7	0.7	9.2	45	85.6	3.5	14.0
eggplant, raw	1.0	0.2	6.1	26	92.0	2.5	6.2
endive (escarole), raw	1.3	0.2	3.4	17	93.8	3.1	10.6
jerusalem artichoke, raw	2.0	0.0	17.4	76	78.0	1.6	0.1
kale, raw	3.3	0.7	10.0	50	84.5	2.0	12.6
kohlrabi, raw	1.7	0.1	6.2	27	91.0	3.6	3.3
kohlrabi, boiled	1.8	0.1	6.7	29	90.3	1.1	3.4
lettuce, butterhead	1.3	0.2	2.3	13	95.6	1.0	15.2
lettuce, iceberg	1.0	0.2	2.1	13	95.9	1.4	13.2
lettuce, romaine	1.6	0.2	2.4	16	94.9	2.4	11.3
mushrooms, raw	1.0	0.2	6.1	26	92.0	2.5	6.2
mushrooms, canned, drained	1.9	0.3	5.0	24	91.1	2.4	10.9

Food : Vegetables	Pro	Fat	Carb	Cal	Water	Fiber	Fat %Cal
onions, raw	1.2	0.2	8.6	38	89.7	1.8	3.8
parsnip, raw	1.2	0.3	18.0	75	79.5	4.9	3.6
peas, edible pod, boiled	3.3	0.2	7.1	42	88.9	2.8	4.9
peppers, sweet, raw	0.9	0.2	6.4	27	92.2	1.8	6.3
potato, with skin, baked	2.3	0.1	25.2	109	71.2	2.4	0.8
pumpkin, raw	1.0	0.1	6.5	26	91.6	1.8	3.5
pumpkin, canned	1.1	0.3	8.1	34	90.0	2.8	7.4
radishes, raw	0.6	0.5	3.6	17	94.8	1.6	28.6
rhubarb, raw	0.9	0.2	4.5	21	93.6	1.8	8.6
squash, crookneck, raw	0.9	0.2	4.0	19	94.2	0.0	11.4
squash, hubbard, raw	2.0	0.5	8.7	40	88.0	0.0	11.3
squash, zucchini, raw	1.2	0.1	2.9	14	95.3	1.2	9.0
spinach, raw	2.9	0.4	3.5	22	91.6	2.7	14.3
spinach, boiled	3.0	0.3	3.8	23	91.2	2.4	10.2
sweet potato, raw	1.7	0.3	24.3	105	72.8	3.0	2.6
tomato, red, ripe, raw	0.9	0.3	4.6	21	93.8	1.1	14.1
turnips, raw	0.9	0.2	6.4	27	92.2	1.8	6.3
water chestnut, raw	1.4	0.1	23.9	106	73.5	3.0	0.8
yam, mountain, raw	3.3	0.2	10.5	47	84.9	5.4	2.9

Food : Fruits	Pro	Fat	Carb	Cal	Water	Fiber	Fat %Cal
apple, with skin	0.2	0.4	15.3	59	83.9	2.7	5.5
apple, dried	0.9	0.3	65.9	243	31.8	8.7	1.2
apple juice	0.1	0.1	11.7	47	87.9	0.1	2.1
applesauce, sweetened	0.2	0.2	19.9	76	79.6	1.2	2.1
applesauce, unsweetend	0.2	0.1	11.3	43	88.3	1.2	1.0
apricot	1.4	0.4	11.1	48	86.4	2.4	7.3
apricot, dried	3.7	0.5	61.8	238	31.1	9.0	1.7
banana	1.0	0.5	23.4	92	74.3	2.4	4.7
blackberries	0.7	0.4	12.8	52	85.6	5.0	6.8
blueberries	0.7	0.4	14.1	56	84.6	2.7	6.1
cherry, sour, red	1.0	0.3	12.2	50	86.1	1.2	5.4
cherry, sweet	1.2	1.0	16.6	72	80.8	2.3	12.0
cranberry, raw	0.4	0.2	12.7	49	86.5	4.2	3.7
cranberry sauce, canned	0.2	0.2	38.9	151	60.7	1.0	0.9
currant, black	1.4	0.4	15.4	63	82.0	0.0	5.9

Food : Fruits	Pro	Fat	Carb	Cal	Water	Fiber	Fat %Cal
currant, red	1.4	0.2	13.8	56	84.0	4.3	3.2
dates, domestic, dry	2.0	0.5	73.5	275	22.5	7.5	1.5
elderberies	0.7	0.5	18.4	73	79.8	7.0	6.2
figs	0.8	0.3	19.2	74	79.1	3.3	3.6
figs, dried	3.1	1.2	65.3	255	28.4	9.3	4.1
gooseberries	0.9	0.6	10.2	44	87.9	4.3	11.9
grapes, american	0.6	0.4	17.2	63	81.3	1.0	5.0
grape juice	0.6	0.1	15.0	61	84.1	0.1	1.2
grapefruit	0.7	0.1	8.4	33	90.5	1.1	2.7
grapefruit juice, unsweetened	0.5	0.1	9.0	38	90.1	0.1	2.4
kiwi	1.0	0.4	14.9	61	83.1	3.4	6.5
lemon without peel	1.1	0.3	9.3	29	89.0	2.8	9.3
melon, cantaloup	0.9	0.3	8.4	35	89.8	0.8	7.2
melon, honeydew	0.5	0.1	9.2	35	89.7	0.6	2.6
nectarine	0.9	0.5	11.8	49	86.3	1.6	8.4
orange, all varieties	0.9	0.1	11.8	47	86.8	2.4	2.3
orange juice	0.7	0.2	10.4	45	88.3	0.2	4.0
peach	0.7	0.1	11.1	43	87.7	2.0	1.9
peach, dried	3.6	0.8	61.3	239	31.8	8.2	2.9
pears	0.4	0.4	15.1	59	83.8	2.4	6.1
pears, asian	0.5	0.2	10.7	42	88.3	3.6	4.9
persimmon, native	0.8	0.4	33.5	127	64.4	0.0	2.8
pineapple, raw	0.4	0.4	12.4	49	86.5	1.2	7.9
plums	0.8	0.6	13.0	55	85.2	1.5	10.1
prunes	2.6	0.5	62.7	239	32.4	7.1	2.0
prunes, canned, heavy syrup	0.9	0.2	27.8	105	70.7	3.8	1.7
quince	0.4	0.1	15.3	57	83.8	1.9	1.6
raisins, golden, seedless	3.4	0.5	79.5	302	15.0	4.0	1.4
raspberries	0.9	0.6	11.6	49	86.6	6.8	10.1
strawberries	0.6	0.4	7.0	30	91.6	2.3	11.1
tangerines	0.6	0.2	11.2	44	87.6	2.3	3.9
watermelon	0.6	0.4	7.2	32	91.5	0.5	12.1

Food : Cereal & Grain Products	Pro	Fat	Carb	Cal	Water	Fiber	Fat %Cal
bagels, plain	10.5	1.6	53.4	275	32.6	2.1	5.2
barley, pearled	9.9	1.2	77.7	352	10.1	15.6	3.1

Food : Cereal & Grain Products	Pro	Fat	Carb	Cal	Water	Fiber	Fat %Cal
barley, pearled, cooked	2.3	0.4	28.2	123	68.8	3.8	2.9
barley, raw	12.5	2.3	73.5	354	9.4	17.3	5.8
bread, italian	8.8	3.5	50.0	271	35.7	3.1	11.6
bread, italian, fresh*	9.1	0.8	56.4	276	31.8	0.2	2.6
bread, pumpernickel	8.7	3.1	47.5	250	37.9	5.9	11.2
bread, rye	8.5	3.3	48.3	259	37.3	6.2	11.5
bread, white	8.2	3.6	49.5	267	36.7	2.3	12.1
bread, whole wheat	9.7	4.2	46.1	246	37.7	6.9	15.4
corn bran	8.4	0.9	85.4	224	4.7	86.1	3.6
corn flour, yellow, whole	6.9	3.9	76.9	361	10.9	13.4	9.7
corn meal, yellow, degermed	8.5	1.7	77.7	366	11.6	7.4	4.2
corn meal, yellow, whole	8.1	3.6	76.9	362	10.3	7.3	9.0
macaroni, cooked	4.8	0.7	28.3	141	66.0	1.3	4.5
oat bran, cooked	3.2	0.9	11.4	40	84.0	2.6	19.4
oat bran, raw	17.3	7.0	66.2	246	6.6	15.4	25.6
oatmeal, cooked	2.6	1.0	10.8	62	85.3	1.7	14.5
oatmeal, dry	16.0	6.3	67.0	384	8.8	10.6	14.8
pancakes; plain; dry mix	10.0	1.7	73.6	355	9.1	2.7	4.3
pancakes; prepared without fat*	5.5	0.9	44.2	197	50.0	1.5	4.0
pancakes; whole-wheat; mix	12.8	1.5	71.0	344	8.8		3.9
pncks; whole-wheat without fat*	9.1	1.1	50.4	244	50.0		4.1
rice, brown, long, cooked	2.6	0.9	23.0	111	73.1	1.8	7.3
rice, brown, long, raw	7.9	2.9	77.2	370	10.4	3.5	7.1
rice, white, long, cooked	2.7	0.3	28.2	130	68.4	0.4	2.1
rice, white, long, raw	7.1	0.7	80.0	365	11.6	1.3	1.7
rye	14.8	2.5	69.8	335	11.0	14.6	6.7
rye flour, medium	9.4	1.8	77.5	354	9.9	14.6	4.6
semolina	12.7	1.1	72.8	360	12.7	3.9	2.8
spaghetti, cooked	4.8	0.7	28.4	141	66.0	1.7	4.5
spaghetti, dry	12.8	1.6	74.7	371	10.3	2.4	3.9
waffles; dry mix*	9.0	1.4	75.6	351		2.2	3.6
wheat bran	15.6	4.3	64.5	216	9.9	42.8	17.9
wheat flour, white	10.3	1.0	76.3	364	11.9	2.7	2.5
wheat flour, whole	13.7	1.9	72.6	339	10.3	12.2	5.0
wheat, durum	13.7	2.5	71.1	339	10.9		6.6
wheat, hard, red, spring	15.4	1.9	68.0	329	12.8	12.6	5.2
wheat, soft, red, winter	10.4	1.6	74.2	331	12.2	12.6	4.4

Food : Breakfast Cereals	Pro	Fat	Carb	Cal	Water	Fiber	Fat %Cal
100% bran cereal	12.5	5.0	72.9	269	3.0	29.6	16.7
All-bran cereal	14.3	1.8	74.4	249	3.0	35.6	6.5
All-bran extra fiber*	13.3	3.3	50.0	175		50.0	18.0
Cheerios	15.1	6.4	69.1	391	5.0	7.0	14.7
corn bran cereal	6.8	3.5	84.3	346	2.5	19.0	9.1
corn flakes	8.1	0.3	86.1	389	2.6	2.6	0.7
corn grits, cooked	1.4	0.2	13.0	60	85.3	0.2	3.0
corn grits, dry	8.8	1.2	79.6	371	10.0	1.6	2.9
farina, cooked	1.4	0.1	10.6	50	87.9	1.4	1.8
farina, dry	10.6	0.5	78.0	369	10.5	1.9	1.2
Fiber one*	10.0	3.3	80.0	200		46.7	16.7
Grape-nuts cereal	11.7	0.4	82.0	357	3.2	10.0	1.0
oat bran, cooked	3.2	0.9	11.4	40	84.0	2.6	19.4
oat bran, raw	17.3	7.0	66.2	246	6.6	15.4	25.6
oatmeal, cooked	2.6	1.0	10.8	62	85.3	1.7	14.5
oatmeal, dry	16.0	6.3	67.0	384	8.8	10.6	14.8
oats, instant, cooked	2.5	1.0	10.2	59	85.5	1.7	15.3
oats, instant, dry	15.5	6.1	64.0	369	9.3	10.9	14.9
oats, instant, apple/cinnamon, cooked	2.6	1.1	17.7	91	77.8	2.0*	10.9
oats, instant, apple/cinnamon, dry	10.9	4.5	74.3	382	6.6	8.6*	10.6
Post bran flakes*	10.5	1.4	77.9	309	3.2	20.0	4.1
Ralston, cooked*	1.9	0.4	11.5	56		1.9	6.0
Ralston, dry*	11.9	2.4	73.8	357		11.9	6.0
Roman meal, cooked	2.7	0.4	13.7	61	82.7		5.9
Roman meal, dry	14.4	2.2	72.0	322	9.1	17.9	6.1
Shop-rite bran flakes*	10.0	1.7	80.0	333		16.7	4.6
shredded wheat	10.9	1.3	79.8	352	6.4	9.8	3.3
Shredded white & bran*	11.9	1.7	80.0	339		13.6	4.6
Total cereal	10.0	2.1	78.8	352	4.0	12.9	5.4
Wheat chex*	10.0	2.0	82.0	380		10.0	5.2
Wheatena, cooked*	1.9	0.4	12.1	57		1.9	5.9
Wheatena, dry*	12.2	2.4	78.0	366		12.2	5.9

Food : Legumes	Pro	Fat	Carb	Cal	Water	Fiber	Fat %Cal
bean, baked, canned, plain	4.8	0.5	20.5	93	72.7	5.0	4.4
bean, black, raw	21.6	1.4	62.4	341	11.0	15.2	3.7

Food : Legumes	Pro	Fat	Carb	Cal	Water	Fiber	Fat %Cal
bean, black, cooked	8.9	0.5	23.7	132	65.7	8.7	3.7
bean, great northern, raw	21.9	1.1	62.4	339	10.7		3.0
bean, great northern, cooked	8.3	0.5	21.1	118	69.0	7.0	3.4
bean, kidney, raw	23.6	0.8	60.0	333	11.8	24.9	2.2
bean, kidney, cooked	8.7	0.5	22.8	127	66.9	6.4	3.5
bean, kidney, red, raw	22.5	1.1	61.3	337	11.8	15.2	2.8
bean, kidney, red, cooked	8.7	0.5	22.8	127	66.9	7.4	3.5
bean, navy, raw	22.3	1.3	60.7	335	12.4	24.4	3.4
bean, navy, cooked	8.7	0.6	26.3	142	63.2		3.6
bean, pinto, raw	20.9	1.1	63.4	340	11.0	24.4	3.0
bean, pinto, cooked	8.2	0.5	25.7	137	64.3	8.6	3.4
bean, small white, raw	21.1	1.2	62.3	336	11.7		3.2
bean, small white, cooked	9.0	0.6	25.8	142	63.2		4.1
bean, white, raw	23.4	0.9	60.3	333	11.3	15.2	2.3
bean, white, cooked	9.7	0.4	25.1	139	63.1	6.3	2.3
bean, white, canned	7.3	0.3	21.9	117	70.1	4.8	2.2
broadbean, raw	26.1	1.5	58.3	341	11.0	25.0	4.0
broadbean, cooked	7.6	0.4	19.7	110	71.5		3.3
carob flour	4.6	0.7	88.9	383	3.6	39.8	1.5
chickpea, raw	19.3	6.0	60.7	364	11.5	17.4	14.9
chickpea, cooked	8.9	2.6	27.4	164	60.2		14.2
chickpea, canned	5.0	1.1	22.6	119	69.7	4.4	8.6
lentils, raw	28.1	1.0	57.1	338	11.2	30.5	2.6
lentils, cooked	9.0	0.4	20.1	116	69.6	7.9	2.9
lima, baby, cooked	8.0	0.4	23.3	126	67.2	7.7	2.7
lima, large, raw	21.5	0.7	63.4	338	10.2	19.0	1.8
lima, large, cooked	7.8	0.4	20.9	115	69.8	7.0	3.0
mung beans, cooked	7.0	0.4	19.1	105	72.7	7.6	3.3
pea, split, raw	24.6	1.2	60.4	341	11.3	25.5	3.1
pea, split, cooked	8.3	0.4	21.1	118	69.5	8.3	3.1

Food : Snacks & Sweets	Pro	Fat	Carb	Cal	Water	Fiber	Fat %Cal
apple butter	0.1	0.3	47.7	184	51.7	1.3	1.5
candy, hard	0.0	0.0	98.2	373	1.3	0.0	0.0
gumdrops	0.0	0.0	98.9	386	1.0	0.0	0.0
ice pop	0.0	0.0	18.9	72	80.0	0.0	0.0

Food : Snacks & Sweets	Pro	Fat	Carb	Cal	Water	Fiber	Fat %Cal
ices, water	0.4	0.0	32.6	78	66.9	0.0	0.0
jams & preserves, average	0.7	0.2	64.4	242	34.5	1.1	0.7
jellybeans	0.0	0.0	98.9	386	1.0	0.0	0.0
marmalade, orange	0.3	0.0	66.3	246	33.2	0.2	0.0
popcorn, plain	12.0	4.2	77.9	382	4.1	15.1	9.9
pretzel, hard, salted	9.1	3.5	79.2	381	3.3	3.2	8.3
pretzl, soft, frozen*	9.4	0.0	57.8	266		3.1	0.0
sorbet, Sharons fruit*	0.0	0.0	20.8	83		0.0	0.0

Appendix 3:
Ultraviolet and
Other Radiation

Ultraviolet rays, visible light, infrared, X-rays, gamma rays, and radio waves are all electromagnetic radiation. They differ quantitatively, namely in the wavelength or — what is saying the same thing — the frequency of the radiation. But this difference extends over many orders of magnitude, as illustrated below. The wavelength of visible light, for example, is about a million times shorter than that of radio waves; the wavelength of gamma rays is about a million times shorter than that of visible light. As a result, their properties and interaction with matter, including living tissue, differ enormously.

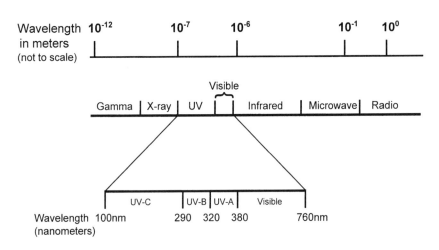

The Electromagnetic Spectrum

Gamma rays are produced through the radioactive decay of unstable atomic nuclei; X-rays also arise from such nuclear interactions but can also be produced artificially by electronic means. Gamma and X-rays interact with tissue primarily by the ionization they produce in the tissue. That is, they knock an electron off an

152

atom, resulting in an ion — an atom with a net charge. This generates free radicals, which can interact with and damage various cellular components, including the genetic material, DNA. Such damage sometimes is repaired by the cell, sometimes kills the cell, and sometimes results in the cell becoming precancerous. (It is thought that cancer arises in a two- or three-step process: *Initiation* permanently alters a cell's DNA; in *promotion* and *progression*, which might take place many years later, the cell divides and grows into an actual malignancy.) This is why such radiation is so dangerous. Longer-wavelength radiation, like infrared, microwaves, and radio waves, does not have sufficient energy, no matter how intense it is, to produce ionization. So longer wavelengths do not present such a hazard. Beta rays, which are electrons (negatively charged particles), and alpha rays, which carry a positive charge, are also included in the term "ionizing radiation," even though they are not electromagnetic radiation at all. Like gamma rays, these particles are commonly produced in the decay of unstable nuclei like carbon-14 and uranium.

Luminous bodies like the sun or an ordinary incandescent lightbulb emit electromagnetic radiation in a continuous spectrum of wavelengths. Such bodies appear red or yellow or white, or they are invisible, depending upon what wavelength radiation they are emitting the most. This wavelength depends on the surface temperature of the object, becoming shorter (more energetic radiation) as the temperature becomes higher. But whether the sun or a lightbulb, they are radiating across a broad spectrum of wavelengths. Fluorescent bulbs, on the other hand, are radiating not because of their temperature, but by entirely different means. Their radiation consists of a number of very specific, discrete wavelengths, including a significant proportion in the ultraviolet. They have been designed to fool the eye into interpreting their radiation as white sunlight. The wavelengths of visible light extend from about 380nm (nanometers, or billionths of a meter), which is violet light, to red at about 760nm. Very intense visible light or infrared can damage several structures of the eye, essentially by burning them. Ultraviolet light has its own special set of hazards. It is absorbed strongly by proteins and DNA, which can be damaged considerably in the process. This sort of damage results in cataract formation in the lens of the eye, various manifestations of skin aging, and, potentially, the transformation of normal cells into precancerous ones. Ultraviolet light is classified into one of three types — UV-A, UV-B, and UV-C — according to its wavelength. UV-A extends from 320nm to the edge of the visible spectrum, about 380nm; UV-B from 290nm to 320nm; UV-C from about 100nm to 290nm. The shortest and most energetic portion in sunlight, UV-C, is potentially the most dangerous but is completely absorbed by the earth's atmosphere, primarily in the ozone layer. None of the wavelengths less than 290nm reach the earth's surface. UV-B is much more energetic than UV-A, but UV-A is about 10 to 100 times as intense in sunlight. The longer wavelength UV-A also penetrates more deeply into the skin, and therefore plays a more important role in sun-induced damage to connective tissue. The pigment melanin absorbs both UV-A and UV-B, as well as visible light. The ultraviolet in artificial lighting is at most marginally dangerous because it is so much weaker than sunlight.

Appendix 4:
Table of Body Weights

These tables of body weights were generated from established values of the body mass index for 20% underweight, low normal weight, high normal weight, and 20% overweight. Such values of the body mass index correlate well with body fat for people of average musculature; they may not be accurate in people with a significantly greater proportion of muscle mass. The tables list body weights in pounds (lbs) and kilograms (kg) for men and women over a range of body heights.

MEN

height		20% under		low normal		high normal		20% over	
in	cm	lbs	kg	lbs	kg	lbs	kg	lbs	kg
60	152	83	37.6	102	46.5	128	58.1	139	63.2
61	155	86	38.9	106	48.0	132	60.0	144	65.3
62	157	88	40.2	109	49.6	136	62.0	148	67.5
63	160	91	41.5	113	51.2	141	64.0	153	69.6
64	163	94	42.8	116	52.9	145	66.1	158	71.9
65	165	97	44.2	120	54.5	150	68.1	163	74.1
66	168	100	45.5	124	56.2	155	70.3	168	76.4
67	170	103	46.9	127	57.9	159	72.4	173	78.8
68	173	106	48.3	131	59.7	164	74.6	179	81.1
69	175	109	49.8	135	61.4	169	76.8	184	83.5
70	178	113	51.2	139	63.2	174	79.0	189	86.0
71	180	116	52.7	143	65.0	179	81.3	195	88.5
72	183	119	54.2	147	66.9	184	83.6	200	91.0
73	185	123	55.7	151	68.8	189	86.0	206	93.5
74	188	126	57.2	155	70.7	194	88.3	211	96.1
75	191	129	58.8	160	72.6	200	90.7	217	98.7
76	193	133	60.4	164	74.5	205	93.2	223	101.4
77	196	136	62.0	168	76.5	210	95.6	229	104.0
78	198	140	63.6	173	78.5	216	98.1	235	106.8

WOMEN

height		20% under		low normal		high normal		20% over	
in	cm	lbs	kg	lbs	kg	lbs	kg	lbs	kg
58	147	72	32.6	90	40.8	114	51.7	128	58.4
59	150	74	33.7	93	42.2	118	53.5	133	60.4
60	152	77	34.8	96	43.7	122	55.3	137	62.5
61	155	79	36.0	99	45.1	126	57.1	142	64.6
62	157	82	37.2	103	46.6	130	59.0	147	66.7
63	160	85	38.4	106	48.1	134	60.9	152	68.9
64	163	87	39.6	109	49.7	138	62.9	156	71.1
65	165	90	40.9	113	51.2	143	64.9	161	73.3
66	168	93	42.2	116	52.8	147	66.9	166	75.6
67	170	96	43.4	120	54.4	152	68.9	171	77.9
68	173	98	44.7	123	56.1	156	71.0	177	80.2
69	175	101	46.1	127	57.7	161	73.1	182	82.6
70	178	104	47.4	131	59.4	166	75.2	187	85.0
71	180	107	48.8	135	61.1	170	77.4	192	87.5
72	183	110	50.2	138	62.9	175	79.6	198	90.0
73	185	113	51.6	142	64.6	180	81.8	203	92.5
74	188	117	53.0	146	66.4	185	84.1	209	95.0
75	191	120	54.4	150	68.2	190	86.4	215	97.6
76	193	123	55.9	154	70.1	195	88.7	221	100.2

Appendix 5:
Desserts, Treats, and Fast Food
Ranked by Fat Content

Most of the foods in these categories have a relatively high fat and low nutritional content and should therefore not constitute a significant portion of your diet. But there are exceptions: Some are quite low in fat, and there is a wide variation among the others. It's debatable whether it is the percentage of fat in a food or the percentage of calories from fat that is more important in judging a food. There is only a rough correlation between these two measures. You want to keep fat to as low a percentage of your diet as possible, but in choosing an occasional treat it is the actual amount of fat in it that you are more concerned with. Furthermore, if a food has a relatively low calorie content, its percentage of calories from fat will be higher than a similar food with more calories. I have therefore ranked these items by actual fat content in 100 grams — that is, the percentage of fat in the food rather than the percentage of calories from fat, but I have also listed the latter as well as the calorie content, since these are also important considerations. Keep in mind that the figures for percentage of fat in a food tend to significantly understate the proportion of calories from fat that you are getting. These values were calculated from data in the USDA nutrient database, except where noted otherwise by a star (*). Foods that have "(recipe)" in their description were prepared following a typical recipe for that type of food, rather than purchased ready to eat, "(comm)" indicates an item purchased commercially, generally ready to eat. These clarifications are included only where uncertainty about this may occur or where there is a significant difference between the commercial and recipe-prepared types. Some food items are listed more than once to show that several varieties differing in composition are available.

Food:	Fat	Calories	Fat%Cal
Fast Foods			
salad w/shrimp	1.1	45	21.0
corn on cob w/margarine	2.4	106	20.0
chili	3.3	101	29.1
frijoles w/cheese	4.7	135	31.1
salad w/pasta & seafood	5.0	91	49.5

Food: Fast Foods	Fat	Calories	Fat%Cal
taco salad w/chili	5.0	111	40.8
pizza w/cheese	5.1	223	20.6
potato, baked w/cheese & chili	5.5	122	40.8
ice milk, vanilla soft cone	5.9	159	33.6
pancakes, commercial w/syrup	6.0	224	24.2
potato salad	6.0	114	47.6
burrito w/beans	6.2	206	27.2
burrito w/beans cheese	6.3	203	27.9
potato, baked, w/cheese broccoli	6.3	119	47.8
tostada, beans cheese	6.9	155	39.8
burrito w/beans peppers	7.2	202	32.0
potato, baked w/sour cream & chives	7.4	130	51.2
taco salad	7.5	141	47.6
english muffin w/margarine	9.1	300	27.4
pizza w/pepperoni	9.8	255	34.6
corndog	10.8	263	37.0
sub, tuna salad	10.9	228	43.1
coleslaw	11.1	148	67.4
enchilada, cheese	11.6	196	53.1
taco	12.0	216	50.1
fish filet, breaded fried	12.3	232	47.7
cheeseburger w/condiments	12.5	261	43.2
potatoes, hash brown	12.8	210	54.9
burrito with fruit	12.9	312	37.1
egg and cheese sandwich	13.3	233	51.4
animal crackers	13.4	446	27.1
scallops, breaded fried	13.5	268	45.2
chicken pieces w/bbq sauce	13.8	254	49.0
french toast w/butter	13.9	264	47.4
biscuit w/egg ham	14.1	230	55.1
hot dog, plain	14.8	247	54.1
biscuit with egg	14.9	232	57.6
hush puppies	14.9	329	40.7
shrimp, breaded fried	15.2	277	49.3
chicken pieces w/honey	15.3	286	48.0
potatoes, french fries	16.1	309	46.9
chicken filet sandwich, plain	16.2	283	51.5

Food:	Fat	Calories	Fat%Cal
Fast Foods			
egg, scrambled	16.2	212	68.7
biscuit w/ham	16.3	342	42.9
hamburger, plain	16.7	311	48.4
brownie	16.8	405	37.4
nachos w/cheese	16.8	306	49.3
danish, fruit	17.0	356	42.9
crab cake	17.3	266	58.4
chicken, fried, no bone	17.4	284	55.0
cheeseburger, plain	17.8	329	48.8
danish, cinnamon	19.0	397	43.1
biscuit w/egg & steak	19.2	277	62.4
croissant w/egg cheese	19.5	290	60.4
biscuit w/egg bacon	20.7	305	61.2
biscuit w/egg & sausage	21.5	323	59.9
biscuit w/egg cheese bacon	21.8	331	59.3
croissant w/egg cheese bacon	22.0	320	61.8
chocolate chip cookies	22.1	423	47.0
croissant w/egg cheese ham	22.1	312	63.7
croissant w/egg cheese sausage	23.9	327	65.6
biscuit with sausage	25.6	391	59.0
cheese danish	27.1	388	62.8
nachos w/cinnamon sugar	33.0	543	54.7
Desserts/Bakery & Related			
angelfood cake	0.3	257	1.1
pancake, plain, prepared w/o fat*	0.9	197	4.0
pancake, whole wheat, prepared w/o fat*	1.1	244	4.1
crispbread crackers, rye	1.3	366	3.2
matzo crackers, plain	1.4	395	3.2
crackermeal	1.7	383	4.0
english muffin, plain	1.8	235	6.9
english muffin, plain, toasted	2.0	255	7.1
english muffin, wheat	2.0	223	8.1
english muffin, wheat, toasted	2.1	243	7.8
tortillas, corn	2.5	222	10.1
fortune cookies	2.7	378	6.4
english muffin, raisin-cinnamon	2.7	243	10.0

Food: Desserts/Bakery & Related	Fat	Calories	Fat%Cal
english muffin, raisin-cinnamon, toasted	2.9	264	9.9
melba toast crackers, plain	3.2	390	7.4
fudge cake cookies	3.7	349	9.5
sponge cake (recipe)	4.3	297	13.0
french roll	4.3	277	14.0
hard roll	4.3	293	13.2
popovers	4.5	202	20.0
hamburger/hot dog roll	5.1	286	16.0
blueberry muffin (comm)	6.5	277	21.1
croutons, plain	6.6	407	14.6
ice cream cones, wafer type	6.9	417	14.9
tortillas	7.1	325	19.7
fig bars	7.3	348	18.9
dinner roll (comm)	7.3	300	21.9
oat bran muffin	7.4	270	24.7
cornbread, whole-milk (recipe)	7.7	271	25.6
chocolate cake, diet (recipe)	7.7	305	22.7
corn muffin (comm)	8.4	305	24.8
boston cream pie (comm)	8.5	252	30.4
apple croissants	8.7	254	30.8
lemon meringue pie (comm)	8.7	268	29.2
egg custard pie (recipe)	8.9	206	38.9
fruitcake (comm)	9.1	324	25.3
ladyfingers	9.1	365	22.4
wheat-bran muffin	9.2	276	30.0
pumpkin pie (comm)	9.5	210	40.7
coffee cake, cinnamon-crumb topping	9.6	318	27.2
pancake, plain, traditional (recipe)	9.7	227	38.5
gingersnaps	9.8	416	21.2
blueberry pie (comm)	10.0	232	38.8
peach pie	10.0	223	40.4
graham crackers	10.1	423	21.5
gingerbread cake, prepared from dry mix	10.2	309	29.7
coffee cake, fruit	10.2	311	29.5
corn muffin	10.2	321	28.6
coffee cake, chocolate-frosting	10.8	331	29.4
mince pie (recipe)	10.8	289	33.6

Food: Desserts/Bakery & Related	Fat	Calories	Fat%Cal
apple pie (comm)	11.0	237	41.8
cherry pie (comm)	11.0	260	38.1
brownies (recipe)	11.1	384	26.0
apple strudel	11.2	274	36.8
french toast (recipe, w/whole milk)	11.3	232	43.8
corn muffin (toaster)	11.3	346	29.4
fruitcake (recipe)	11.5	360	28.8
egg custard pie (comm)	11.6	210	49.7
chocolate cake (recipe)	11.7	305	34.5
saltines	11.8	434	24.5
pineapple upside-down cake	12.1	319	34.1
corn muffin, (recipe, 2% milk)	12.3	316	35.0
brownies, diet (recipe)	12.5	426	26.4
apple pie (recipe)	12.5	265	42.5
molasses cookies	12.8	430	26.8
sweetroll (recipe, raisin & nuts)	12.8	344	33.5
lemon meringue pie (recipe)	12.9	285	40.7
hush puppies (recipe)	13.5	337	36.1
raisin cookies, soft	13.6	401	30.5
banana-cream pie (recipe)	13.6	269	45.5
animalcrackers	13.8	446	27.8
waffles, plain (recipe)	14.1	291	43.6
chocolate wafer cookies	14.2	433	29.5
butterscotch pie (recipe)	14.3	279	46.1
vanilla-cream pie (recipe)	14.4	278	46.6
yellow cake (recipe)	14.6	361	36.4
chocolate cake, no frosting (recipe)	15.1	358	38.0
cheese coffee cake	15.2	339	40.4
vanilla wafers (lower fat)	15.2	441	31.0
chocolate chip cookies (lower fat)	15.4	453	30.6
chocolate mousse pie	15.4	260	53.3
custard creampuff (recipe)	15.5	258	54.1
carrot cake, no frosting	15.7	342	41.3
eclairs	15.7	262	53.9
chocolate-cream pie (recipe)	16.1	282	51.4
oatmeal raisin cookies (recipe)	16.2	435	33.5
gingerbread cake (recipe)	16.4	356	41.5

Food: Desserts/Bakery & Related	Fat	Calories	Fat%Cal
cinnamon-raisin sweetroll (comm)	16.4	372	39.7
marshmallow coated cookies	16.9	421	36.1
fruit danish	17.0	356	42.9
marble cake	17.0	347	44.1
pound cake (comm)	17.9	389	41.4
oatmeal cookies (recipe)	17.9	447	36.0
oatmeal cookies (comm)	18.1	450	36.2
croutons, seasoned	18.3	465	35.4
french cruller, glazed	18.3	412	40.0
jelly donut	18.7	340	49.5
butter cookies (comm)	18.8	467	36.2
cinnamon danish	19.0	397	43.1
vanilla wafers (higher fat)	19.4	473	36.9
chocolate-cream pie (comm)	19.4	304	57.4
brownies (recipe)	19.9	423	42.3
chocolate donut, cake type, glazed	19.9	417	42.9
vanilla sandwich cream cookies	20.0	483	37.3
cheese croissants	20.9	414	45.4
butter croissants	21.0	406	46.6
pecan pie (recipe)	22.2	412	48.5
cheesecake (comm)	22.5	321	63.1
chocolate-chip cookies (higher fat)	22.6	481	42.3
taco shells, baked	22.6	468	43.5
glazed donut	22.8	403	50.9
donut, cake type, glazed	22.9	426	48.4
donut, cake type, plain	22.9	421	49.0
cheese & peanut butter crackers	23.2	482	43.3
peanut butter cookies (comm)	23.6	477	44.5
shortbread cookies, plain	24.1	502	43.2
cream donut	24.5	361	61.1
nut danish	25.2	430	52.7
cheese crackers	25.3	503	45.3
creampuff	25.9	362	64.4
carrot cake, w/cream cheese frosting	26.4	436	54.5
cheese danish	27.1	388	62.8
pie crust, baked from mix	30.4	501	54.6
puff pastry, baked	38.5	558	62.1

Food: Snacks and Sweets	Fat	Calories	Fat%Cal
gumdrops	0.0	386	0.0
hard candy	0.0	373	0.0
honey, strained	0.0	304	0.0
ice pops	0.0	72	0.0
ices, water, lime	0.0	78	0.0
marmalade, orange	0.0	246	0.0
molasses blackstrap	0.0	235	0.0
sugar, brown	0.0	376	0.0
sugar, granulated	0.0	387	0.0
syrup, corn, dark	0.0	282	0.0
syrup, corn, hi-fructose	0.0	281	0.0
syrup, pancake	0.0	287	0.0
frozen fruit & juice bars	0.1	82	1.1
jellies	0.1	271	0.3
molasses	0.1	266	0.3
pie filling, canned apple	0.1	101	0.9
sugar, powdered	0.1	389	0.2
topping, pineapple	0.1	253	0.4
topping, strawberry	0.1	254	0.4
jams and preserves	0.2	242	0.7
marshmallows	0.2	318	0.6
pie filling, canned cherry	0.2	115	1.6
chewing gum	0.3	341	0.8
fruit butter, apple	0.3	184	1.5
jellybeans	0.5	367	1.2
y & s twizzlers, strawberry	1.6	370	3.9
sherbet, orange	2.0	138	13.0
pudding, chocolate, regular	2.1	361	5.2
y & s nibs, cherry candy	2.3	374	5.5
corn cakes	2.4	387	5.6
caramel chocolate-flavor roll	2.5	360	6.3
ice milk, vanilla soft-serve	2.6	126	18.6
ices, pineapple-coconut	2.6	113	20.7
rice cake, brown rice, plain	2.8	387	6.5
fruit leather rolls	3.0	350	7.7
skittles	3.0	392	6.9
popcorn cakes	3.1	384	7.3

Food: Snacks and Sweets	Fat	Calories	Fat%Cal
taffy (recipe)	3.3	376	7.9
butterscotch	3.5	395	8.0
pretzel, hard plain salted	3.5	381	8.3
apple crisp (recipe)	3.6	163	19.9
pudding, chocolate whole milk	3.6	141	23.0
pudding, tapioca	3.7	119	28.0
popcorn, air-popped	4.2	382	9.9
ice milk, vanilla	4.3	139	27.8
frozen pudding pop, vanilla	4.4	159	24.9
egg custards, baked (recipe)	4.7	105	40.3
fruit leather bars	5.3	351	13.6
fudge, vanilla (recipe)	5.4	369	13.2
frozen yogurt, vanilla, soft	5.6	159	31.7
yogurt, chocolate soft	6.0	160	33.8
fruit leather pieces	7.2	341	19.0
popcorn, caramel-coated, w/peanuts	7.8	400	17.6
Bit-o-honey chews	8.0	387	18.6
caramels	8.1	382	19.1
Fruit leather bars w/cream	8.2	372	19.8
starburst fruit chews	8.3	396	18.9
ice cream, strawberry	8.4	192	39.4
York peppermint patty	9.1	346	23.7
cocoa powder, unsweetened, European	9.6	198	43.6
ice cream, chocolate	11.0	216	45.8
ice cream, vanilla	11.0	201	49.3
popcorn, caramel-coated	12.8	431	26.7
3 Musketeers bar	12.9	416	27.9
beef jerky	13.0	338	34.6
ice cream, vanilla soft-serve	13.0	215	54.4
cocoa, dark unsweetened	13.1	222	53.1
syrup, chocolate fudge type	13.4	346	34.9
After Eight mints	13.7	358	34.4
cocoa, dry powder, unsweetened	13.7	229	53.8
milk chocolate-coated raisins	14.8	390	34.2
Mars Milky Way bar	15.2	419	32.6
tortilla chip nacho light	15.2	445	30.7
Raisinets	15.9	412	34.7

Food: Snacks and Sweets	Fat	Calories	Fat%Cal
fudge, chocolate w/nuts (recipe)	16.1	426	34.0
ice cream, vanilla, rich	16.2	241	60.5
granola bar, hard chocolate-chip	16.3	438	33.5
mousse, chocolate (recipe)	16.3	221	66.4
fudge, chocolate-marshmallow	16.9	422	36.0
Oh Henry! bar	16.9	431	35.3
trail mix, tropical	17.1	407	37.8
Chex mix	17.3	425	36.6
Butterfinger bar	18.5	437	38.1
Doo Dads original flavor	18.5	456	36.5
peanut brittle (recipe)	19.1	453	37.9
Combos, cheddar pretzel	19.5	478	36.7
100 GRAND bar	19.8	454	39.3
granola bar, hard, plain	19.8	471	37.8
crisped rice bar, almond	20.4	458	40.1
Reese's Pieces candy	20.7	469	39.7
potato chips, light	20.8	471	39.7
5th Avenue bar	21.2	466	40.9
Rolo caramels, milk chocolate	21.8	475	41.3
Baby ruth bar	22.2	461	43.3
Snickers bar	22.3	455	44.1
corn snacks, onion flavor	22.6	500	40.7
Mars almond bar	23.0	467	44.3
Twix caramel cookie	23.5	478	44.2
tortilla chip, ranch flavor	23.8	490	43.7
praline recipe	24.3	454	48.2
Taro chips	24.9	498	45.0
Caramello candy bar	25.3	489	46.6
granola bar, hard almond	25.5	495	46.4
tortilla chip, nacho flavor	25.6	498	46.3
Whatchamacallit	25.9	503	46.3
Nestle Crunch milk chocolate	26.0	494	47.4
tortilla chip, plain	26.2	501	47.1
potato chips, cheese flavor	27.2	496	49.4
Almond Joy candy bar	27.7	464	53.7
Demet's turtles	27.8	485	51.6
Krackel chocolate bar	27.8	502	49.8

Food: Snacks and Sweets	Fat	Calories	Fat%Cal
popcorn, oil-popped	28.1	500	50.6
Kit Kat wafer bar	28.5	510	50.3
Twix peanut butter cookie	29.0	506	51.6
Chunky bar	29.2	495	53.1
trail mix, regular	29.4	462	57.3
semisweet chocolate	29.7	477	56.0
milk chocolate	30.6	513	53.7
Reese's peanut butter cups	31.1	485	57.7
pork skins, plain	31.3	545	51.7
corn cones, nacho-flavor	31.7	536	53.2
pork skins, bbq-flavor	31.8	538	53.2
Trail mix, chocolate chip	31.9	484	59.3
Mr. Goodbar chocolate bar	32.3	514	56.6
potato chips, bbq-flavor	32.4	491	59.4
Symphony milk chocolate bar	32.4	522	55.9
corn chips, bbq-flavor	32.7	523	56.3
toffee (recipe)	32.8	542	54.5
carob	33.0	533	55.7
Golden III chocolate bar	33.0	518	57.3
popcorn, cheese-flavor	33.2	526	56.8
sesame crunch	33.3	517	58.0
corn chips, plain	33.4	539	55.8
Goobers chocolate-covered peanuts	33.5	513	58.8
milk chocolate–coated peanuts	33.5	519	58.1
peanut bar	33.7	522	58.1
Bar None candy bar	33.9	521	58.6
sweet chocolate	34.2	505	61.0
truffles (recipe)	34.3	488	63.3
corn puffs, cheese flavor	34.4	554	55.9
milk chocolate w/almonds	34.4	526	58.9
potato sticks	34.4	522	59.3
Skor toffee bar	34.4	527	58.7
potato chips, plain, salted	34.6	536	58.1
Alpine white bar almond	36.9	564	58.9
Golden almond Solitaires	37.0	535	62.2
Golden almond chocolate bar	37.8	548	62.1
baking chocolate, unsweetened, squares	55.3	522	95.3

Appendix 6:
Further Resources

Books for the General Reader

The 120-Year Diet. Roy L. Walford, MD. Simon and Schuster (Pocket Books), New York, 1986. Roy Walford is the noted UCLA gerontologist who did much of the recent work on caloric restriction and aging. This book discusses a number of ways of avoiding disease and living longer, but the emphasis is on caloric restriction.

Maximum Life Span. Roy L. Walford, MD. Norton, New York, 1983. Discusses more of the scientific background, theories of aging, and issues related to increasing longevity. It does contain practical advice on life extension, almost all of it still valid.

Food for Life. Neal Barnard, MD. Crown Publishing, New York, 1993. Good discussion of diet, disease, overall health, and weight control. Also contains recipes and tips on changing your diet.

On Food and Cooking. Harold McGee. Collier Books (Macmillan), New York, 1984. A comprehensive survey of what foods are, where they come from, and what happens to them during preparation and cooking. Scientifically detailed, yet understandable. Highly recommended.

Foods and Nutrition Encyclopedia. 2 vols. 2nd ed. Audrey H. Ensminger et al., eds. CRC Press, Boca Raton, FL, 1993. A very comprehensive reference; contains alphabetical listing covering almost all aspects of food and nutrition.

The Good Heart Diet Cook Book. Ellen Stern and Jonathan Michaels. Ticknor & Fields, New Haven, CT, 1982. Low-fat and nonfat recipes of many kinds, similar to the type we have discussed; also some interesting cooking tips. The book is remarkable in that all the recipes have no added fat, sugar, salt, meat, or eggs. Out of print but available in some libraries.

Health, United States, 1993. (New editions periodically). National Center for Health Statistics, Public Health Service, Hyattsville, MD, 1994. Interesting and useful reference on causes of death and disease, plus other health-related statistics.

Internet Resources

United States Department of Agriculture Nutrient Database

Large compilation of nutrients in foods. These include protein, fat, carbohy-drate, ash, calories, alcohol, water, caffeine, fiber, calcium, iron, magnesium, phos-phorus, potassium, sodium, zinc, copper, manganese, cholesterol, all the individual vitamins, most of the essential amino acids, the types of fatty acids, and some other trace nutrients for some foods (compilation is ongoing). It covers almost all unpro-cessed foods (apples, celery, nuts, etc.) and many prepared and processed foods like breakfast cereals, cakes, and pizza. Formerly accessible via gopher, lynx, or anony-mous ftp, you can now go directly via the World Wide Web to http://www.nal. usda.gov/fnic/foodcomp (formerly http://www.inform.umd.edu/EdRes/Topic/ AgrEnv/USDA). Most of the data is in the directory USDA Nutrient Database for Standard Reference, Release 11-1 (frequently referred to as SR11-1), organized by food groups into 22 files. These are listed as 0100 (Dairy and Egg Products) through 2200 (Mixed Dishes), plus a few accessory files. Note that these files contain up to 1.4 megabytes. You can download the files for use on your own computer, in which case you will also need the file nutr_def.txt, the "Standard Reference Man-ual," which gives the keys for interpreting the lines and fields in all the files. For example, lines beginning with 203 specify grams of protein in 100 grams edible portion (along with related statistical data such as number of measurements and standard error). There is also some data in the directory "Food Composition Pro-ducts," instead of SR11. These include vitamin D, vitamin K, selenium, and sugar. There is also related information such as retention of nutrients during preparation and an abbreviated database (HG-72) listing the most common nutrients in typ-ical portions of foods. (The menu path to these files has been changed on occasion; if you run into any problems, you can ask for help from ndlinfo@rbhnrc.usda.gov.)

If you download the files, you will have to do some serious programming if you want to organize large sections into neat tables. To pull out particular items and nutrients you could look up the three-digit number corresponding to the nutrient (203 for protein, for example), and use (in UNIX) the egrep command to find and save each food and the nutrient you are looking for in a new file. The USDA provides a simple search program, good enough for most purposes, on the Website. This will search for whatever food you enter (pizza, oatmeal, etc.) and display a list of items in the database that match it. You can then select one, and its nutrient composition will be displayed. This search program is also available for downloading.

The information was formerly available in print, in 21 volumes correspond-ing to the 21 food group files then in the database. The title of the print version is *Agricultural Handbook No. 8, Composition of Foods*. Older versions were only one volume. Printed versions can no longer be ordered, but copies are commonly avail-able in libraries. Since there is no copyright, you are free to make additional copies. The USDA plans to offer a CD-ROM version in the future.

Relevant USENET newsgroups include:

sci.life-extension	All aspects of life extension, including supplements, diet, and some more exotic speculative ideas
alt.food.fat-free	News, discussion, recipes of fat-free or very low-fat foods
rec.food.veg	Discussions of vegetarianism, including health aspects
rec.food.veg.cooking	Vegetarian cooking and recipes
sci.med.nutrition	News and discussion of nutrition and health
alt.support.diet	Support and tips on diets and sticking to a diet
misc.fitness	Physical fitness and all types of exercise;
misc.fitness.weights	many related matters like exercise
misc.fitness.aerobic	equipment, diet, and supplements.

You have to take most of what you read in these groups with a large grain of salt, of course, but people are frequently very helpful. If you've heard of a recent interesting study, for example (the regular news reports usually garble things), you may be able to find the actual scientific reference from someone here.

Collections of fat-free and/or vegetarian recipes are available via gopher at

gopher.geod.emr.ca

Follow the menu path Vegetarian Info/Recipes. Under Recipes/FatFree, there are over 50 directories corresponding to categories of recipes from beans to desserts to tofu. Each of these contains a variety of very low-fat recipes. Also in the Recipes menu is the directory CADAdmin, under which you will find another directory of fat-free recipes, plus directories for the various vegetarian diets — vegan, lacto, and ovolacto. You can also access this resource via anonymous ftp to

ftp.geod.emr.ca

in the directory pub/Vegetarian/Recipes. This collection is also available via anonymous ftp to ftp.halcyon.com in the directory pub/recipes.

A considerable amount of health information, especially on cancer, is available on-line through the National Institutes of Health. This can be accessed via gopher to

gopher.nih.gov

or through the World Wide Web at

http://www.nih.gov

For information on cancer follow the menu path

Health and clinical information/CancerNet

Under "PDQ Information" are files on treatments for the various cancers written for patients or for physicians — two separate files for each specific cancer. You can access the "PDQ Treatment for Physician" files, of course; they are much more technical and contain references to the scientific literature if you should want to pursue it further. Also under "PDQ Information" are files on screening and prevention for each individual cancer. Bulletins and full-text publications on such related matters as chemotherapy, pain management, and diet are available under "CancerNet News."

If you follow the menu path
**Health and clinical information/NIH Consensus Conferences/
Individual Consensus Development Conferences**
you will be presented with a listing of articles on a variety of health topics from calcium intake to ovarian cancer to the significance of blood lipids. Full text (they probably average something like 15 single-spaced pages) is available on-line by selecting the appropriate article. The NIH convenes public conferences that include presentations by experts working in the specific area, followed by question and answer sessions and discussion, and finally closed deliberation by the panel of experts at which a consensus report is written. These do not represent an official position or policy of the NIH, but are intended to convey some of the latest thinking on a topic to scientists, physicians, or anyone else who is interested. Since they are arrived at by consensus, they tend to stick mainly to well-established facts, but usually at least mention or review briefly some of the controversial areas on the edge of research. Consensus statements are reviewed periodically by the NIH and may be updated or flagged as out-of-date.

Some interesting information on food, agriculture, and related matters (e.g., pesticides and food safety) can be found through the Cooperative State-USDA gopher
esusda.gov
If you follow the path
**USDA & Other Federal Agency Information/ Food
Labeling Information-FDA Regulations**
there are files on the latest regulations governing what must and what can be placed on food labels. This can be useful because it's not always clear what the terms allowed on labels mean or how the regulations apply.

Periodicals

Unfortunately, there are almost no really useful and reliable general periodicals in this field. A number of medical schools publish newsletters on general health and/or nutrition, but they are so bland and conservative as to be almost worthless. *Life Extension Report*, published by the Life Extension Foundation, Hollywood, Florida, frequently has informative and timely articles, but in recent years it has also begun to carry a good deal of political and sociological discussions. *MEDNEWS*, a health information newsletter, is available via E-mail or on the World Wide Web at
http://mednews.nus.sg
A relatively recent commercial newsletter that you can receive by E-mail is *International Health News*, published by Hans R. Larsen, 1320 Point St., Victoria BC, Canada V8S 1A5. It essentially collects and condenses some important recent reports. US $19.95/year via E-mail. Inquire to above address or
**health@DataFlux.BC.CA or
http://vvv.com/healthnews/**
If you have access to a medical library, you can get your information first hand

by looking up the original published studies in the journals. Most public medical school libraries are open to the citizens of their home state on a limited basis. Looking up most of the relevant studies and interpreting them will take a fair amount of effort unless you are familiar with this procedure and with scientific and medical jargon. It's the best way to go if you are really interested in deciding for yourself how good the evidence is, but it's probably not a very practicable alternative for most people. However, many journals also sometimes publish review articles in which the studies on a particular topic (say beta-carotene and cancer) in recent years are reviewed and summarized. This is as close to reading the original reports as you can get without actually looking them all up. Some of the journals that could be checked in this regard are

Advances in Cancer Research (annual)
Advances in Internal Medicine
American Journal of Clinical Nutrition
American Journal of Epidemiology
Geriatrics
Journal of the American Dietetic Association
Journal of Nutrition
Medicine and Science in Sports and Exercise
Nature
New England Journal of Medicine
Nutrition and Cancer
Nutrition Reviews
Postgraduate Medicine
Preventive Medicine
Progress in Cardiovascular Disease

If you are really ambitious about keeping current, you can set up to do your own searches of biomedical and related scientific journals from your own microcomputer. The National Library of Medicine maintains MEDLARS (MEDical Literature And Retrieval System), which includes a number of medical/scientific databases. There's one on AIDS, one on cancer, and so on. The most popular and extensive is MEDLINE, which covers 3,700 biomedical and related journals. It is updated weekly to monthly. Abstracts (summaries) of most articles are available on-line, and you can also arrange to order the full text on-line through agreements with local medical libraries. Formerly, you needed to open an account with the National Library of Medicine, although you were charged only for actual usage. The software commonly used for such searches is called "Grateful Med" and is available for PCs and Apple Macs. Grateful Med provides an input screen, allows you to search by menus, and helps you to select the appropriate search terms. Any combination of terms can be selected for the search, so you can look for studies relevant to, for example, both exercise and cancer. Partially because the search criteria are set up before connecting to the database, the costs are relatively low — typically a few dollars for a search. Grateful Med can be purchased from the National Library of Medicine; price as of this writing is $29.95.

Order forms for Grateful Med and to set up a MEDLINE account, as well as more general information on this service, are available on-line. You can connect by gopher to

gmedserv.nlm.nih.gov

and follow the menu path

NLM Fact Sheets, Newsletters, Agreements, and Forms/
NLM Agreements and Forms/Online Databases and Databanks/

The files are:

> Application for MEDLARS User ID
> Grateful Med Fact Sheet
> Order Form for Grateful Med

Or connect via the World Wide Web to http://www.nlm.nih.gov and select Online Information Services. Forms and information are available under MEDLARS.

You will also need either direct connection to the Internet or a good modem; a list of local telephone numbers is provided with your account number.

In 1997, the National Library of Medicine began a trial program allowing free MEDLINE access. The Website for this is

http://www.nlm.gov/databases/freemedl.html

You do not need any special software for searches other than your Web browser. As long as this continues, it is unnecessary to go through the trouble of opening a personal account and installing special software.

Glossary

This glossary is intended to clarify words and terms used in this book and closely related terms that may not be familiar to nonscientists or to scientists in other fields. The items are explanations rather than rigorous definitions.

ACUTE   Of short duration; short and relatively severe. Frequently used in describing illness.

ADIPOSE TISSUE   Tissue composed of fat cells.

AFLAVTOXINS   Toxins produced by a widely distributed fungus, which can damage the liver and cause cancer.

ALPHA-TOCOPHEROL   Most potent chemical form of vitamin E.

AMINO ACIDS   Nitrogen-containing organic compounds that link together in many different combinations to form the various proteins. Chemically, amino acids contain the amino group (NH_2) and the carboxyl ($COOH$) group.

ANABOLISM   Metabolic processes that synthesize or build up (see CATABOLISM).

ANALGESIC   Relieving pain.

ANECDOTAL   Based on isolated observations rather than controlled scientific studies.

ANEMIA   Abnormal blood condition characterized by low number of red blood cells, low hemoglobin, or both.

ANGINA   Pain in upper chest and choking feeling caused by lack of oxygen being delivered to the heart. The pain usually radiates down the inner side of the left arm.

ANOREXIA   Loss of appetite resulting in decreased consumption of food.

ANTIBODY   Specialized protein produced by the immune system to fight a foreign substance by binding to a specific portion of it, called an antigen.

ANTIGEN   The portion of a foreign substance (almost always a protein) that the immune system recognizes and reacts to.

ANTIOXIDANT   Any substance that prevents oxidation or interrupts an oxidative sequence. This can be by: removing oxygen; inactivating key intermediaries; removing a metal essential to the sequence; scavenging the initiating or intermediate free radicals.

AORTA   The large artery directly connected to the heart.

ARTERY   Any of the vessels through which the heart pumps blood to the various tissues of the body.

ASCORBIC ACID   Most common form of vitamin C.

ATHEROSCLEROSIS   Deposition of lipid with proliferation of cells in the inner walls of the arteries.

AUTOIMMUNE DISEASE   Any of the diseases in which the body's immune system attacks the body's own tissue, as in rheumatoid arthritis and lupus.

B CELL   A type of lymphocyte that changes into an active cell upon encountering a foreign substance (antigen); it then manufactures specific proteins, called antibodies, against that antigen, and interacts with other immune cells in ways critical to immune function.

BASAL METABOLIC RATE   The amount of energy produced or needed by the body to maintain life when at rest.

BERIBERI   Disease caused by insufficient thiamin (vitamin B1) in the diet.

BETA-CAROTENE   Widely distributed carotenoid that is converted into vitamin A in the human intestine; also of interest as an antioxidant and for possible therapeutic purposes.

BHA   Butylated hydroxyanisole; a lipid-soluble, synthetic antioxidant, commonly used as a preservative.

BHT   Butylated hydroxytoluene; a lipid-soluble, synthetic antioxidant, commonly used as a preservative.

BIOFLAVONOID   A group of chemically related, colored substances found in many fruits, essential for the body's utilization of ascorbic acid (vitamin C).

BLOOD PLASMA   The liquid portion of blood, containing no blood cells or platelets.

BLOOD SERUM   The liquid portion of blood, containing no blood cells, platelets, or clotting proteins.

BODY MASS INDEX (BMI)   A mathematical construct that measures how close a person is to normal weight for his or her height; equal to body weight in kilograms divided by the square of the height in meters.

BRAN   The outer shell covering each individual grain of cereals such as wheat, rye, and oats; removed when whole grains are processed into white flour. Contains substantial amounts of dietary fiber, plus other nutrients.

BUFFER   A substance that prevents a solution from becoming too acid or too alkaline.

CALORIE   1) In science, the amount of energy needed to raise the temperature of one gram of water one degree C. 2) In common usage, one thousand of the units as defined in 1, used as a measure of the energy available from food; abbreviated Cal or kcal.

CAPILLARY   The smallest of the blood vessels; oxygen, nutrients, and other substances are exchanged between the bloodstream and tissues through capillary walls, which are just one cell thick.

CANCER   A disease characterized by uncontrolled growth of cells that tend to invade surrounding tissue.

CANTHAXANTHIN   Carotenoid widely distributed in plants. Has antioxidant properties like beta-carotene, but cannot be converted into vitamin A in the body. Sometimes used as an orange food coloring or an oral suntanning agent.

CARBOHYDRATES   Any of the group of organic compounds composed of carbon, hydrogen, and oxygen, including sugars, starches, and cellulose.

CARBON   Chemical element, symbol C, that binds to other carbon atoms and to other elements, so forming the basis of all life.

CARCINOGEN   Anything that causes cancer.

CARCINOMA   Cancer arising from any of the epithelial tissues of the body.

CARDIAC   Pertaining to the heart.

CARDIAC OUTPUT   The volume of blood expelled by the heart per unit of time.

CARDIOVASCULAR   Pertaining to the heart and blood vessels.

CARDIOVASCULAR DISEASE   Any of the diseases of the heart or blood vessels, including atherosclerosis, systemic hypertension, and rheumatic heart disease.

CAROTENOID   Any of a group of red, yellow, or orange pigments chemically related to retinoids and found in many plants, including carrots, sweet potatoes, and many leafy vegetables.

CASE-CONTROL STUDY   A technique used in epidemiologic studies in which cases are those individuals who have a certain disease, and controls are individuals from the same population who do not have the disease. Differences between the groups are then analyzed to find possible causes of the disease.

CATABOLISM   Metabolic processes that break down substances (see ANABOLISM).

CATALASE   An antioxidant enzyme produced naturally in humans, plants, and many other organisms as one of the prime defenses against free radical damage.

CATARACT   An opacity in the normally transparent lens of the eye that impairs the transmission of light through the lens.

CELL   The fundamental unit of all living things; in higher organisms, specialized into many different types depending on the tissue and the cell's place in it.

CELL DIVISION   The process by which a cell divides in two, and thus by which cells proliferate; the resultant cells may grow and divide themselves, or differentiate into specialized functional units.

CELLULOSE   The main polysaccharide in living plants, forming the plant cell wall; a common dietary fiber.

CHRONIC   Long-continued; of long duration.

COLLAGEN   Protein that makes up a large part of the connective tissue throughout the body.

CONGESTIVE HEART FAILURE   Condition that results when the heart is unable to pump enough blood to meet the body's needs; frequently characterized by fluid collecting in various parts of the body, commonly the lungs and legs.

CORONARY ARTERY   Either of two arteries that branch from the aorta to supply blood to the heart itself.

CORONARY ARTERY DISEASE   Any abnormal condition in the arteries of the heart, especially those that result in narrowing of the artery and reduced delivery of oxygen and nutrients to the heart.

CORTICOSTEROID   Steroid hormones secreted by the cortex of the adrenal gland to regulate the metabolism of nutrients, electrolytes, and water.

CROSSOVER EXPERIMENT   A study during which the treatment being given any particular group is changed to the treatment of another group until all groups have received all treatments; in its simplest form, if there are two groups, group A being given a drug and group B a placebo, group A would be switched to the placebo and group B to the drug.

CRUDE FIBER   Obsolescent term for the nondigestible portion of food; refers to the part of food remaining after harsh chemical treatments to extract the digestible portions, which only approximates actual dietary fiber, the more modern term.

DHEA (DEHYDROEPIANDROSONE)   Steroid hormone produced naturally by the body. Its concentration in the blood declines steadily and sharply with age.

DIASTOLIC BLOOD PRESSURE   Blood pressure when the large chambers of the heart are filling with blood between contractions; the lower figure of the two numbers given in a blood pressure reading.

DIETARY FIBER   The nondigestible part of food.

DIURETIC   A substance that increases the volume of urine.

DNA   The very large molecules that carry genetic information and specify how each cell functions.

DYSPLASIA   Abnormal development or condition of tissue and cells.

EDEMA   Swelling caused by the excessive transfer of fluid from the bloodstream into surrounding tissue.

ELASTIN   An elastic protein found especially in connective tissue.

EMULSIFIER   A substance that breaks down large fat globules into many smaller ones, thus producing a finer, uniform mixture of fat in water (not a true solution). This process is used by the body during digestion to give the digestive enzymes a greater area of fat to work on; it is also common in the preparation of commercial packaged foods.

ENZYMES   Organic molecules that specify and enable the many different chemical reactions essential to life in cells through the organism, without being changed themselves in the process.

EPIDEMIOLOGY   The study of the frequencies of occurrence of diseases and related conditions among natural populations (i.e., outside a laboratory, experimental setting); frequently makes use of sophisticated statistical analysis to extract relations from large amounts of data.

EPITHELIAL   Referring to the layer of tissue covering the internal and external organs of the body, including the lining of the blood and other vessels; includes the skin, the linings of the gastrointestinal tract, mucous membranes, the lining of the bladder, etc.

ESOPHAGUS   The tube through which food passes from the back of the throat to the stomach.

ESSENTIAL   As applied to nutrients, any substance required by an animal for normal function that must be supplied in the diet. Some vitamins, for example, can be made by the body but not at a rate sufficient for its requirements; other nutrients, such as some amino acids, are required but can be synthesized from other chemicals by the body in sufficient quantities to meet its needs, so are nonessential.

ESTROGENS   Steroid hormones that promote the development of female sex characteristics. Human estrogen is produced in the ovaries and, to some extent, in the adrenal glands. Smaller amounts are produced in the male testes.

ETHANOL (ethyl alcohol)   The common, potable alcohol found in alcoholic beverages, and also used as a topical disinfectant.

ETIOLOGY   The cause or factors involved in the development of a disease.

FATTY ACID   A component of a molecule of fat, consisting of carbon atoms bound to each other in a chain and hydrogen atoms bound to the carbons. The carbons can all be connected by single bonds, or the chain can include one or more double bonds, leaving fewer bonds for hydrogens; in the latter case the fatty acid is said to be unsaturated.

FERMENTATION   Chemical transformation, usually of carbohydrates, accompanied by release of a gas such as carbon dioxide; this process is usually due to the activity of microorganisms like bacteria, yeasts, or mold.

FOLACIN   B vitamin (therefore water soluble), sometimes referred to as folate or folic acid, required for cell division and the maturation of new cells.

FREE RADICAL   An atom or molecule having an unpaired electron, and hence highly reactive chemically.

FRUCTOSE   A monosaccharide, or simple sugar, consisting of just one of the basic units of carbohydrates; found in fruits, honey, and other natural substances.

FRUIT   In botany, a fully matured plant ovary that contains the seeds capable of growing into a new plant. The common fruits, such as apples and peaches, are included in this classification, and also items like squash, cucumbers, eggplant, and tomatoes, which, while usually thought of as vegetables, are essentially the same as other fruits.

GASTRIC   Pertaining to the stomach.

GASTROINTESTINAL   Pertaining to the organs of the digestive tract, including therefore the stomach and intestines.

GERIATRICS   The branch of medicine that deals with the treatment of elderly people.

GERONTOLOGY   The study of the aging process in living things.

GLUCAGON   A hormone that raises blood glucose levels by promoting the conversion of stored carbohydrates in the liver into glucose.

GLUCOSE   A monosaccharide, or simple sugar, consisting of just one of the basic units of carbohydrates; found naturally in many foods and in the bloodstream, where it is transported to cells as their normal energy source.

GLUTATHIONE   A short chain of just three amino acids, including a sulfur-hydrogen group; a part of the glutathione peroxidase enzyme protective system, and an antioxidant in itself.

GLUTATHIONE PEROXIDASE   A widely distributed intracellular enzyme containing selenium as an essential component. Its functions are to protect against oxidative damage by removing hydrogen peroxide and lipid peroxides, and to detoxify other potentially harmful substances.

GLUTEN   A class of proteins occurring in the seeds of certain cereals; it is the high gluten content of wheat that gives bread its elastic texture.

GLYCOGEN   A carbohydrate found in muscle and liver cells of humans and other animals; it serves as the body's immediate reserve of energy, being converted to blood sugar as needed.

GRAM   A measure of small weights, equal to 0.0353 ounces, about the weight of two small paper clips.

GUMS   A common soluble dietary fiber derived from plant cell secretions.

HEMICELLULOSE   A common type or group of dietary fiber, mostly insoluble, derived from plant cell walls and secretions.

HEMOGLOBIN   Iron-containing protein in red blood cells that transports oxygen.

HEMORRHAGE   Rapid loss of a large amount of blood, either externally or internally.

HEPATITIS   Inflammation of the liver, which may be caused by viral, bacterial, or parasitic infection or by drugs, excess alcohol, or toxins.

HIGH-DENSITY LIPOPROTEIN (HDL)   A blood protein containing about 50 percent protein, with cholesterol and triglycerides; involved in transporting cholesterol and other lipids from the blood to certain organs.

HYDROXYL RADICAL   The combination of oxygen and hydrogen with an unpaired electron, highly chemically reactive and thought to be involved in many damaging reactions and disease processes.

HYPERTENSION   A disease in which the blood pressure is persistently high.

IMMUNE SYSTEM   The system or group of specialized organs, tissues, and cells in humans and other organisms that protects the organism by recognizing foreign proteins and consequently destroying bacteria, viruses, and, in some cases, cancer cells.

INCONTINENCE   Inability to retain urine or other excretions.

INFARCT   An area of dead tissue, usually caused by an interruption in the blood supply to that area.

INFARCTION   An infarct; the development of an infarct.

INORGANIC   In chemistry, a compound that does not contain carbon.

INSULIN   A hormone that regulates glucose levels in the blood by promoting its transfer from the blood into muscle and other cells.

INTESTINE   The long, tubular portion of the digestive tract extending from the stomach to the anus; digestion and absorption of nutrients are completed in the small intestine, which is smaller in diameter but much longer than the large intestine.

ION   An atom or molecule with a net electric charge.

IONIZING RADIATION   Particles or electromagnetic waves that have sufficient energy to produce ionization, that is, to knock an electron off an atom in passing through a material; in cells, this results in the formation of free radicals that can damage DNA and other components.

ISCHEMIA   Decreased blood supply to some portion of tissue, often accompanied by pain.

ISOTRETINOIN   A retinoid (13-*cis*-retinoic acid) used to treat severe acne and being investigated as an anticancer agent.

LACTOSE   The sugar that constitutes the carbohydrate portion of milk; a disaccharide formed from the monosaccharides glucose and galactose.

LECITHIN   One of a group of lipidlike substances called phospholipids, composed of fatty acids and glycerol, choline, and phosphoric acid. A molecule of lecithin consequently has a lipid-soluble portion and a water-soluble portion. Found in a number of plant and animal tissues, it is used commercially as an emulsifier.

LENS   Transparent structure at front of the eye that focuses incoming light much like the lens of a camera.

LEUKOCYTES   White blood cells, which are actually colorless, the primary effectors of the immune system.

LIGNIN   An insoluble fiber and the only common fiber that is not a carbohydrate.

LIPIDS   Fats and fatlike substances, including: 1) the common fats, or triglycerides, 2) sterols like cholesterol, steroid hormones, and bile acids, 3) similar substances like waxes and forms of vitamin A and vitamin D.

LIPID-SOLUBLE   Property of a substance by which it dissolves readily in lipids (like oils), and generally implying that the substance dissolves little if at all in water and similar solvents.

LINOLEIC ACID   One of the most common unsaturated fatty acids in plants and an essential nutrient for humans.

LIPOFUSCIN   A yellow-brown substance that accumulates with age in cells in the skin, heart muscle, and other tissues, giving rise to the "age spots" common in the elderly.

LOW-DENSITY LIPOPROTEIN (LDL)   A blood protein containing relatively more cholesterol and triglycerides than protein; thought to be involved in the deposition of lipids in blood vessels that occurs in atherosclerosis.

LYMPH   Fluid containing white blood cells, mainly lymphocytes, that circulates throughout the body via the lymphatic system.

LYMPHATIC SYSTEM   A large, complex network of thin vessels, valves, ducts, and nodes through which lymph is transported throughout the body. It includes specialized organs such as the tonsils and the spleen, and connects with the blood circulation at a duct in the upper chest.

LYMPHOCYTES   A group of white blood cells (leukocytes), including T and B cells, and natural killer (NK) cells, that constitutes a major part of the immune system.

MACROPHAGE   Immune system cell that engulfs and "eats" foreign cells and substances; macrophages also secrete many chemical mediators of immune function. Some circulate throughout the body in the blood and lymph, while others take up residence in certain organs.

MACULA (macula lutea)   Area of the retina of the eye with maximum visual acuity.

MAXIMUM OXYGEN UPTAKE   The maximum rate at which oxygen can be delivered and utilized by the body, usually normalized to body weight (i.e., milliliters of oxygen per minute per kilogram). A measure of overall fitness.

MEAN   A common measurement of the average, computed by adding all measurements and dividing by the number of measurements. As applied to life span of a group, the age at death of each individual is added, and this sum is divided by the number of individuals in the group.

MEDIAN   Measurement of average by the 50th percentile; there are as many points above this value as below it. As applied to life span of a group, the age at which half of its members have died and half are still alive.

MELATONIN   Hormone produced by the pineal gland, which is located in the brain. It is known to be related to proper sleep, and may have other functions.

MERCAPTOETHANOL   A sulfhydryl compound commonly used in laboratories as an antioxidant.

MET   Metabolic equivalent; the energy expended by the body while sitting quietly, equivalent to about 3.5mL of oxygen uptake per kilogram of body weight per minute for an adult.

Energy expenditures can be measured in terms of MET as an alternative to calories per hour per unit of body weight.

METABOLISM   The physical and chemical processes by which nutrients are transformed into simple substances and synthesized into complex ones, thereby making energy available to the organism.

METASTASIS   The process by which tumor cells spread to distant parts of the body by being transported through the lymphatic circulation or in the bloodstream.

MICROGRAM (μg or mcg)   One millionth of a gram; unit used to measure very small quantities such as nutrients needed in trace amounts.

MILLIGRAM (mg)   One thousandth (milli) of a gram; unit commonly used to measure vitamins, minerals, and other small quantities.

MILLILITER (mL)   One thousandth of a liter, a measure of small volumes; 15mL are equivalent to 1 tablespoon; 29.6mL = 1 fluid ounce.

MINERAL   An inorganic substance having a fairly definite chemical and physical structure; in nutrition, usually referred to by the name of the essential element in the mineral, such as iron or calcium, which is almost always combined with other elements.

MORBIDITY   The incidence of an illness or abnormality in a population; that is, the number of people with the condition divided by the total number of people in the population.

MORTALITY   The death rate; the number of deaths per unit of population in a given time period.

MUCILAGES   Type of soluble dietary fiber similar to gums.

MUTAGEN   Anything that alters the genetic material (DNA), thereby increasing the rate of genetic change.

MYOCARDIAL INFARCTION   An occlusion (blockage) of a coronary artery, caused by atherosclerosis or a clot (embolism).

NATURAL KILLER (NK) CELL   A type of white blood cell that recognizes and kills cancer cells, virus-infected cells, and other kinds of abnormal cells. Unlike most immune system cells, NK cells do not need specific sensitization by prior exposure to foreign proteins; they will attack cells that they recognize as foreign at their first encounter. NK cells are also able to proliferate in response to such encounters and are thought to be one of the body's main defenses against cancer.

NEOPLASM   Any abnormal growth of new tissue, benign or malignant (cancerous).

NIACIN   B vitamin needed in the body's metabolic processes; water soluble, as are all the B vitamins.

ORGANIC   In chemistry, any compound containing carbon.

OSTEOPOROSIS   A disorder characterized by loss of bone mass; as the bones become more porous, fractures, pain in the lower back, and various deformities may occur.

PANTOTHENIC ACID   B vitamin needed in metabolic processes; water soluble, as are all the B vitamins.

PANCREAS   Glandular organ situated below the stomach; produces digestive juices that are funneled to the small intestine, plus the hormones insulin and glucagon, which regulate blood sugar levels.

PAP TEST   A screening test for cervical cancer in which cells are scraped from the surface of the cervix, prepared on a slide, and examined under a microscope.

PECTIN   A dietary fiber, mostly soluble, abundant in plant cell walls.

PELLAGRA   Disease caused by deficiency of niacin, characterized by dermatitis, diarrhea, and dementia.

PLACEBO   A therapeutically inactive substance such as salt, water, or sugar usually used as a control in place of a substance being tested.

PLASMA   See BLOOD PLASMA.

PLATELETS   A type of cell fragment essential for the clotting of blood that circulates in the bloodstream.

POLYSACCHARIDE   A carbohydrate composed of many simple carbohydrate units (monosaccharides) linked together.

POLYUNSATURATED FATTY ACID   A fatty acid in which two or more of the bonds between carbon atoms are double bonds. This leaves one less bond available on each of these carbon atoms to bind hydrogen, so the fatty acid has fewer hydrogen atoms at each of these bonds and fewer overall than an equal-length saturated fatty acid or one with just one double bond.

PROGESTERONE   Hormone produced in the female during the menstrual cycle to prepare the uterus for pregnancy; natural and synthetic types are used therapeutically in the treatment of menstrual disorders and other conditions.

PROSTATE   A gland associated with the male reproductive system that frequently undergoes enlargement, benign or malignant, in later life.

PROTEIN   Organic compound composed of amino acids joined by peptide bonds into a chain, which usually curves into a specific shape; proteins make up the building materials and regulatory molecules of living things.

RECOMMENDED DIETARY ALLOWANCE (RDA)   The average daily amount of a nutrient that a healthy person should consume in the diet to maintain normal health. In the United States, the RDA has been traditionally determined by a committee of the National Academy of Sciences.

RELATIVE RISK   The ratio of the incidence of a disease or condition in a certain group to the incidence in some control group; for example the incidence of lung cancer among smokers divided by the incidence in nonsmokers.

RETIN-A   The brand name of the topical preparation of tretinoin used to treat skin disorders and photoaged skin.

RETINA   The structure covering the back of the eye onto which light is focused; the retina converts this light into nerve impulses and relays it to the brain.

RETINOIC ACID   Retinoid that can satisfy some, but not all, of the body's requirements for vitamin A. The term is sometimes used to refer to all-*trans*-retinoic acid, which is one form of retinoic acid.

RETROSPECTIVE STUDY   A study in which a search is made for a relationship between a current disease or condition and one that occurred in the past (e.g., a study of cancer incidence in the population now and the dietary habits of those studied over the past ten years).

RIBOFLAVIN   B vitamin needed especially for the metabolism of proteins.

SARCOMA   Cancer arising from the soft tissue, bone, or connective tissue, including muscle and fatty tissue; much less common than carcinomas.

SCURVY   Deficiency disease caused by lack of vitamin C in the diet, characterized by weakness, bleeding gums, tenderness to touch, and many small hemorrhages.

SELENATE   Common shorthand for the inorganic compound sodium selenate (Na_2SeO_4).

SELENITE   Common shorthand for the inorganic compound sodium selenite (Na_2SeO_3), probably the most extensively studied form of selenium.

SELENOCYSTEINE   An organic compound consisting of the amino acid cysteine with selenium incorporated into it; this is the chemical form in which selenium is utilized in the important enzyme glutathione peroxidase.

SELENOMETHIONINE   An organic compound consisting of the amino acid methionine with selenium incorporated into it; this is a very common form in which selenium is found in foods and other organic matter.

SERUM   See BLOOD SERUM.

SKELETAL MUSCLE   Any of the muscles that are attached to bone, under voluntary control, and used to move the body parts, as distinct from heart muscle and the smooth muscle around many structures, which usually function without voluntary control.

SODIUM SELENITE   See SELENITE.

STROKE   Loss of consciousness followed by paralysis caused by a clot cutting off the blood supply to the brain, or by rupture of a blood vessel with resulting hemorrhage into or around the brain.

SYSTOLIC BLOOD PRESSURE   Blood pressure when the large chambers of the heart are contracting and therefore pumping blood into the arteries; the higher figure in a blood pressure reading.

SUCROSE   Common table sugar; a disaccharide formed from the monosaccharides glucose and fructose.

SULFHYDRYL   An atom of sulfur bound to an atom of hydrogen, or a compound containing such a combination; this arrangement occurs in many substances of biological importance, such as glutathione and the amino acid cysteine.

T CELL   A type of lymphocyte extremely important in immune function, especially its response to foreign cells. For example, viral infection of the body triggers the generation of a population of T cells that specifically kill cells infected with that virus.

THIAMIN   Water-soluble vitamin, sometimes called vitamin B1, essential to the body's metabolic processes in which energy is extracted from food.

THIOL   A compound containing a sulfhydryl group.

THROMBOSIS   An abnormal condition in which a thrombus develops.

THROMBUS   A blood clot attached to the interior wall of a vein or artery, thus partially or completely blocking the blood vessel.

THYMUS   Immune system gland located in the upper chest behind the breastbone, crucial in the maturation of T cells; large in young adults, it shrinks steadily after maturity.

TISSUE CULTURE   The growth of cells in a nutritive medium in the laboratory, that is, outside of any animal or other organism. Cells derived from a tissue sample from an animal, including human, can be grown to many times their original number, providing a simple, clearly defined model for many studies.

TRACE ELEMENT   An element essential to normal body function but only needed in very small amounts in the diet.

TRETINOIN   A retinoid (all-*trans*-retinoic acid) used to treat skin disorders. The topical preparation can reverse photodamage of the skin. See RETIN-A.

TRIGLYCERIDE   The common fat molecule, formed from glycerol and three fatty acids.

UNSATURATED FATTY ACID   A fatty acid in which at least one of the bonds between carbon atoms is a double bond. This leaves one less bond available on each of these two carbon atoms to bind hydrogen, so the fatty acid has fewer hydrogen atoms, or is "unsaturated."

VERTEBRA   Any of the bony segments of the spinal column (plural vertebrae).

VIRUS   A particle consisting of genetic material (DNA or RNA) usually wrapped in protein and sometimes lipid. Outside a cell, a virus does not have any metabolism or any of the processes associated with life; once it penetrates a living cell, it uses the cell's chemical machinery to produce more viruses, usually killing or incapacitating the cell in the process.

VITAL CAPACITY   A measurement of the amount of air that can be expelled from the lungs after a maximum inhalation.

VITAMIN   An organic compound present in very small quantities in foods and essential for the normal processes of the body.

VITAMIN A   A fat-soluble vitamin essential for growth, maintenance of healthy skin and other epithelial tissues, and vision. Chemically consists of several retinols with various levels of vitamin A potency. For this reason, vitamin A is measured in international units (IU), defined as 0.3µg of all-*trans*-retinol, or in "retinol equivalents" (RE), defined as 1µg of all-*trans*-retinol. Humans can convert beta-carotene into vitamin A as needed, 6µg of beta-carotene being equivalent to 1µg of retinol.

VITAMIN B6   Water-soluble vitamin needed in many metabolic processes and thought to have an essential role in a number of other functions; sometimes referred to as pyridoxine, the most common form.

VITAMIN B12   Water-soluble vitamin, sometimes called cobalamin, best known for its essential role in the formation of red blood cells.

VITAMIN C   Water-soluble vitamin essential for the maintenance of the body's connective tissue and for many other crucial biochemical processes.

VITAMIN D   Fat-soluble vitamin related to the steroids; essential to the formation of bones and teeth, and for the absorption of calcium; the common form is calciferol.

VITAMIN E   A group of fat-soluble substances, including alpha-tocopherol, the most common, and other tocopherols, which function as antioxidants in the body.

VITAMIN K   Fat-soluble vitamin necessary for blood clotting.

Bibliography

Ader, R. On the clinical relevance of psychoneuroimmunology. *Clin Immunol Immunopathol* 64:6–8, 1991.

Albanes, D. Caloric intake, body weight and cancer: a review. *Nutr Cancer* 9:199–217, 1987.

Alpha-tocopherol, Beta-carotene Cancer Prevention Study Group. The effect of vitamin E and beta-carotene on the incidence of lung cancer and other cancers in male smokers. *N Engl J Med* 330:1029–1035, 1994.

American College of Sports Medicine. The recommended quantity and quality of exercise for developing and maintaining cardiorespiratory and muscular fitness in healthy adults. *Med Sci Sports Exercise* 22:265–274, 1990.

American Dietetic Association. Position on the use of nutritive and nonnutritive sweeteners. *J Am Diet Assoc* 93:816–821, 1993.

Ames, B.N. Dietary carcinogens and anticarcinogens. *Science* 221:1256–1264, 1983.

_____; Shigenaga, M.K.; and Hagen, T.M. Oxidants, antioxidants, and the degenerative diseases of aging. *Proc Natl Acad Sci USA* 90:7915–7922, 1993.

Anderson, J.W., et al. Bakery products lower serum cholesterol concentrations in hypercholesterolemic men. *Am J Clin Nutr* 54:836–840, 1991.

_____, et al. Hypocholesterolemic effects of oat-bran or bean intake for hypercholesterolemic men. *Am J Clin Nutr* 40:1146–1155, 1984.

_____, and Gustafson, N.J. Hypocholesterolemic effects of oat and bean products. *Am J Clin Nutr* 48:749–753, 1988.

Arsenian, M.A. Magnesium and cardiovascular disease. *Prog Cardiovasc Dis* 35:271–310, 1993.

Artand-Wild, S.M., et al. Differences in coronary mortality can be explained by differences in cholesterol and saturated fat intakes in 40 countries but not in France and Finland: a paradox. *Circulation* 88:2771–2779, 1993

Avioli, L.V. Calcium supplementation and osteoporosis. In *Nutritional Intervention in the Aging Process*. H.J. Armbrect, J.M. Prendergast, and R.M. Loe, eds. New York: Springer-Verlag, 1984.

Bak, A.A., and Grobee, D.E.. Caffeine, blood pressure and serum lipids. *Am J Clin Nutr* 53:971–975, 1991.

Barkan, G.A., et al. Body weight and coronary disease risk: patterns of risk factor change associated with long-term weight change. *Am J Epidemiol* 124:410–419, 1986.

Barrows, C.H., and Roeder, L.M. Nutrition. In: *Handbook of the Biology of Aging*. C.E. Finch and L. Hayflick, eds. New York: Van Nostrand, 1977.

Batist, G., et al. Selenium-induced cytotoxicity of human leukemic cells: interaction with reduced glutathione. *Cancer Res* 46:5482–5485, 1986.

Beilin, L.J. Dietary salt and risk factors for cardiovascular disease. *Kidney Int Suppl* 37:S90–S96, 1992.

Bendich, A. Carotenoids and the immune response. *J Nutr* 119:112–115, 1989.

_____. Symposium conclusions: biological actions of carotenoids. *J Nutr* 119:135–136, 1989.

_____. Vitamin C and immune responses. *Food Technol* 41:112–114, 1987.

Berlin, J.A., and Colditz, G.A. A meta-analysis of physical activity in the prevention of coronary heart disease. *Am J Epidemiol* 132:612–628, 1990.

Berstein, L., et al. Physical exercise and reduced risk of breast cancer in young women. *JNCI* 86:1403–1408, 1994.

Bjorksten, J. The crosslinkage theory of aging. *J Am Geriat Soc* 16:408–427, 1968.

Bjorntorp, P., and Evans, W.J. The effect of exercise and diet on body composition. In *Body Composition: The Measure and Meaning of Changes With Age.* J. Watkins et al., eds. Boston: Foundation for Nutritional Advancement, 1992.

Blair, S.N., et al. Physical fitness and all-cause mortality: a prospective study of healthy men and women. *JAMA* 262:2395–2401, 1989.

Block, G. The data support a role for antioxidants in reducing cancer risk. *Nutr Rev* 50:207–213, 1992.

———. Vitamin C and cancer prevention: the epidemiologic evidence. *Am J Clin Nutr* 53: 270S–282S, 1991.

Blodgett, D.J.; Schurig, G.G.; and Kornegay, E.T. Immunomodulation in weanling swine with dietary selenium. *Am J Vet Res* 47:1517–1519, 1986.

Blot, W.J., et al. Nutrition intervention trials in Linxian, China: supplementation with specific vitamin/mineral combinations, cancer incidence, and disease-specific mortality in the general population. *JNCI* 85:1483–1492, 1992.

Bomhard, E.M.; Bremmer, J.N.; and Herbold, B.A. Review of the mutagenicity/genotoxicity of butylated hydroxytoluene. *Mutation Res* 277:187–200, 1992.

Breitman, T.R.; Selomick, S.E.; and Collins, S.J. Induction of differentiation of the human promyelocytic leukemia cell line (HL-60) by retinoic acid. *Proc Natl Acad Sci USA* 77: 2936–2940, 1980.

Brenner, B.M.; Meyer, T.W.; and Hostetter, T.H. Dietary protein intake and the progressive nature of kidney disease. *N Eng J Med* 307:652–659, 1982.

Bunker, M.L., and McWilliams, M. Caffeine content of common beverages. *J Am Diet Assoc* 74:28–32, 1979.

Bunker, V.W., and Clayton, B.E. Selenium status in disease: the role of selenium as a therapeutic agent. *Br J Clin Pract* 44:401–403, 1990.

Burton, G.W. Antioxidant action of carotenoids. *J Nutr* 119:109–111, 1989.

Butchko, H.H., and Kotsonis, F.N. Acceptable intake vs actual intake: the aspartame example. *J Am Coll Nutr* 10:258–266, 1991.

Butterworth, C.E., et al. Folate deficiency and cervical dysplasia. *JAMA* 267:528–533, 1992.

Caderni, G.; Bianchina, F.; Dolara, P.; and Kriebel, D. Proliferation activity in the colon of the mouse and its modulation by dietary starch, fat and cellulose. *Cancer Res* 49: 1655–1659, 1989.

Calcium and vitamin D intakes influence the risk of bowel cancer in men. *Nutr Rev* 43: 170–172, 1985.

Calvo, M.S. Dietary phosphorus, calcium metabolism and bone loss. *J Nutr* 123:1627–1633, 1993.

Casaburi, R. Physiologic responses to training. *Clin Chest Med* 15(2):215–227, 1994.

Castelli, W.P., et al. Summary estimate of cholesterol used to predict coronary artery disease. *Circulation* 67:730–734, 1983.

Centers for Disease Control and Prevention. Public health focus: physical activity and the prevention of coronary heart disease. *JAMA* 270:1529–1530, 1993.

Chesnut, C.H. Bone mass and exercise. *Am J Med* 95(5A):34S–36S, 1993.

Chipault, J.R., et al. Antioxidant properties of spices in oil-in-water emulsions. *Food Res* 20:443–446, 1955.

Chopra, J.G.; Forbes, A.L.; and Habicht, J.P. Protein in the U.S. diet. *J Am Diet Assoc* 72:253–258, 1978.

Chu, J,; Schweid, A.; and Weiss, N.S. Survival among women with endometrial cancer; a comparison of estrogen users and non-users. *Am J Obstet Gynecol* 143:569–575, 1982.

Clapp, N.K.; Satterfield, L.C.; and Bowles, N.D. Effects of the antioxidant butylated hydroxytoluene (BHT) on mortality in BALB/c mice. *J Gerontol* 34:497–501, 1979.

Clifford, C., and Kramer, B. Diet as risk and therapy for cancer. *Med Clin North Am* 77: 725–744, 1993.

Cohn, S.H., et al. Changes in body chemical composition with age measured by total-body neutron activation. *Metabolism* 25:89–96, 1976.

Colditz, G.A., et al. The use of estrogen and progestins and the risk of breast cancer in post-menopausal women. *N Engl J Med* 332:1589–1593, 1995.

Combs, C.F., and Combs, S.B. The nutritional biochemistry of selenium. *Ann Rev Nutr* 4:257–280, 1984.

Comfort, A. Effect of ethoxyquin on the longevity of C3H mice. *Nature* 229:254–255, 1971.

Dalen, J.E. An apple a day or an aspirin a day? *Arch Intern Med* 151:1066–1069, 1991.

Davidson, D.M., and Gold, K.V. Cardiovascular effects of n-3 fatty acids. *N Engl J Med* 319:580, 1988.

Devine, J., and Williams, P.N. *The Chemistry and Technology of Edible Oils and Fats.* Permagon Press, New York, 1961.

Di Mascio, P.; Murphy, M.E.; and Sies, H. Antioxidant defense systems: the role of carotenoids, tocopherols, and thiols. *Am J Clin Nutr* 53:194S–200S, 1991.

Diplock, A.T. Antioxidant nutrients and disease prevention: an overview. *Am J Clin Nutr* 53:189S–193S, 1991.

Doll, R. Tobacco: an overview of health effects. In *Tobacco: A Major International Health Hazard.* D.G. Zaridze and R. Peto, eds. Lyon: IARC, 1986.

Dorgan, J.F.; Brown, C.; and Barrett, M., et al.. Physical activity and risk of breast cancer in the Framingham Heart Study. *Am J Epidemiol* 139:662–669, 1994.

Dreon, D.M.; Vranizan, K.M.; and Krauss, R.M., et al. The effects of polyunsaturated vs. monounsaturated fat on plasma lipoproteins. *JAMA* 263:2462–2466, 1990.

Edington, D.; Cosmas, A.; and McCafferty, W. Exercise and longevity: evidence for a threshold age. *J Gerontol* 27:341–343, 1972.

Eichner, E.R. Exercise, lymphokines, calories and cancer. *Physician Sportsmed* 15:109–116, 1987.

Ellis, C.N., et al. Sustained improvements with prolonged topical tretinoin (retinoic acid) for photoaged skin. *J Am Acad Dermatol* 23:629–637, 1990.

Esterbauer, H.; Dieber-Rotheneder, M.; Striegel, G.; and Waeg, G. Role of vitamin E in preventing the oxidation of low-density lipoprotein. *Am J Clin Nutr* 53:314S–321S, 1991.

Evans, W.J. Exercise, nutrition and aging. *J Nutr* 122:796–801, 1992.

Fan, A.M., and Kizer, K.W. Selenium. Nutritional, toxilogic, and clinical aspects. *West J Med* 153:160–167, 1990.

Farnes, S.W., and Setness, P.A. Retinoid therapy for aging skin and acne. *Postgrad Med* 92 (6):191–200, 1992.

Fentem, P.H. Exercise in prevention of disease. *Br Med Bull* 48:630–650,1992.

Fico, M.E., and Poirier, K.A., et al. Differential effects of selenium on normal and neoplastic canine mammary cells. *Cancer Res* 46:3384–3388, 1986.

Frei, B.; England, L.; and Ames, B.N. Ascorbate is an outstanding antioxidant in human blood plasma. *Proc Natl Acad Sci USA* 86:6377–6381, 1989.

Ganger, K.F.; Cust, M.; and Whitehead, M.I. Controversies in the use of hormone replacement therapy. In *New Techniques in Metabolic Bone Disease.* J.C. Stevenson, ed. London: Wright, 1990.

Gersten, J.W. Effect of exercise on muscle function decline with aging. *West J Med* 154: 579–582, 1991.

Gey, K.F.; Puska, P.; Jordan, P.; and Moser, U.K. Inverse correlation between plasma vitamin E and mortality from ischemic heart disease in cross-cultural epidemiology. *Am J Clin Nutr* 53:326S–334S, 1991.

Gilchrest, B.A. *Skin and Aging Processes.* Boca Raton FL: CRC, 1984.

Giovannucci, E., et al. Folate, methionine, and alcohol intake and risk of colorectal adenoma. *JNCI* 85:875–884, 1993.

_____, et al. A prospective study of dietary fat and risk of prostate cancer. *JNCI* 85: 1571–1579, 1993.

Glinsmann, W.H.; Irausquin, H.; and Park, Y.K. Evaluation of health aspects of sugars contained in carbohydrate sweeteners. *J Nutr* 116:S5–S216, 1986.

Golczewski, J.A., and Frenkel, G.D. Cellular selenoproteins and the effects of selenite on cell proliferation. *Biol Trace Elem Res* 20:115–126, 1989.

Goldfarb, R.H., and Herberman, R.B. Natural killer cell reactivity: regulatory interactions among phorbolester, interferon, cholera toxin, and retinoic acid. *J Immunol* 126:2129–2135, 1981.

Gonzales. M.J., et al. Lipid peroxidation products are elevated in fish oil diets even in the presence of added antioxidants. *J Nutr* 122:2190–2195, 1992.

Goodman, D.S. Vitamin A and retinoids in health and disease. *N Eng J Med* 310:1023–1031, 1984.

Goodrick, C.L. Effects of long-term voluntary wheel exercise on male and female Wistar rats. *Gerontology* 26:22–33, 1980.

_____, et al. Differential effects of intermittent feeding and voluntary wheel exercise on body weight and lifespan in adult rats. *J Gerontol* 38:36–45, 1983.

Graziano, J.M.; Manson, J.E.; and Buring, J.E., et al. Dietary antioxidants and cardiovascular disease. *Ann NY Acad Sci* 669:249–259, 1992.

Greeder, G.A., and Milner, J.A. Factors influencing the inhibitory effect of selenium on mice inoculated with Ehrlich ascites tumor cells. *Science* 209:825–827, 1980.

Greenwood, M.R.C., and Pittman-Waller, V.A. Weight control: a complex, various, and controversial problem. In *Obesity and Weight Control.* R.T. Frankle, and M. Yang, eds. Rockville MD: Aspen, 1988.

Guercio-Hauer, C.; Macfarlane, D.F.; and Delea, V.A. Photodamage, photoaging, and photoprotection of the skin. *Am Fam Physician* 50:327–334, Aug. 1994.

Hakama, M., and Saxen, E.A. Cereal consumption and gastric cancer. *Int J Cancer* 2:265–268, 1967.

Halliwell, B. Free radicals and antioxidants: a personal view. *Nutr Rev* 52:253–265, 1994.

Ham, W.T., et al. The involvement of the retinal pigment epithelium. In *Optical Radiation and Visual Health.* M. Waxler, and V.M. Hitchins, eds. Boca Raton FL: CRC, 1986.

Hammond, E.C., et al. Tar and nicotine content of cigarette smoke in relation to death rates. *Environ Res* 12:263–274, 1976.

D Harman. The aging process. *Proc Natl Acad Sci USA* 78:7124–7128, 1981.

_____. Free radical theory of aging. *Mutat Res* 275:257–266, 1992.

_____. Free radical theory of aging: effect of free radical inhibitors on the mortality of male LAF1 mice. *J Gerontol* 23:476–482, 1968.

Harris, S.B.; Weindruch, R.; Smith, G.S.; Mickey, M.R.; and Walford, R.L. Dietary restriction alone and in combination with oral ethoxyquin/2-mercaptoethylamine in mice. *J Gerontol* 45:B141–147, 1990.

Harward, M.P. Nutritive therapies for osteoporosis. the role of calcium. *Med Clin North Am* 77:889–898, 1993.

Hasling, C., et al. Calcium metabolism in postmenopausal osteoporotic women is determined by dietary calcium and coffee intake. *J Nutr* 122:1119–1126, 1992.

Heaney, R.P. Calcium, bone health and osteoporosis. In *Bone and Mineral Research, Annual 4.* W.A. Peck, ed. New York: Elsevier, 1986.

_____; Recker, R.R. and Saville, P.D. Menopausal changes in calcium balance performance. *J Lab Clin Med* 92:953–963, 1978.

Hegsted, D.M., and Ausman, L.M. Diet, alcohol and coronary heart disease in men. *J Nutr* 118:1184–1189, 1988.

Heidrick, M.L.; Hendricks, L.C.; and Cook, D.C. Effect of dietary 2-mercaptoethanol on the life span, immune system, tumor incidence and lipid peroxidation damage in spleen lymphocytes of aging BC3F1 mice. *Mech Ageing Dev* 27:341–358, 1984.

Hertog, M.G.L., et al. Intake of potentially anticarcinogenic flavonoids and their determinants in adults in The Netherlands. *Nutr Cancer* 20:21–29, 1993.

Hochschild, R. Effect of membrane stabilizing drugs on mortality in *Drosophilia melanogaster. Exp Gerontol* 6:133–151, 1971.

Hofman, S.L. Southwestern internal medicine conference: retinoids — differentiation agents for cancer treatment and prevention. *Am J Med Sci* 304:202–213, 1992.

_____; Strickland, S.; and Mahdavi, V. The induction of differentiation in teratocarcinoma cells by retinoic acid. *Cell* 15:393–403, 1978.

Hollenberg, N.K. Management of hypertension and cardiovascular risk. *Am J Med* 90(2A): 2S–6S, 1991.

Imaida, K.; Fukushima, S.; and Inoue, K., et al. Modifying effects of concomitant treatment with butylated hydroxyanisole or butylated hydroxytoluene on N,N-dibutylnitrosamine-induced liver, forestomach and urinary bladder carcinogenesis in F344 male rats. *Cancer Lett* 43:167–172, 1988.

Ip, C. The chemopreventive role of selenium in carcinogenesis. *J Am Coll Toxicol* 5:7–20, 1988.

_____. Susceptibility of mammary carcinogenesis in response to dietary selenium levels: modification by fat and vitamin intake. In *Selenium in Biology and Medicine.* G.F. Combs et al., eds. New York: Van Nostrand, 1987.

Iwasaki, K.; Gleiser, C.A.; and Masoro, E.J., et al. Influence of the restriction of individual dietary components on longevity and age-related disease of Fisher 344 rats. *J Gerontol* 43:B13–21, 1988

_____; _____; and _____; et al. The influence of dietary protein source on longevity and age-related disease processes of Fischer rats. *J Gerontol* 43:B2–12, 1988.

Jackson, R.; Scragg, R.; and Beaglehole, R. Alcohol consumption and risk of coronary heart disease. *Br Med J* 303:211–216, 1991.

Jacobs, L.R. Role of dietary factors in cell replication and colon cancer. *Am J Clin Nutr* 48: 775–779, 1988.

Jacobsen, B.K.; Bjelke, E.; Kvale, G.; and Heuch, I. Coffee drinking, mortality, and cancer incidence: results from a Norwegian prospective study. *JNCI* 76:823–831, 1986.

Jain, M.; Miller, A.B.; and To, T. Premorbid diet and the prognosis of women with breast cancer. *JNCI* 86:1390–1397, 1994.

Jenkins, D.J.A., et al. Glycemic index of foods: a physiological basis for carbohydrate exchange. *Am J Clin Nutr* 34:362–366, 1981.

Kagawa, Y. Impact of westernization on the nutrition of Japanese: changes in physique, cancer, longevity and centenarians. *Preve Med* 7:205–217, 1978.

Kark, J.D., et al. Serum vitamin A (retinol) and cancer incidence in Evans County, Georgia. *JNCI* 66:7–16, 1981.

Kashtan, H., et al. Wheat-bran and oat-bran supplements effects on blood lipids and lipoproteins. *Am J Clin Nutr* 55:976–980, 1992.

King, M.M., and McCay, P.B. Modulation of tumor incidence and possible mechanisms of inhibition of mammary carcinogenesis by dietary antioxidants. *Cancer Res* 43:248S–2490S, 1983.

Kirkpatrick, D.C., and Lauer, B.H. Intake of phenolic antioxidants from foods in Canada. *Food Chem Toxicol* 24:1035–1037, 1986.

Klatsky, A.; Armstrong, M.A.; and Friedman, G.D. Alcohol and mortality. *Ann Int Med* 117:646–654, 1992.

Kligman, L.H. Photoaging: manifestations, prevention, and treatment. *Dermatol Clin* 4:517–528, 1986.

Knekt, P., et al. Antioxidant vitamin intake and coronary mortality in a longitudinal population study. *Am J Epidemiol* 139:1180–1189, 1994.

Koller, L.E., et al. Immune responses in rats supplemented with selenium. *Clin Exp Immunol* 63:570–576, 1986.

_____, and Exon, J.H. The two faces of selenium — deficiency and toxicity — are similar in animals and man. *Can J Vet Res* 50:297–306, 1986.

Kolonel, L.N.; Hankin, J.H.; and Lee, J., et al. Nutrient intakes in relation to cancer incidence in Hawaii. *Br J Cancer* 44:332–339, 1981.

Krinsky, N.I. Carotenoids and cancer in animal models. *J Nutr* 119:123–126, 1989.

Kris-Etherton, P.M.; Krummel, D.; Russel, M.E., et al. The effect of diet on plasma lipids, lipoproteins, and coronary heart disease. *J Am Diet Assoc* 88:1373–1400, 1988.

Kritchevsky, D. Dietary guidelines: the rationale for intervention. *Cancer* 72:1011–1014, 1993.

Kushi, L.H.; Lenart, E.B.; and Willet, W.C. Health implications of Mediterranean diets in light of contemporary knowledge. 2: Meat, wine, fats, and oils. *Am J Clin Nutr* 61 *(suppl)*:1416S–1427S, 1995.

LaBella, F.S., and Paul, G. Structure of collagen from human tendon as influenced by age and sex. *J Gerontol* 20:54–59, 1965.

Lane, H.W.; Butel, J.S.; and Medina, D. Selenium, lipid peroxidation, and murine mammary tumorigenesis. In *Selenium in Biology and Medicine, Part B.* G.F. Combs et al., eds. New York: AVI/Van Nostrand, 1987.

LaVecchia, C.; Harris, R.E.; and Wyander, E.L. Comparative epidemiology of cancer between the United States and Italy. *Cancer Res* 48:7285–7293, 1988.

_____; Franceschi, S.; and Dolara, P., et al. Refined-sugar intake and the risk of colorectal cancer in humans. *Int J Cancer* 55:386–389, 1993.

Leaf, A., and Weber, P.C. Cardiovascular effects of n-3 fatty acids. *N Engl J Med* 318:549–557, 1988.

Leibovitz, B.; Hu, M.; and Tappel, A.L. Dietary supplements of vitamin E, beta-carotene, coenzyme Q10 and selenium protect tissues against lipid peroxidation in rat tissue slices. *J Nutr* 120:97–104, 1990.

Lemann, J.; Pleuss, J.A.; and Gray, R.W. Potassium causes calcium retention in healthy adults. *J Nutr* 123:1623–1626, 1993.

Levi, F. Selected physical activity and the risk of endometrial cancer. *Br J Med* 67:846–851, 1993.

Lewis, H.D.; David, J.D.; and Archibald, D.G., et al. Protective effects of aspirin against myocardial infarction and death in men with unstable angina. *N Engl J Med* 309:396–403, 1983.

Lindsay, R. The pathogenesis, prevention and treatment of osteoporosis. In *New Techniques in Metabolic Bone Disease.* J.C. Stevenson, ed. London: Wright, 1990.

Lippman, S.M.; Kessler, J.F.; and Meyskens, F.L. Retinoids as preventive and therapeutic anticancer agents (part I). *Cancer Treat Rep* 71:391–405, 1987.

_____; _____; and _____. Retinoids as preventive and therapeutic anticancer agents (part II). *Cancer Treat Rep* 71:493–515, 1987.

Lupton, J.R., and Jacobs, L.R. Fiber supplementation results in expanded proliferative zones in rat gastric mucosa. *Am J Clin Nutr* 46:980–984, 1987.

McGee, H. *On Food and Cooking.* Macmillan, New York, 1984.

Masoro, E.J. Dietary restriction and metabolic diseases. In *Nutritional Intervention in the Aging Process.* H.J. Armbrecht, J.M. Prendergast, and R.M. Coe, eds. New York: Springer-Verlag, 1984.

_____, and McMahan, C.A. Nutritional influences on aging of Fischer 344 rats: I. physical, metabolic, and longevity characteristics. *J Gerontol* 40:657–670, 1985.

Massey, L. Dietary factors influencing calcium and bone metabolism: introduction. *J Nutr* 123:1609–1610, 1993.

Massey, L.K., and Whiting, S.J. Caffeine, urinary calcium, calcium metabolism and bone. *J Nutr* 123:1611–1614, 1993.

Massie, H.R., and Aiello, V.R. The effect of dietary methionine on the copper content of tissues and survival of young and old mice. *Exp Gerontol* 19:393–399, 1984.

Mattson, F.H. A changing role for dietary monounsaturated fatty acids. *J Am Diet Assoc* 89:387–391, 1989.

Meredith, C.N., et al. Body composition and aerobic capacity in young and middle-aged endurance trained men. *Med Sci Sports Exercise* 19:557–563, 1987.

Mertz, W. Chromium in human nutrition: a review. *J Nutr* 123:626–633, 1993.

Mervaala, E.M., et al. Beneficial effects of a potassium- and magnesium-enriched salt. *Hypertension* 19:535–540, 1992.

Miller, A.B. Cancer and obesity. In *Obesity and Weight Control*. R.T. Frankle, and M. Yang, eds. Rockville MD: Aspen, 1988.

_____, and Risch, H.A. Diet and lung cancer. *Chest* 96:85–95, 1985.

Milner, J.A., and Hsu, C.Y. Inhibitory effects of selenium on the growth of L1210 leukemic cells. *Cancer Res* 41:1652–1656, 1981.

Moon, R.C. Comparative aspects of carotenoids and retinoids as chemoprotective agents for cancer. *J Nutr* 119:127–134, 1989.

Morales, A.J.; Nolan, J.J.; Nelson, J.C., and Yen, S.S.C. Effects of replacement dose of dehydro-epiandrostone in men and women of advancing age. *J Clin Endocrin Metab* 78:1360–1367, 1994.

Morehouse, L.E. *Total Fitness in 30 Minutes*. New York: Simon and Schuster, 1990.

Morel, I., et al. Antioxidant and iron-chelating activities of the flavonoids catechin, quercetin and diosmetin on iron-loaded rat hepatocyte cultures. *Biochem Pharmacol* 45(1):13–19, 1993.

Moriguchi, S.; Werner, L.; and Watson, R.R. High dietary vitamin A (retinyl palmitate) and cellular immune functions in mice. *Immunology* 56:169–177, 1985.

Muntzel, M., and Drueke, T. A comprehensive review of the salt and blood pressure relationship. *Am J Hyperten* 5:1S–42S, 1992.

National Cancer Institute. *Artificial Sweeteners*. http://www.nih.gov/Health & Clinical Information/CancerNet Information/Fact Sheets from the NCI/Risk Factors & Possible Causes.

National Center for Health Statistics. *Health, United States 1993*. Hyattsville MD: Public Health Service, 1994.

National Research Council. *Diet and Health*. Washington DC: National Academy Press, 1989.

National Research Council, Food and Nutrition Board. *Recommended Dietary Allowances*. 10th ed. Washington DC: National Academy Press, 1989.

Negri, E.; LaVecchia, C.; and Franceschi, S., et al. Vegetable and fruit consumption and cancer risk. *Int J Cancer* 48:350–354, 1991.

Nelson, M.E., et al. Effects of high-intensity strength training on multiple risk factors for osteoporotic fractures. A randomized control trial. *JAMA* 272:1909–1914, 1994.

Neve, J.; Vertongen, F.; and Molle, F. Selenium deficiency. *Clin Endocrinol Metab* 14:629–656, 1985.

Nomura, A. Stomach. In *Cancer Epidemiology and Prevention*. D. Schottenfeld, and J.F. Fraumeni, eds. Philadelphia: Saunders, 1982.

Nyman, I.; Larsson, H.; and Wallentin, L., et al. Prevention of serious cardiac events by low-dose aspirin in patients with silent myocardial ischaemia. *Lancet* 340:497–501, 1992.

Olson, O.E. Selenium toxicity in animals with emphasis on man. *J Am Coll Toxicol* 5:45–69, 1986.

Paffenbarger, R.S.; Hyde, R.T.; and Wing, A.L. Physical activity and incidence of cancer in diverse populations: a preliminary report. *Am J Clin Nutr* 45:312–317, 1987.

Paffenbarger, Jr., R.S., et al. The association of changes in physical-activity level and other lifestyle characteristics with mortality among men. *N Engl J Med* 328:538–545, 1993.

Palmore, E.B. *Social Patterns in Normal Aging: Findings from the Duke Longitudinal Study*. Durham NC: Duke University Press, 1981.

Palozza, P., and Krinsky, N.I. Beta-carotene and alpha-tocopherol are synergistic antioxidants. *Arch Biochem Biophys* 297:184–187, 1992.

Panel on Dietary Sugars. *Dietary Sugars and Human Disease*. HMSO, London, 1989.

Pearson, D., and Shaw, S. *Life Extension, A Practical Scientific Approach*. New York: Warner, 1982.

Pelton, R.B., and Williams, R.J. Effect of pantothenic acid on the longevity of mice. *Proc Soc Exp Biol Med* 99:632–633, 1958.

Peng, A., et al. Beta-carotene and canthaxanthin inhibit chemically and physically induced neoplastic transformation in 10T1/2 cells. *Carcinogenesis* 9:1533–1539, 1988.

Pennington, J.A.T. *Bowes and Church's Food Values of Portions Commonly Used*. 16th ed. Philadelphia: Lippincott, 1994.

Perneger, T.V.; Whelton, P.K.; and Klag, M.J. Risk of kidney failure associated with the use of acetaminophen, aspirin, and nonsteroidal antiinflammatory drugs. *N Engl J Med* 331 (25):1675–1679, 1994.

Peterson, H.B.; Lee, N.C.; and Rubin, G.L. Genital neoplasia. In *Menopause: Physiology and Pharmacology*. D.R. Mishell, ed. Chicago: Year Book, 1986.

Peto, R., et al. Can dietary beta-carotene materially reduce human cancer rates? *Nature* 290: 201–208, 1981.

Physicians' Health Study Research Group, Steering Committee. Final report on the aspirin component of the ongoing Physicians' Health Study. *N Engl J Med* 321:129–135, 1989.

Pienta, K.J., and Esper, P.S. Risk factors for prostate cancer. *Ann Intern Med* 118:793–803, 1993.

Poulter, N.; Chang, C.L.; Cuff, A.; and Poulter, C., et al. Lipid profiles after the daily consumption of an oat-based cereal: a controlled crossover trial. *Am J Clin Nutr* 58:66–69, 1993.

Powell, K.E.; Thompson, P.D.; Caspersen, C.J.; and Kendrick, J.S. Physical activity and the incidence of coronary heart disease. *Annu Rev Public Health* 8:253–287, 1987.

Pryor, W.A. The antioxidant nutrients and disease prevention — what do we know and what do we need to find out? *Am J Clin Nutr* 53:391S–393S, 1991.

Ravussin, E., et al. Determinants of 24-hour energy expenditure in man. *J Clin Invest* 78: 1568–1578, 1986.

Reddy, B.S. Dietary fat and colon cancer: animal models. *Prev Med* 16:460–467, 1987.

_____; Burrill, C.; and Rigotty, J. Effects of diets high in omega-3 and omega-6 fatty acids on initiation and postinitiation stages of colon carcinogenesis. *Cancer Res* 51:487–491, 1991.

Retzlaff, E.; Fontaine, J.; and Futura, W. Effect of daily exercise on life-span of albino rats. *Geriatrics* 21:171–177, March, 1966.

Rimm, E.B.; Stampfer, M.J.; and Ascherio, A. et al. Vitamin E consumption and the risk of coronary heart disease in men. *N Engl J Med* 328:1450–1456, 1993.

Risch, H.A., et al. Dietary fat intake and risk of epithelial ovarian cancer. *JNCI* 86:1409–1415, 1994.

Romm, P.A.; Green, C.E.; Reagan, K.; and Rackley, C.E. Relation of serum lipoprotein cholesterol levels to presence and severity of angiographic coronary artery disease. *Am J Cardiol* 67:479–483, 1991.

Roy, M.E., et al. Selenium and immune cell functions. II. Effect on lymphocyte-mediated cytotoxicity. *Proc Soc Exp Biol Med* 193:143–148, 1990.

Rudkin, D., and Felix, C. *The Omega-3 Phenomenon*. New York: Rawson Associates, 1987.

Schwartz, A.G., et al. Dehydroepiandrostone and structural analogs: a new class of cancer chemopreventive agents. *Adv Cancer Res* 51:391–424, 1988.

Science News 114 (No.24): 408, 1978.

Seelig, M.S. Interrelationship of magnesium and estrogen in cardiovascular and bone disorders, eclampsia, migraine and premenstrual syndrome. *J Am Coll Nutr* 12:442–458, 1993.

Seifter, E., et al. Regression of C3HBA mouse tumor due to X-ray therapy combined with beta-carotene or vitamin A. *JNCI* 71:409–417, 1983.

Shekelle, R.B., et al. Dietary vitamin A and risk of cancer in the Western Electric study. *Lancet* 2:1185–1190, 1981.

Shibata, A., et al. Intake of vegetables, fruits, beta-carotene, vitamin C and vitamin supplements and cancer incidence among the elderly: a prospective study. *Br J Can* 66:673–679, 1992.

Shinnick, F.L., et al. Oat fiber: composition versus physiologic function in rats. *J Nutr* 118:144–151, 1988.

Simopoulis, A.P. Omega-3 fatty acids in health and disease and in growth and development. *Am J Clin Nutr* 54:438–463, 1991.

Singh, V.N., and Gaby, S.K. Premalignant lesions: role of antioxidant vitamins and beta-carotene in risk reduction and prevention of malignant transformation. *Am J Clin Nutr* 53:386S–390S, 1991.

Slater, T.F. Disturbances of free radical reactions: a cause or consequence of cell injury? In *Medical, Biochemical and Chemical Aspects of Free Radicals*. Vol.1. O. Hayaishi, et al., eds. Amsterdam: Elsevier, 1989.

Snow-Harter, C.M. Bone health and prevention of osteoporosis in active and athletic women. *Clin Sports Med* 13:389–404, 1994.

Snowdon, D.A. Animal product consumption and mortality because of all causes combined, coronary heart disease, stroke, diabetes, and cancer in Seventh-day Adventists. *Am J Clin Nutr* 48:739–748, 1988.

Sperduto, R.D., et al. The Linxian cataract studies: two nutrition intervention trials. *Arch Ophthalmol* 111:1246–1253, 1993.

Sporn, M.B., and Roberts, A.B. The role of retinoids in differentiation and carcinogenesis. *Cancer Res* 43:3034–3040, 1983.

Staehelin, H.B., et al. Beta-carotene and cancer prevention: the Basel study. *Am J Clin Nutr* 53:265S–269S, 1991.

Stampfer, M.J.; Hennekens, C.H.; and Manson, J.E., et al. Vitamin E consumption and the risk of coronary heart disease in women. *N Engl J Med* 328:1444–1449, 1993.

Stein, P.P., and Black, H.R. The role of diet in the genesis and treatment of hypertension. *Med Clin North Am* 77(4):831–847, 1993.

Steinmetz, K.A., and Potter, J.D. Vegetables, fruit, and cancer: I. epidemiology. *Cancer Causes and Control* 325–357, 1991.

_____, and _____. Vegetables, fruit, and cancer: II. mechanisms. *Cancer Causes and Control* 427–441, 1991.

Stellman, S.D. Cigarette yield and cancer risk: evidence from case-control and prospective studies. In *Tobacco: A Major International Health Hazard*. D.G. Zaridze and R. Peto, eds. Lyon: IARC, 1986.

Stich, H.F. The beneficial and hazardous effects of simple phenolic compounds. *Mutat Res* 259:307–324, 1991.

Sunde, R.A., and Hoekstra, W.G. Structure, synthesis and function of glutathione peroxidase. *Nutr Rev* 38:265–273, 1980.

Superko, H.R., et al. Caffeinated and decaffeinated coffee effects on plasma lipoprotein cholesterol, apolipoproteins, and lipase activity: a controlled, randomized trial. *Am J Clin Nutr* 54:599–605, 1991.

Swain, J.F., et al. Comparison of the effects of oat bran and low-fiber wheat on serum lipoprotein levels and blood pressure. *N Engl J Med* 322:147–152, 1990.

Swecker, W.S., et al. Influence of supplemental selenium on humoral immune responses in weaned beef calves. *Am J Vet Res* 50:1760–1763, 1989.

Talamini, R., et al. Diet and prostate: a case-control study in northern Italy. *Nutr Cancer* 18:277–286, 1992.

Taylor, A. Role of nutrients in delaying cataracts. *Ann NY Acad Sci* 669:111–123, 1992.

Taylor, H.R., et al. The long-term effects of visible light on the eye. *Arch Ophthalmol* 110: 99–104, 1992.

Thompson, H.J., et al. Effect of type and amount of dietary fat on the enhancement of rat mammary tumorigenesis by exercise. *Cancer Res* 49:1904–1908, April, 1989.

Tominaga, S. Smoking and cancer patterns and trends in Japan. In *Tobacco: A Major International Health Hazard.* D.G. Zaridze and R. Peto, eds. Lyon: IARC, 1986.

Tomita, Y., et al. Augmentation of tumor immunity against syngeneic tumors in mice by beta-carotene. *JNCI* 78:679–680, 1987.

Tribble, D.L., and Krauss, R.M. HDL and coronary artery disease. *Adv Intern Med* 38:1–29, 1993.

Trout, D.L. Vitamin C and cardiovascular risk factors. *Am J Clin Nutr* 53:322S–325S, 1991.

Tuyns, A.J. Epidemiology of alcohol and cancer. *Cancer Res* 39:2840–2843, 1979.

Tzankoff, S.P., and Norris, A.H. Longitudinal changes in basal metabolic rate in man. *J Appl Physiol* 33:536–539, 1978.

U.S. Department of Health and Human Services. *Osteoporosis Research, Education, and Health Promotion.* Bethesda MD: Public Health Service, 1991.

Wald, N., et al. Low serum-vitamin A and subsequent risk of cancer: preliminary results of a prospective study. *Lancet* 2:813–815, 1980.

Walford, R.L. *The 120 Year Diet.* New York: Simon and Schuster, 1986.

Wannamethee, G.; Shaper, A.G.; and Macfarlane, P.W. Heart rate, physical activity, and mortality from cancer and other noncardiovascular diseases. *Am J Epidemiol* 137:735–748, 1993.

Wardlaw, G.M.; Snook, J.M.; and Lin, M., et al. Serum lipid and apolipoprotein concentrations in healthy men on diets enriched in either canola oil or safflower oil. *Am J Clin Nutr* 54:104–110, 1991.

Wargovich, M.J.; Bear, A.R.; Hu, P.J.; and Sumiyoshi, H. Dietary factors and colorectal cancer. *Gastroenterol Clin North Am* 17:727–745, 1988.

_____, and Mastromarino, A.J. Dietary factors in the etiology and prevention of colon cancer. *Cancer Bull* 46:303–308, 1994.

Watrach, A.M.; Milner, J.A.; Watrach, M.A.; and Poirier, K.A. Inhibition of human breast cancer cells by selenium. *Cancer Lett* 25:41–47, 1984.

Waxler, M. Long-term visual health problems: optical radiation risks. In *Optical Radiation and Visual Health.* M. Waxler and V.M. Hitchins, eds. Boca Raton FL: CRC, 1986.

Weidruch, R., and Walford, R.L. Dietary restriction in mice beginning at 1 year of age. *Science* 215:1415–1418, 1982.

_____, and _____. *The Retardation of Aging by Dietary Restriction.* New York: Raven, 1987.

_____; _____; Fliegiel, S.; and Guthrie, D. The retardation of aging in mice by dietary restriction. *J Nutr* 116:641–654, 1986.

Weimann, B.J., and Weiser, H. Functions of vitamin E in reproduction and in prostacyclin and immunoglobulin synthesis in rats. *Am J Clin Nutr* 53:1056S–1060S, 1991.

Weisburger, J.H. Nutritional approach to cancer prevention with emphasis on vitamins, antioxidants, and carotenoids. *Am J Clin Nutr* 53:226S–237S, 1991.

Willet, W.C., and Stampfer, M.J. Selenium and cancer. *Br Med J* 297:573–574, 1988.

Willett, W.C., et al. Dietary fat and fiber in relation to risk of breast cancer: an 8-year follow-up. *JAMA* 268:2037–2044, 1992.

_____; Stampfer, M.J.; and Colditz, M.J., et al. Moderate alcohol consumption and risk of breast cancer. *N Eng J Med* 316:1174–1180, 1987.

Williams, S.R. *Basic Nutrition and Diet Therapy.* St Louis: Mosby–Year Book, 1992.

Yang, G.Q. Research on Se-related problems in human health in China. In *Proceedings of the Third International Symposium on Selenium in Biology and Medicine.* C.F. Combs, J.E. Spallholz, and O.A. Levander, eds. Westport CT: AVI, 1986.

Yu, B.P.; Masoro, E.J.; and McMahan, C.A. Nutritional influences on aging of Fisher 344 rats. *J Gerontol* 40:657–670, 1985.

Yudkin, J. Dietary factors in atherosclerosis. *Lipids* 13:370–372, 1978.

_____. Report of the COMA panel on dietary sugar and human disease: discussion paper. *J Ro Soc Med* 83:627–628, 1990.

_____. Sucrose, coronary heart disease and obesity. do hormones provide a link? *Am Heart J* 115:493–498, 1988.

Ziegler, R.E. A review of the epidemiologic evidence that carotenoids reduce the risk of cancer. *J Nutr* 119:116–122, 1989.

Index

DATE DUE

JUN 0 1 2000		
MAY 0 9 2001		
NOV 0 6 2003		
NOV 2 5 2007		
GAYLORD		PRINTED IN U.S.A.